I

To all who have 'discovered' John with me,
at Aberdeen, Cuddesdon, and Oxford

Discovering John

Ruth Edwards

SPCK

First published in Great Britain in 2003 by
Society for Promoting Christian Knowledge
Holy Trinity Church
Marylebone Road
London NW1 4DU

British Library Cataloguing-in-Publication Data
A catalogue record for this book is available from the British Library

ISBN 0-281-05403-7

1 3 5 7 9 10 8 6 4 2

Typeset by Avocet Typeset, Chilton, Aylesbury, Bucks
Printed in Great Britain by MPG Books Ltd, Bodmin, Cornwall

Contents

	Preface	vii
	Principal Abbreviations	ix
1	Introduction: A Distinctive Gospel	1
2	The Reception of John's Gospel	8
3	The Question of Authorship	18
4	Traditions, Sources, and the Nature of John's Writing	27
5	Purpose, Audience, Place and Date of Composition	37
6	Jesus' Miracles as Narrative Theology	49
7	Christological Confessions and Titles for Jesus	61
8	Jesus' Passion and Resurrection	73
9	Jesus: Word Incarnate and Father's Son	84
10	Characters in John's Story	98
11	'Anti-Semitism'/'Anti-Judaism' in John's Gospel?	112
12	'Replacement Theology' and Jewish Monotheism	122
13	Conclusions: The Value of John's Gospel Today	135
	Appendix 1 The Structure of John's Gospel	148
	Appendix 2 Jesus' Burial and Resurrection in the Gospels	150
	Notes	152
	Bibliography	164
	Indexes: Biblical References	180
	Ancient Authors and Texts	187
	Names and Subjects	188

Preface

John's Gospel has been loved, interpreted and reinterpreted by Christian believers since it was first composed. It has also been the subject of intense academic study by scholars from within and outside the Church. This book seeks to make available to academics, students, clergy, teachers and a wider public insights from this scholarship and my own reflections, resulting from some twenty-five years of New Testament teaching and research. It is written as far as possible in simple language, with technical terms explained and Greek and Hebrew transliterated; at the same time, it regularly interacts with professional scholarship and the unending stream of new publications in danger of engulfing the would-be writer on John.

A. T. Hanson once suggested that older scholars who attempt to write anything substantial on John take their lives into their hands. From Origen in the fourth century to Ernst Haenchen in the twentieth, Johannine experts have died before completing their books. The commentaries of Bernard, Hoskyns, Sanders and Haenchen were all published posthumously, as was Robinson's *The Priority of John*. Raymond Brown died while revising his great commentary. This untoward 'mortality' may perhaps be caused by a tendency among scholars to wait until their later years before writing on John – a task often seen as the crown of their endeavours. But a further factor must surely be the complexity and range of Johannine scholarship and the sheer depth of John's theology.

My own interest in John goes back to school days and early years as a professional Greek scholar. I am immensely grateful to Robin Barbour, then Professor of New Testament Exegesis at Aberdeen University, for first inviting me, in the late 1970s, to lecture to second-year theological students on John, and for the impetus this gave me to pursue Johannine studies in greater depth. Under Howard Marshall, his successor in the Aberdeen chair, further courses followed at honours level and beyond. Later, when I was working at Ripon College, Cuddesdon, Professor Christopher Rowland invited me to give lectures on John's Gospel at the University of Oxford. To these colleagues, to my former doctoral and master's students, and to all whom I taught at undergraduate level and in summer schools, I extend my sincere thanks for their enthusiasm for John, and their indirect contribution to this book through shared thoughts and questions. The book is dedicated to them.

I should also like to express appreciation for all the scholars whose works are discussed in this volume, and the many others too numerous to cite who have helped form its thought. Although I may differ from them in places, this book is the richer for the stimulus of their contributions. Special thanks go to those colleagues who have discussed John with me at the Johannine Seminar of the British New Testament Society and other scholarly gatherings.

In these days of reader-response criticism we are particularly conscious of ways in which personal and social background influences interpretation of texts. I have written this book as a critical scholar who is also a committed Christian and a priest in the Scottish Episcopal Church. The Bible and the life of the Church have shaped my faith, as has the process of intellectual enquiry, including the study of other cultures and faiths. From my first study of John's Gospel I have admired it and been inspired by it; but over the years I have become increasingly aware of the problems it poses for Jewish readers and others who see the New Testament as responsible for fostering anti-Semitism, intolerance and bigotry. I have tried to face these difficulties honestly while continuing to recognize the immense potential for good within the Bible and this Gospel in particular.

In interpreting John I have striven to be as conciliatory as possible towards those of other faiths, while remaining faithful to the text. To this end, the expressions 'Hebrew Bible' and 'Jewish Scriptures' have been used in preference to 'Old Testament', and 'BCE' (before the Common Era) and 'CE' (of the Common Era) instead of 'BC' (before Christ) and 'AD' (*anno Domini*). I am well aware that a fully objective analysis is impossible; but truth has been the first priority, even if this means challenging some traditional understandings. I have worked primarily from the Greek and Hebrew texts, although I have regularly consulted the standard translations. Unless otherwise stated, all biblical renderings are my own; they make no attempt at elegance or 'dynamic equivalence', but are designed to bring out the text's structure and basic meaning.

I should like to thank the staff of SPCK for their patience and courtesy, and Ruth McCurry, the commissioning editor, for her enthusiasm for the project. Most of all I want to thank my husband, Patrick Edwards – *vir optimus et eruditus* – for his unfailing support and help from the book's first inception to the final stages. He has read every chapter, in more than one draft, and devoted untold hours to checking and indexing biblical references. I am deeply grateful to him for his comments, constructive criticisms and encouragement.

Ruth B. Edwards
Aberdeen, August 2003

Principal Abbreviations

Abbreviations of journals and series are those used regularly in the scholarly literature. For details please see *The SBL Handbook of Style*, ed. P. H. Alexander *et al.* (Peabody, Mass., Hendrickson, 1999), pp. 121–52. Help can also be found in the lists printed annually in the *Catholic Biblical Quarterly* (end of pt 4) and *New Testament Abstracts* (start of pt 1).

ANF	*Ante-Nicene Christian Library*, ed. A. Roberts and J. Donaldson
AV	Authorized Version (King James Version)
Bib. Inst.	Biblical Institute Press (Pontificio Istituto Biblico, Rome)
ET	English translation
et al.	*et alibi* (and other places), *et alii* (and others)
f.	and page/verse/etc. immediately following
GNB	Good News Bible
ISBE	*International Standard Bible Encyclopedia* (rev. edn), ed. G. W. Bromiley
JB	Jerusalem Bible
LSJ	Liddell and Scott, *Greek-English Lexicon* (rev. H. S. Jones and R. McKenzie)
LXX	Septuagint (Old Testament in Greek)
NEB	New English Bible
NIV	New International Version
NJB	New Jerusalem Bible
NPNF	*Nicene and Post-Nicene Fathers*, ed. P. Schaff
par.	and parallel(s)
RGG	*Die Religion in Geschichte und Gegenwart*, ed. K. Galling
RSV	Revised Standard Version
TDNT	*Theological Dictionary of the New Testament*, ed. G. Kittel (tr. and ed. G. W. Bromiley)
v.l.	*varia lectio* (variant reading)

1

Introduction: A Distinctive Gospel

Over the centuries John's Gospel[1] has inspired artists and musicians, theologians, poets and thinkers, and countless ordinary Christians. It has sustained faith, aroused love, and encouraged heroism. Viewed as the high point of New Testament theology, it has profoundly shaped Christian doctrine. In patristic and medieval times John was symbolized as an eagle, 'the spiritual bird, fast-flying, God-seeing' (Eriugena),[2] an image still used in Church art. His Gospel has been seen as both speaking tellingly to the simple believer, and plumbing the depths of the Christian faith for the sophisticated (cf. Marsh, 1968, p. 81). But John has been criticized as 'world-denying' and 'sectarian', 'androcentric', and 'anti-Jewish' – 'a Gospel of Christian love and Jew hatred' (Kohler, 1905, p. 251). While in the past it was seen as painting 'a perfect portrait of Jesus' (Temple, 1939, p. xvi), today some view it as historically inaccurate, 'a presentation of falsehood', and responsible for stimulating and supporting the vilest anti-Semitism (Casey, 1996, esp. pp. 198, 218–29).

What is this writing that has provoked such diverse responses? Who wrote it, and why was it written? Can a study of its context and circumstances of composition help us understand it? It has been said that the questions asked of a text are as important as the answers given (Malbon, 2000, p. 1). Readers with a historical bent may be stimulated by the questions just posed; those with more literary interests may be intrigued by the Gospel as 'story'. How does its 'plot' work? How does its author use characters, and what literary devices are employed? Their questions and motivation for study will be different from those of the first set of readers. Others will be more interested in John's theology. How does John relate to the religious thought of its day? What is distinctive about its message? Many people study biblical texts to deepen their personal faith, or find guidance for living. Some of these are inspired by John; for others, it raises problems. Does its message need to be re-interpreted for today's world? How should Christians respond to recent criticisms of it? Does John still have meaning for the Church and contemporary society?

This book is intended for those interested in any of these aspects of John. It will not answer all their questions, but it is hoped that it may help them to think out for themselves where they stand. Chapters 1–2 outline the shape of the Gospel and review its interpretation over the centuries. Chapters 3–5 investigate authorship and composition, including the questions of John's sources and audience. Chapters 6–9 focus more sharply on theology, especially John's christology (understanding of Christ). They explore the different methods by which he seeks to convey Jesus' identity through miracles, faith confessions, Jesus' words and actions, and personal reflection. Chapter 10 discusses John's use of characters, both from a literary angle, and to see how they illuminate John's understanding of faith in Jesus. Chapters 11–12 tackle different facets of the question whether John's Gospel is 'anti-Jewish' (or 'anti-Semitic'),[3] and how John's belief in Jesus' divinity relates to Jewish monotheism. Chapter 13 draws together the threads of this study, centring on whether John's Gospel has any abiding value for today.

Reading John's Story

At this point you are invited to read John's Gospel for yourself in the same way as you would read any book, following its story-line and enjoying its shape. As you read, you may like to refer to Appendix 1, which summarizes the themes of the following discussion.

I. Proem: Prologue and Testimony

The Gospel opens with a proem (Greek *prooimion*, 'opening'), consisting of an elevated 'Prologue' followed by a plain prose narrative, called the 'Testimony' (Dodd, 1953, p. 292). The Prologue (1.1–18) is mysterious, not readily grasped on a quick reading, or even on several readings, conveying its message through images of light, darkness, life, birth, grace, truth, and glory. It meditates on Jesus as the divine, preexistent Word, who became flesh to make God known to humankind. Apart from Jesus, only one historical personage is mentioned: John (the Baptist), sent by God as a witness (1.6, 15).

The Testimony (1.19–51) takes us from eternity to time: different characters are shown who testify to Jesus through christological confessions. He is acknowledged in turn as God's 'lamb', 'son', 'messiah' and 'Israel's king'. But although the Testimony seems to be historical narrative, being marked off by clear indications of time (e.g. 1.29), it too is preparatory for the main story. Its purpose, like that of the Prologue, is to herald themes which will be important for John – not just 'titles' for Jesus, but also motifs like 'water' (1.26), 'Spirit' (1.32), and 'witness' (1.7f., 34). It also anticipates future events, e.g. the recognition of Jesus as 'messiah' (1.41), placed much later by the other Gospels (cf. Mk 8.29 par.).

II. Jesus' Self-Revelation and Ministry

The main narrative is generally divided into two sections, with further subdivisions (cf. Appendix 1). John 2—12, sometimes called 'the Book of Signs' (Dodd, 1953, p. 297; cf. Brown, 1966, p. cxxxviii), reflects on Jesus' disclosure of himself and his ministry. Interest centres on his miracles and teaching, and controversies arising from them. Only a few miracles are related, but those chosen have a significant role. Beginning with that at Cana (2.1–11), they are called 'signs' (Greek *sēmeia*) and function as pointers to Jesus' identity. Their climax is the raising of Lazarus (11.1–44), demonstrating Jesus' control over death and looking forward to his own resurrection. These miracles are often associated with dialogues bringing out their meaning. Jesus also discloses his identity through his actions in the Temple (2.13–22), in his dialogue with Nicodemus (3.1–15), and in his meeting with the Samaritan woman (4.4–42). Particularly intriguing are the references forward to Jesus' passion, e.g. 'Destroy this temple and in three days I will raise it up' (2.19), 'As Moses lifted up the serpent in the wilderness, so must the Son of Man be lifted up' (3.14). These grow in frequency and intensity as the narrative advances.

Another prominent theme of these chapters is Jesus' relationship to Moses, flagged in 1.17 and 1.45. By his miracles and teaching, Jesus shows himself to be like Moses, and yet as greater than Moses (6.4–59, esp. 41–51; cf. Boismard, 1993). Jesus is also presented as greater than Jacob (4.12) and greater than Abraham (8.53–8). This interest in Moses and the patriarchs, together with numerous allusions to the Jewish Scriptures, raises questions about how John saw Christianity's relation to Judaism. Some (e.g. Moloney, 1996; Brown, 1997, p. 334) have suggested that by giving prominence to Jewish religious feasts – Sabbath, Passover, Dedication, Tabernacles – John depicts Jesus as superseding (for Christians) many aspects of Judaism, including both Temple and festivals.

By his words and actions Jesus antagonizes 'the Jews', and their leaders 'the Pharisees' and 'High Priests'. These are represented as misunderstanding Jesus, 'persecuting' him, and seeking to kill him. Some scholars (notably Harvey, 1976; Lincoln, 2000) see John as presenting Jesus 'on trial', or rather as the focus of a juridical controversy (Asiedu-Peprah, 2001). 'The Jews' make charges, and Jesus defends himself and makes counter-accusations. The Baptist, the disciples, the crowd, all bear witness to him, as do the Scriptures, and, most importantly, the Father (8.18). Readers find themselves drawn into the process and having to make up their own minds about Jesus. This stylized presentation, though dramatic, presents problems: by using 'the Jews' to stand for opposition to Jesus, John lays himself open to 'anti-Jewish' readings of his text, with dire consequences. Another feature of this section is

Jesus' 'elusiveness' (Stibbe, 1991). The Pharisees send officers to arrest him (7.32), but they are so impressed by his words they fail to do so (7.45f.). After Jesus' statement that he existed before Abraham, 'the Jews' try to stone him, but he hides himself (8.59). Again they attempt to stone him, or arrest him, but he escapes (10.31, 39). Jesus is also 'elusive' in the sense that he speaks enigmatically, and is often misunderstood. This 'elusiveness' is also part of the pattern of John's plot.

Throughout John 2—12 Jesus is not only life-giver, but also judge. By coming as a 'light' to the world, Jesus shows up the darkness (3.19–21): by speaking the truth, he makes people come to a decision between truth and falsehood, 'light' and 'darkness', himself and 'the world'. His coming separates people into those who accept him and those who reject him. This recurring dichotomy climaxes in John 11, where Jesus raises Lazarus after Martha has confessed him as the Christ. 'The Jews' are divided into those who put their faith in Jesus and those who inform on him to the Pharisees, leading to the plot to kill him (11.45f.). Chapter 12 acts as a transition between Jesus' public ministry and his passion. Mary anoints his feet, and a crowd acclaims him 'Israel's king'. He speaks allusively of his death, agonizing over his 'hour' (12.23–33), and tells of the casting out of 'the ruler of this world' (12.31). This section ends with a sombre quotation from Isaiah about God blinding eyes and hardening hearts, and an appeal from Jesus to believe, with a warning of judgement and promise of eternal life (12.37–50).

III. Passion and Resurrection Narrative

This part is sometimes called 'the Book of Glory' (Brown, 1966), because John sees Jesus' suffering and death not as his humiliation, but rather as his 'lifting up' or 'glorification'. Jesus' death, resurrection, and return to the Father are presented as part of a single movement. Thus the 'hour' of his death is also the 'hour' of his glory (13.31f.; 17.1, etc.). Chapter 13 both introduces the passion and provides a key to its understanding. At his last meal, on the eve of the Passover, Jesus washes his disciples' feet as an example of love and humble service; by this act he foreshadows his loving 'to the end' (cf. Edwards, 1994). The emotional tension grows as he gives Judas a morsel from the common dish, and Satan enters him. Judas leaves to betray Jesus, 'and it was night' (13.30).

Jesus' tender farewell to his disciples and his 'High-Priestly Prayer'[4] occupy John 14—17. The pace is slow and reflective, as the Evangelist mingles reassurances for the future, promises of the Paraclete (Holy Spirit), and injunctions to love. He calls the disciples his 'friends'; warns them that 'the world' will hate them; speaks of his 'departure', and promises to return. But there is also a note of triumph: Jesus' farewell ends with the words, 'Be of good cheer. I have overcome the world'

(16.33). He has fulfilled his mission: he has made God known to those given him. He now consecrates himself and his disciples, praying that they may be one. His closeness to the Father is intensely expressed as he prays that the disciples may know the love with which God loves him.

The pace quickens with the narrative of Jesus' trial and death. Roman soldiers and Jewish officers arrest him. He appears first before Annas, then Caiaphas, and finally Pilate, who wishes to release him; but the High Priests and their officers call for his death and 'the Jews' likewise insist that he must die 'because he made himself the Son of God' (19.6f.). Pilate complies, and Jesus is crucified, having carried his own cross to Golgotha, the place of execution. Soldiers cast lots for his seamless robe, in fulfilment of Scripture (19.23f.); Jesus commends his mother and 'the disciple whom he loved' to one another (19.26f.). He 'thirsts' (again in fulfilment of Scripture), and 'yields up his spirit' (19.30). He dies on the day of preparation for Passover. In another Scripture fulfilment, a soldier pierces his side, from which blood and water flow. Meditation on the Hebrew Bible clearly helps interpret these painful events.

In his account of Jesus' passion John stresses his autonomy and kingly authority. Jesus identifies himself to those who come to arrest him with his majestic 'I am'; they step back and fall to the ground (18.6). In his dialogue with Pilate he discusses kingship and truth. The soldiers dress him in purple, crown him with thorns, and mockingly hail him as king (19.2f.). Even Pilate refers to him as 'king'; but his kingship is 'not of this world' (18.36–9). He dies beneath a superscription, 'Jesus of Nazareth, the king of the Jews' (19.19), which Pilate refuses to change despite the request of the High Priests. In contrast to Mark (15.34), where his last words are a cry of dereliction, 'My God, my God, why have you forsaken me?', Jesus dies with the triumphant words, 'It is accomplished' (19.30). He is buried with vast quantities of spices supplied by Joseph of Arimathea and Nicodemus, a member of the Jewish Sanhedrin, who had earlier come to Jesus by night. John 20 tells the powerful end of the story – resurrection! This is depicted in a series of vivid scenes: the encounter with Mary Magdalene, Peter and 'the disciple whom Jesus loved' running to the tomb, appearances to the disciples, and Thomas' recognition of Jesus as 'My Lord and my God' (20.28). It concludes with a statement on the purpose of the Gospel (20.31).

IV. Epilogue or Appendix
John's story is completed by a further appearance of Jesus and a final miracle when the disciples catch a huge draught of fish. Peter, who had earlier denied Jesus three times (18.15–18, 25–7), is restored and commissioned. His future destiny and that of the 'beloved disciple' is predicted. The Gospel ends with a second conclusion (21.25).

The Distinctiveness of John

Although at first sight this Gospel appears much like the first three, the 'Synoptics' (so called because of their common viewpoint), attentive readers cannot fail to observe differences, which sometimes earn it the epithet 'maverick' (e.g. Kysar, 1976). Unlike Matthew and Luke, John gives no account of Jesus' birth or human ancestry. He relates fewer miracles, and those included function as signs pointing to his identity. In contrast to the Synoptists, he describes no exorcisms, whereby individual sufferers are freed from the grip of demonic forces, possibly because his whole Gospel represents a confrontation of Jesus with the powers of evil, culminating in their defeat on the cross.

Until the last week of Jesus' life the Synoptics picture his ministry as taking place largely in Galilee,[5] whereas John describes regular visits to Jerusalem. Jesus' Temple action occurs at the start of his ministry, rather than just before his passion as in the Synoptics. John mentions three Passovers, indicating at least two years of active ministry, contrasting with the apparent single year of the Synoptics. He also differs from them in his chronology of the Last Supper and crucifixion. He narrates incidents not found in them (wine miracle, raising of Lazarus, coming of the 'Greeks', foot-washing), and omits others. These omissions include some significant episodes, e.g. Jesus' temptation, his baptism (only referred to indirectly), his agony in the garden, his words of interpretation over the bread and the wine at the Last Supper (though note 6.51–8).

The disciples are also handled differently. Their call follows a different pattern; they are never called 'apostles',[6] and are not sent out until after the resurrection (contrast Mk 6.7–13; Mt.10.1, 5–15; Lk. 9.1–6). The names of the Twelve are not listed, and they are rarely mentioned as a group (only at 6.67, 71; 20.24). Neither Levi/Matthew, nor Bartholomew, nor Simon the Zealot, nor James and John are mentioned by name (though note 21.2); but other disciples appear, including Nathanael, Lazarus, and the mysterious 'beloved disciple'. Several disciples take a more active part than in the Synoptics – Philip, Andrew, Thomas, and Judas (not Iscariot). Women too feature quite prominently, notably the Samaritan woman (not in the Synoptics), Martha and Mary of Bethany, Jesus' mother, and Mary Magdalene. This has raised questions about the role of women in John's 'community'.

John's Passion Narrative also differs considerably from the Synoptics. Jesus appears before Annas as well as Caiaphas, but not before the Sanhedrin. He has a long dialogue with Pilate, whereas in the Synoptics he is virtually silent. He carries his own cross instead of having it carried for him. Only John tells of the seamless robe, Jesus' thirst, his spear wound, and his final cry, 'It is accomplished'. John alone relates the generous anointing of his body by Nicodemus and Joseph of Arimathea (contrast Mk 16.1, where the women go to the tomb on Easter morning to anoint the body). There are also substantial differences in the Resurrection Narratives. These differences also call for an explanation. Does John preserve independent traditions, or is he retelling familiar stories creatively to bring out his theological message? Is he seeking to 'correct' the Synoptics and improve on their accounts?

There are also more subtle differences of style and emphasis between John and the Synoptics. Jesus' speech is more enigmatic and repetitive, especially in the Supper Discourses. Contrasting abstractions like truth and falsehood, 'above' and 'below', 'of this world' and 'not of this world', regularly appear. Has John fresh sources from a different cultural background? Has he deliberately transposed Jesus' teaching into a new key? There can be no doubt that it is presented differently from in the Synoptics. The Kingdom of God is mentioned only in 3.3–5. Ethical teaching is very limited, with nothing on poverty and wealth (contrast Mt. 5—7; Lk. 6.20–49); no 'eschatological discourse' (contrast Mk 13; Mt. 24; Lk. 17.22–37; 21.5–36). There are no narrative parables with their vivid illustrations from everyday peasant life. Their function is fulfilled by symbolic images – light and darkness, flesh and spirit, etc. – or metaphors of water, bread, shepherd, and vine. Jesus' memorable, pithy 'wisdom' sayings, like 'Seek and you shall find', 'You cannot serve God and money', are replaced by reflective discourses. The focus on Jesus' person is intense, and the christology 'high': Jesus is the pre-existent divine Word, the revealer of God's nature, endowed with supernatural knowledge and authority to give life and to judge. Whereas the Synoptics attribute hardly any explicit christological claims to Jesus, John represents him as aware of his divine origin, and claiming unity with God. It is this picture of Jesus' own self-awareness that has most troubled scholars concerned with John's historical accuracy.

Much depends on what sort of work John is writing. Is he attempting a 'blow by blow' factual account of what Jesus said and did? Is he giving an imaginative reflection on Jesus' life and ministry with little relationship to 'the historical Jesus'? Or is it something in between? It will help us in considering these questions to examine how John has been interpreted in the past, and some of the different approaches current today.

2

The Reception of John's Gospel

In recent years interest has grown in how texts have historically been interpreted and in their influence. Such study (known in German as *Wirkungsgeschichte*) is important for biblical texts, which have had a major impact on scholarship, the Church, and society. This chapter explores (a) how John was interpreted from earliest days to the Reformation; (b) how scholarly understanding was transformed by historical-critical analysis; (c) John's reception in recent literary, feminist, and other studies. It concludes by outlining the approach of the present work.

Church Fathers to the Reformation

The story of this Gospel's influence begins within the New Testament itself, since the Epistles of John appear to comment on some of its themes. Written probably by a different author, before *c.* 100 CE, these writings apply the Gospel's teaching on truth, love, and the person of Jesus to a new situation involving a split arising out of different interpretations of its christology (1 Jn 2.19; 2 Jn 7–9). A little later, Ignatius (d. *c.* 107 CE), bishop of Syrian Antioch, echoed phrases from John, speaking of Jesus as 'the door of the Father' (*Phld.*, 9.1; cf. Jn 10.9) and the Spirit knowing whence it comes and whither it goes (*Phld.*, 7.1; cf. Jn 3.8). Justin Martyr (mid-2nd cent.) spoke of Jesus as the Word who 'became flesh', and interpreted being 'born again' (Jn 3.3–5) as referring to baptism (*1 Apol.*, 32, 61). Around the same time, Tatian, a Syrian writer who was converted to Christianity while studying rhetoric at Rome, indicated his acceptance of John as Scripture by including it in his *Diatessaron*, 'Through Four', harmonizing the Gospels. John was also cited by Theophilus of Antioch (later 2nd cent.), an apologist who sought to commend Christianity to outsiders. He used Stoic terminology to expound the Christian faith, making much play with the concept of the *logos* and distinguishing the *logos endiathetos* ('immanent word'), present in God before creation, from the *logos prophorikos* ('expressed word') after creation. He quotes directly from the Prologue, attributing it explicitly to 'John' (*Autol.*, 2.22).

Other early Christian leaders, known as controversialists, used John to defend what they saw as the correct form of Christianity against 'unorthodox' views. Foremost among these was Irenaeus (*c.* 130–*c.* 200), bishop of Lyons, whose name ironically means 'peaceful'. He saw John as one of four pillars upholding the Church (the other three being the Synoptics), and used it extensively in his treatise *Adversus haereses* ('Against Heresies'). He is the first patristic author known to ascribe John to an eyewitness, identifying its author as 'the disciple of the Lord, who lay in his bosom' (3.11). Among those opposed by Irenaeus were the Phrygian Montanists, whose movement, known as the New Prophecy, was deeply influenced by John's promise of the Paraclete to lead into all truth (16.13), and whose charismatic ideas and practices were seen as a serious threat to 'Catholic' order (Culpepper, 1994, pp. 120f.; Trevett, 1996). Irenaeus also strongly attacked Gnostics, whose name derives from the Greek *gnōsis*, 'knowledge', because they stressed the importance of knowledge of God for salvation. Theirs was a complex system of belief with roots in older oriental thought, combining elements from Greek philosophy, Judaism, and Christianity in elaborate mythological speculation. The Gnostics had a dualistic outlook, seeing a sharp dichotomy between spirit and matter, good and evil, often taking a negative view of creation. In John they found elements that could feed such beliefs, including contrasts between light and darkness, truth and falsehood, flesh and spirit, and negative uses of 'the world'; but other aspects of John's message were neglected.

Ptolemaeus (mid-2nd cent.), an early Valentinian Gnostic, composed a commentary on John's Prologue, while the better-known Heracleon wrote extensively on the Gospel (Pagels, 1973). It was also exploited in other Gnostic writings, including those discovered since 1945 at Nag Hammadi in Egypt (Robinson, 1977). These include the *Gospel of Truth*, ascribed to Valentinus (? *c.* 150 CE), the *Trimorphic Protennoia* (? *c.* 200), and the *Gospel of Philip* (? 3rd cent.). In the face of such extensive use of John by 'heretics', Irenaeus' championship must have played an important role in ensuring its acceptance into the Christian canon.[1] To sum up this early period: John was used for pastoral exhortation, for apologetics to pagans, for polemics against those perceived as heretics, and as a source for Gnostic and Christian teaching.

In the third century two main schools of biblical interpretation dominated: the Alexandrine, which made much use of allegorical exegesis, and the Antiochene, favouring more literal interpretations. Origen (*c.* 185–*c.* 254), former head of the Alexandrine Catechetical School, was immensely learned in theology, philosophy, and grammatical and biblical studies, including Hebrew and textual criticism (cf. his *Hexapla*). He developed a threefold system of exegesis giving passages a literal, moral, and allegorical (or 'spiritual') sense. His commentary on John was apparently written in response to an invitation to refute

Heracleon. It is on a massive scale, and unfinished: after 15 years' work writing 32 'books' of commentary (not all of which have survived) he reached only 13.33; his comments on 1.1–17 fill five books! Believing in verbal inspiration, he wrestled with the problem of differences between John and the other Evangelists by harmonizing their accounts where possible and ingeniously allegorizing. He proposed, for example, allegorical interpretations of Jesus' Temple 'cleansing' in which it symbolized Christ's purging of his Church, and the coming of the Word to the individual soul; the expelled animals stood for different types of human beings, the oxen being the 'earthly', the sheep the 'foolish and sensual', and the doves the 'light-headed and easily-swayed' (Wiles, 1960, pp. 44f.; Trigg, 1983, pp. 151f.).

Another famous allegorizer was Augustine (354–430), who wrote ten volumes of *Tractates*, 'Lectures', on John and a *Harmony of the Gospels* where he systematically sought to reconcile John's differences from the Synoptics, e.g. by postulating two separate Temple cleansings (*Harm.* 2.129). Augustine had a huge admiration for John, seeing him as a preacher of sublime truths, and compared him to a soaring eagle (*Tract. Ev. Jo.*, 36.5 and elsewhere; for examples of his allegorization, see 17.4–7). The chief problem with such allegorical exegesis is exercising control over the imagination: interpreters all too easily give the text the meaning they want. Thus Cyril of Alexandria (d. 444) took Jesus' seamless tunic to stand for the Virgin Birth, whereas Cyprian (d. 258) saw it as symbolizing the unity of the Church, reflecting the unity of the Godhead. John describes it as woven 'without seam, from the top throughout' (19.23); from this Cyprian deduces that the Church's unbreakable bond of unity comes from the top, i.e. from God (*Unit. Eccles.*, 7). In contrast, Theodore of Mopsuestia (*c.* 350–428), an Antiochene scholar, simply comments that seamless garments were once a common form of dress, though they had died out except for soldiers' uniforms (Wiles, 1960, p. 25).

The Antiochenes did not limit themselves to simple grammatical or factual exegesis. They also used the Bible to draw 'spiritual' and churchly lessons. Thus Chrysostom (*c.* 347–407), a leading member of this school, used the paralysed man in John 5 as a model of perseverance for staying so many years by the pool. He saw Jesus' warning to him (5.14) as supporting the doctrine of hell fire (*Hom. Jo.*, 37), and the pool apparently as standing for baptism, as did other Church Fathers (Wiles, 1960, p. 51). He was clearly reading into the text beliefs held for other reasons. Today scholars are wary of such 'eisegesis'; but these Church leaders were not attempting modern historical criticism. They accepted Scripture as divinely inspired, and interpreted it according to the methods of their day; for them it was a natural quarry for moral lessons and doctrine alike. It was also a tool to correct and chastise those with whom they disagreed. A sad feature of some patristic exegesis is the use of John (among other texts) to attack Jews for their 'unbelief': thus Chrysostom cited 12.35 to accuse them of walking in darkness (*Hom. Jo.*, 48), while Cyril used 19.13–16 to charge them with 'murdering' Jesus. Chrysostom, in particular, has been heavily criticized for his sermons *Adversus Ioudaios* (preached between 387 and 389).[2] Yet these were directed not against Jews, but Christian converts from Judaism who were still participating in Jewish festivals and other observances (Wilken, 1983). It is important that such texts are read in their historical context and in the light of the rhetorical conventions of their day.

On the doctrinal side, John's identification of Jesus with the *logos*, existing before creation, and 'only-begotten' Son, simultaneously human and divine, played a vital role in the development of Trinitarian dogma, featuring prominently in Arian and other controversies (Pollard, 1970). John's images of Jesus coming down from heaven and becoming incarnate profoundly influenced the formulation of the creeds: 'Who for us men, and for our salvation came down from heaven, and was incarnate ...' (Nicene, i.e. Niceno-Constantinopolitan, Creed), as did his reference to the Holy Spirit as 'the life-giver' (cf. Kelly, 1972, esp. pp. 139–43, 341).

Some Fathers undertook work more like modern critical scholarship. Dionysius the Great (d. *c.* 264) used linguistic criteria to separate the authorship of Revelation from that of John's Gospel, declining to identify the author of Revelation with 'the disciple who reclined on Jesus' breast' (Eusebius, *HE*, VII.25). Both Jerome (*c.* 345–420) and Origen worked on establishing a sound text; Antiochene scholars studied grammatical usage. Additionally John played a role in popular imagination, in the development of legends (Culpepper, 1994, esp. ch. 7), and in art with the Cana miracle, the Samaritan woman, and the raising of Lazarus featuring in catacomb paintings, early mosaics, and murals.

Devotional, controversial, dogmatic, and imaginative interpretations dominated the understanding of John throughout the medieval period. A type of fourfold exegesis (a development of Origen's threefold system) became common, involving literal, moral, allegorical, and mystical interpretations. The *Glossa Ordinaria*, a standard medieval commentary, included *catenae* (chains of quotations) from Fathers and other scholars. Rupert of Deutz (*c.* 1075–1129) was among those writing new commentaries. He favoured mystical and allegorical interpretations, while Albertus Magnus, Thomas Aquinas, and Bonaventure preferred more literal exegesis (Schnackenburg, 1968, p. 207). An outstanding commentator was Nicolas de Lyra (*c.* 1270–1349), a converted French Jew, who became a Franciscan. He was one of the few medieval Christian scholars to know Hebrew, and made extensive use of rabbinic and other Jewish materials in his *Postillae*, 'Comments' (Krey and Smith, 2000, pp. 223–49).

Alongside such scholarly study came creative interpretations in medieval mystery plays, music, illuminated manuscripts (e.g. the Book of Kells), and other art. Numerous churches possess wooden rood screens depicting Mary and the 'beloved disciple' (understood as the apostle John) flanking Jesus on the cross. A long tradition of religious painting continued through the Renaissance and beyond. Subjects included *The Wedding at Cana* by Gérard David (1503), *Jesus and the Woman of Samaria* by Filippino Lippi, Rembrandt's risen Christ showing his wounds to Thomas (1634) and his appearance to Mary Magdalene dressed as a gardener (1638). Particularly dramatic is Rembrandt's *Raising of Lazarus* (*c.* 1630), where Jesus stands, right arm raised high, gazing with an intent, almost anguished, expression, at the recumbent, half-awakened Lazarus, who grasps the edge of his coffin as if to rise; Martha, Mary, and three elderly Jews look on in amazement.[3] Among music inspired by this Gospel is Bach's *St John Passion* and numerous settings of the *Stabat Mater*.

With the rise of humanism came revived interest in biblical languages and textual criticism, notably by Erasmus (d. 1536). John played its part in Reformation controversies, especially over the interpretation of the Eucharist. The Reformers, led by Luther (1483–1546), saw Scripture as the sole source of authority, rejecting allegory (much used by the Roman Catholic Church) in favour of the 'natural sense' of the words. Several wrote commentaries on John, including Calvin (1509–1564), who saw it as a 'key to open the door' to understanding the other Gospels (Parker, 1959, p. 6); his commentary still offers illuminating insights. Luther also admired John and wrote several volumes of sermons on it; but they do not show him at his best, being marred by tendentious and crudely polemical outbursts against 'the schismatic spirits', 'Papists', 'Turks' (i.e. Muslims), and 'the Jews' (Pelikan, 1957, pp. 17, etc.; 1959, pp. 348f.). His later work, *On the Jews and their Lies* (1543), goes further, directly inciting hatred and violence against Jews, and so frequently maligning them that scholars hesitated to publish it for fear of misuse (Bertram, in Sherman, 1971, p. 123); it shocked even Luther's contemporaries. This was not an exegetical work, but it does cite John along with other New Testament writings in support of its views.

Historical-Critical Analysis

The eighteenth century saw fresh challenges to the interpretation of Scripture from the Enlightenment, with its distrust of authority and tradition, and its application of reason to intellectual enquiry. The rise of historical criticism in Germany is generally traced to this period (Kümmel, 1973, pp. 51–119): it involves interpreting texts as objectively as possible, free from restraints of ecclesiastical control. Practitioners may accept the Bible's truth claims or be agnostic about them. Questions of authorship, genre, purpose, sources, and redaction loom large, but there is also interest in theological content, historicity, and *Sitz-im-Leben*, 'setting in life' (Krentz, 1975; Marshall, 1979).

An early effect of historical criticism was to challenge the long-accepted view of the Apostle John as author, and the Gospel's historical reliability for Jesus' life and teaching (Ashton, 1991, pp. 9–43). John's Gospel tended to be seen as fundamentally 'Hellenistic', indebted to Platonic, Stoic, and Gnostic thought, and its final composition was placed well into the second century CE. It was generally assumed to be dependent on the Synoptics. Detailed literary and source analysis led to the discovery of anomalies (*aporiae*), with resulting theories of displacement (accidental misplacing of sections of text) and multiple sources and editions. In continental Europe, scholars such as Faure (1922) sought to recover an original *Grundschrift*, 'basic document', possibly a *Wunderbuch* or 'miracle book'. Nevertheless, some continued to maintain both apostolic authorship and historical reliability. Outstanding among these was B. F. Westcott, who did much to establish a sound text of the New Testament. He produced a five-stage argument that: (a) the author of John was a Jew; (b) he was a Jew from Palestine; (c) he was an eyewitness; (d) he was an apostle; (e) he was John, the son of Zebedee (1919, pp. v–xxv; orig. edn 1880). Other scholars also affirmed the Jewish character of John in contrast to those who saw its author as a 'Hellenist'. Schlatter (1902) cited numerous parallels in rabbinic literature, as did Odeberg (1929). Thus both radicals and conservatives produced differing results from the same historical-critical method.

An important group around this time was the *Religionsgeschichtliche Schule*, 'History of Religions School', who interpreted New Testament texts in the light of their contemporary religious setting. Reitzenstein and Bousset compared John's ideas with those of Hellenistic 'mystery cults'. Bultmann (1925) drew on newly published Mandaean texts (in Aramaic) to interpret John. The Mandaeans, who lived in the area that is now part of Iraq and Iran, were strongly dualistic in their thought, their beliefs centring on the 'great king of light' ('the great life') and his opponent, the ruler of the realm of darkness. Bultmann made extensive use of their writings in his influential commentary (1971; 1st edn 1941); but in his enthusiasm for the new discoveries he over-estimated their significance. The Mandaean texts date from a much later period than John, their so-called redeemer myth not being securely attested before the eighth century CE, and are 'an extraordinary farrago of theology, myth, fairy-tale, ethical instruction, ritual ordinances, and what purports to be history' (Dodd, 1953, p. 115). Bultmann is also famous for his existential reading of John and for his source-criticism (Fergusson, 1992, pp. 94–106).

Other writings that have influenced Johannine interpretation are the Hermetic tractates from Egypt (*Corpus Hermeticum*), dating to around the second and third centuries CE (though a few texts may be earlier). These were reputedly written by Hermes Trismegistos, 'Thrice-greatest',[4] who dialogues with his sons on topics such as truth, knowledge, light, and rebirth, in language similar to John's. The *Hermetica* speak of *Logos*, 'Word', or *Nous*, 'Mind', as the divine agent in creation and an intermediary between God and humanity, and see salvation as lying in knowledge of God (cf. Jn 17.3: 'This is eternal life, that they may know you, the only true God ...'). Dodd used these writings extensively in his major work *The Interpretation of John* (1953). He also adduced parallels to John from the writings of Philo (*c.* 20 BCE–*c.* 50 CE), an Alexandrine Jew who interpreted Judaism in the light of Greek philosophy. Philo frequently mentions the *logos*, speaking of it as 'divine', and as 'God's first-born son'. Dodd concluded that John was written to commend Christianity to educated pagans and Hellenized Jews familiar with such concepts.

Other texts used to interpret John are the Coptic Gnostic library from Nag Hammadi (already discussed), the *Odes of Solomon*,[5] and the Dead Sea Scrolls, discovered at Qumran from 1947 (Martínez, 1996; Vermes, 1998). The Dead Sea Scrolls, written in Hebrew or Aramaic, are especially important as coming from Palestine itself and definitely pre-dating John (Qumran was destroyed in 70 CE). Like other writings already mentioned, they feature polarities between good and evil, light and darkness, truth and falsehood, and contain verbal parallels to John. Some scholars were so impressed by these that they concluded that John must have had direct links with Qumran.[6] But some of the phrases and ideas which he shares with the Scrolls are found in other Jewish sources, including the Septuagint (LXX or Greek Old Testament) and the *Testaments of the Twelve Patriarchs*.[7] The Dead Sea Scrolls are especially valuable for the light they shed on Jewish exegetical methods, and for providing a Jewish context for aspects of John's christology.

Their publication led to what has been called the 'new look' on John (Robinson, 1962, pp. 94–106; Smalley, 1978, ch. 1), in which it was acclaimed as no longer 'Hellenistic', but truly 'Jewish'.[8] This in turn led to more positive assessments of its historical reliability and fresh support for the idea of apostolic authorship (e.g. Morris, 1969, 1972). Such scholars were strongly influenced by Gardner-Smith (1938), who argued that John was independent of the Synoptics, relying on oral traditions. These ideas were seemingly reinforced by Dodd's second major work (1963). Armed with these materials, Robinson (1976, 1985) argued for a date of composition before 70 CE.

The 'new look' never caught on in continental Europe. Scholars there continued to question John's historical worth, and to maintain his dependence on the Synoptics or other written sources (e.g. Nicol, 1972; Neirynck, 1977; Boismard et al., 1977). In Britain, Barrett (1955, 1978) supported John's dependence on Mark and Luke, while others opted for a compromise that John knew traditions close to the Synoptics, but not the Gospels themselves (e.g. Lindars, 1972). Others, from Germany and the USA, preferred to talk of cross-currents or interlocking connections between the Johannine and Synoptic traditions (Schnackenburg, 1968, p. 42; Carson, 1991, p. 51).

Recent years have witnessed a proliferation of commentaries on John (see Edwards, 1992), including Schnackenburg's magisterial three-volume work (ET 1968–82), and Brown's monumental Anchor Bible Commentary (1966). Both these scholars initially accepted a link between this Gospel and the Apostle John, but later changed their minds; both postulated a long complex tradition-history. Johannine scholarship has also flourished in numerous monographs and articles, some strongly influenced by sociological theory and social-scientific analysis, especially Berger and Luckmann (1967). This has led to a widespread hypothesis that John stems from a small community[9] with a 'sectarian' outlook, locked in bitter conflict with the Jewish Synagogue (the proponents differ over the degree of bitterness and sectarianism).[10] This hypothesis has become so popular that it is often simply assumed. Yet problems remain that have not been properly tackled, including the complexity of the community's hypothetical development, its supposed transfer from Palestine to Asia Minor, and the sociological basis for its isolation and 'sectarianism' (cf. Caird, 1980; King, 1984; Edwards, 1996a, pp. 108–11; Dokka, 1999). Serious questions have also been raised about the nature and dating of the 'Synagogue ban' that is supposed to have triggered the conflict. Not all recent historical-critical work is concerned with such issues. There has also been solid exegetical scholarship and insightful work on broader topics of Johannine theology.

Newer Literary and Other Approaches

Some are dissatisfied with the ostensibly objective historical-critical method. They believe that too much effort has been spent on 'excavating' biblical books as if they were archaeological tells, while failing to appreciate the texts as literary wholes (cf. Alter and Kermode, 1987).

This has given rise to fresh approaches including narrative, reader-response, feminist, and liberationist criticisms (cf. Barton, 1998). Narrative criticism seeks to enable readers to understand texts without reference to their literary development or historical context. One of the first scholars to apply it to John was Culpepper (1983). He analysed the Gospel under headings such as 'narrator', 'plot', and 'characters', drawing attention to many conventions previously taken for granted, for example, the omniscient, omnipresent narrator, and the difference between the real author and the implied author evoked by the text. He and others (e.g. Davies, 1992; Stibbe, 1993a, b, 1994) have also highlighted narrative devices and ironies. Such critics have done much to open people's eyes to the literary artistry of this Gospel, and to redress the balance of more atomistic historical criticism. But their works are sometimes marred by technical jargon and over-elaborate analyses (examples in Mlakuzhyil, 1987, ch. 2).

Reader-response criticism concentrates on how texts are received by readers, whether actual, 'authorial' (the audience assumed by the author), 'narrative', or 'implied'. Its techniques are similar to those of narrative criticism, and are often applied alongside it. Reader-response critics are interested in how readers' prior knowledge affects their understanding. Like narrative critics, they usually reject the concept of authorial intention, assuming that there is no single correct way to read a text. Jasper (1998, p. 31), for example, calls the text 'an intangible substance', which each new reader 'puts on' according to her or his own desires and anxieties. This approach easily leads to idiosyncratic readings (e.g. Staley, 1988). At the same time reader-response critics have done a good task in heightening awareness of the presuppositions all readers bring to texts, as pointed out long ago by Bultmann. It is now widely recognized that interpretation is affected not only by people's religious and philosophical beliefs, but also by their gender, ethnic origins, social class, and life-experience. Reader-response criticism has been applied to John by Davies (1992), Moloney (e.g. 1993), and contributors to Segovia (1996, 1998).

Feminist and liberationist approaches, sometimes called 'advocacy criticism' (Brown, 1997, pp. 27f.), are ideological, proposing ways of reading texts which can change attitudes. Many of them denounce the evils of 'patriarchy', 'hierarchy', and 'imperialism' and actively seek to promote equality and mutuality between women and men, and between people of different 'classes' or cultural and economic backgrounds. Feminist critics are especially interested in how women read texts, and how texts affect women. A leading exponent is Fiorenza, who argues that biblical texts are essentially androcentric (male-centred) and 'kyriocentric' (treating men as dominant in society), and need deconstruction.

She therefore advocates a 'hermeneutic of suspicion', whereby texts are read not just on their surface level, but with a view to uncovering what has been suppressed. She argues that women once played a much larger role in the Jesus movement than one might suppose from the New Testament (e.g. Fiorenza 1983, 1993a, 1995), and that John reflects an inclusive, egalitarian community, some of whose leaders were women (1983, pp. 323–34; for criticisms, see Ng, 2002).

Among other feminist scholars, O'Day (1992), Reinhartz (1994), and Schneiders (1999) all see John's portrayal of women as basically sympathetic. Fehribach (1998), however, is highly critical of his 'androcentric' attitudes, seeing John as using his female characters to advance his portrayal of Jesus as 'the messianic bridegroom'. Schneiders has the most self-conscious methodology, combining literary, feminist, reader-response, and historical-critical approaches. She reads John as essentially a symbolic narrative that can be decoded for spiritual edification (cf. Alexandrine allegorical exegesis). She also argues that its author was a woman. So far only women scholars have been mentioned; but some male scholars show sympathy with feminist perspectives, notably Scott (1992), Maccini (1996), Moloney (e.g. 1985, 1993), and Brown (1979, pp. 183–98).

Liberation theologians (like some feminists) are not concerned with detailed exegesis of texts, but rather their impact on society and ways in which they may be used to foster ideals like justice and freedom. Gutiérrez (1984) is inspired by John's teaching on the Spirit and his image of the 'living water'; Schillebeeckx finds in John a paradigm for a non-hierarchical pattern of Church ministry, seeing the Johannine corpus as 'a biblical admonition against any legalistic garb for church authority' (1981, p. 29). Rensberger interprets John's reference to new birth (3.3–5) as meaning that Christians must identify with those on the borders of society, viewing John's 'community' as a powerless, marginal group struggling against the powerful Synagogue and challenging the values of the world (1988, pp. 113–16; cf. 1998, 1999). One problem with this view, as Rensberger is well aware, is John's depiction of 'the Jews' as Jesus' opponents – a people historically discriminated against and oppressed, their oppression culminating in the Holocaust. In recent years John's underlying 'anti-Jewishness' has become a focus of concern to those seeking to eliminate anti-Semitism and improve Christian–Jewish relations, and has been the subject of academic projects and colloquia (see Farmer, 1999; Bieringer *et al.*, 2001), and much writing.

The Approach of the Present Work

This study is based on the historical-critical method and the belief that knowledge of the literary, social, historical, and religious settings of texts enhances understanding and prevents misconceptions. Its quest is to discover, as far as possible, what the original author(s) of John intended to communicate – the true work of exegesis. Newer criticisms will not be neglected where they are illuminating, but since a Gospel is primarily a theological work, read for its religious message rather than its literary merit, the chief focus will be on content. The task will be not only to expound and clarify its message, but also to assess it critically (what the Germans call *Sachkritik*, 'content criticism'). At the same time it will be recognized that for Christians John is not just a writing of historical, theological, and antiquarian interest, but a Gospel in the full sense of the word – with power to communicate, thrill, and inspire. It is hoped that, from the rather clinical discussion of issues like authorship and sources, and the analysis of how individual passages may be interpreted, a sense will emerge of the original author's aim of conveying a life-enhancing message, still relevant to the Church and the contemporary world. 'These things are written that you may believe that Jesus is the Anointed, the Son of God, and that believing you may have life in his Name' (20.31).

3

The Question of Authorship

Traditionally this Gospel has been ascribed to the Apostle John, the son of Zebedee, identified with the disciple who reclined on Jesus' bosom, also credited with writing Revelation and 1–3 John. Since the rise of critical scholarship, these attributions have been challenged and increasingly rejected. This chapter reviews the evidence for apostolic authorship of John and argues that a more complex theory of composition is necessary.

The 'Beloved Disciple'

The key to the traditional attribution is the figure known as the 'beloved disciple', whom John introduces at the Last Supper with the words, 'There was reclining in Jesus' bosom one of his disciples, whom Jesus loved' (13.23). This figure reappears at the crucifixion, when Jesus commends his mother and the 'beloved disciple' to one another (19.26f.). He is generally assumed to be the same person as the anonymous witness who testifies to the flow of blood and water from Jesus' side (19.35), and the 'other disciple' who, after Jesus' arrest, follows him to the High

Priest's house, and gets Peter admitted to the courtyard (18.15f.). After the resurrection he runs to the tomb with Peter, enters it, 'and believes' (20.2–10). In the Epilogue he is one of the seven fishermen who see the risen Jesus on the shore, being the first to recognize him (21.7). All these references occur in the Passion and Resurrection Narratives. However, some scholars suggest the 'beloved disciple' might also be identified with the anonymous disciple of the Baptist, who became a follower of Jesus along with Andrew (1.35–40). This seems unlikely: there is no hint of this in the text (contrast 20.2) and the reference is widely separated from all the 'beloved disciple's' other appearances.

The most intriguing passage is 21.24, which says of the 'beloved disciple': 'This is the disciple who bears witness about these things and who wrote these things, and we know that his witness is true'. From antiquity it was assumed that this testimony concerns the authorship of the Gospel. But there are problems: the plural 'we know' suggests an authenticating group distinct from the main author. It is widely thought that 21.24 was added to give credibility to John's narrative.[1] Moreover, the episode comes in what appears to be an appendix, with its own conclusion (21.25) separate from that of the main Gospel (20.30f.). One motive for its addition may have been to explain the death of the 'beloved disciple' when some were expecting him to survive until Jesus' second coming. Compare Jesus' words to Peter: 'If I wish him to remain until I come, what is that to you?' (21.22); hence the Evangelist's explanation that a rumour had started that the 'beloved disciple' would not die, but Jesus had never said this (cf. Brown, 1966, pp. 1118f.). The 'beloved disciple' should therefore be regarded as John's 'ideal' author (Bauckham, 1993b, pp. 21–44), rather than its actual author.

However, many scholars believe that the 'beloved disciple' is not a real, historical person at all, but a literary fiction. It seems odd that one individual should be singled out as the disciple whom Jesus loved. Could the 'beloved disciple' symbolize a group, perhaps even all authentic disciples? Bultmann (1971, pp. 484f.) argued that the 'beloved disciple' stands for 'Gentile Christendom' – seen as authentic Christianity – over against 'Jewish Christendom', represented by Peter (and also Jesus' mother). Other scholars have been quick to point out the awkwardness of having a purely symbolic figure interacting with real people. A compromise is to see the 'beloved disciple' as a historical disciple who knew Jesus, idealized as especially loved, and as a model disciple and totally reliable witness.

Possible Identifications

If the 'beloved disciple' was a real person, however idealized, it is legitimate to ask whether he can reasonably be identified with any known figure from early Christianity. Here conjectures become rife: John Mark, Matthias, the Apostle Paul, Apollos, Philip, the rich young man of the Synoptics, Lazarus, Thomas, Judas (not Iscariot), John the son of Zebedee, John 'the Elder' have all been proposed (Charlesworth, 1995). Evidential foundation is lacking for the first six of these, which need not detain us further. Sanders and Mastin (1968, esp. p. 31) argued for Lazarus: he is the only named male individual described elsewhere as loved by Jesus (11.3, 5), and coming from Bethany he could be a possible source for John's unique materials centring on Jerusalem. But once this has been said, there is nothing substantial to add (we can dismiss the pious conjecture that he might have composed the Gospel in gratitude at being raised from the dead). The case for Judas (not Iscariot), mentioned once by name (14.22), has been put by Gunther. He claims that this figure is Jesus' brother of the same name (cf. Mk 6.3; Mt. 13.55), arguing that the reason why the 'beloved disciple' is not mentioned until the Passion Narrative is that Jesus' brother was late in joining the Twelve (1981, p. 127). His proposal falls on three counts: first, John nowhere indicates that this Judas is a relative of Jesus; second, it is unlikely that the Synoptics understood this Judas as Jesus' brother;[2] third, nothing in John specifically links this Judas with the 'beloved disciple'.

Charlesworth himself favours the Apostle Thomas (1995, esp. chs. 4, 7, 10). He argues that Thomas is named as one of the seven fishermen to whom Jesus showed himself (21.2), one of whom must have been the 'beloved disciple' (at least for the author of Jn 21). In 20.27, the risen Jesus invites him to place his finger in the nail-wounds and his hand in Jesus' side; this is because Thomas has said he will not believe unless he does this (20.25). But how, Charlesworth asks, did Thomas know about the spear-wound unless he was the (beloved) disciple who witnessed it? In 11.16 Thomas is willing to die for Jesus. For Charlesworth he is a perfect candidate for the 'beloved disciple', being a witness of both Jesus' death and resurrection, and a model of discipleship, moving from scepticism to full faith in his great confession, 'My Lord and my God' (20.28).

These arguments rest upon a reading of the text that cannot bear close scrutiny. Charlesworth claims that Thomas is never represented as meeting the 'beloved disciple', who left at 20.10, so he cannot know about the spear-wound unless he *is* the 'beloved disciple' (1995, p. 423). But this is absurd. In 20.25 the other disciples tell Thomas about Jesus' appearance to them, an appearance at which he showed them his hands and his side (20.20). Readers can surely imagine for themselves that Thomas heard about Jesus' wounds as well as the fact of his appearance. Nor does Thomas' scepticism in 20.25 fit well with the statement that the 'beloved disciple' 'saw and believed' in 20.8. Charlesworth makes much of apocryphal traditions concerning Thomas as Jesus' twin, but in none of these is there any hint that he was ever identified with the 'beloved disciple' or connected with the authorship of John. In short, readers of the Gospel cannot reasonably be expected to identify the 'beloved disciple' with Lazarus, Judas, or Thomas.

John the Son of Zebedee (and John the 'Elder')

There is, however, one New Testament figure regularly associated with authorship in patristic sources – John, the son of Zebedee, disciple and apostle. How reliable is this tradition? First the external testimonies will be considered, and then the internal evidence. Theophilus of Antioch quotes the opening words of the Prologue, describing it as the work of John, one of the 'spirit-bearing men' (*Autol.*, 2.22). According to Eusebius (*c.* 260–*c.* 340), Irenaeus specifically identifies its author as 'John, the disciple of the Lord, who also rested on his breast', adding that he published the Gospel while staying at Ephesus in Asia (*HE*, V.8.4; cf. III.23.1). Eusebius also attests that Polycrates (2nd cent. CE), bishop of Ephesus, described John as a priest, martyr, and teacher, who slept (i.e. was buried) at Ephesus (*HE*, III.31.3; V.24.3f.). The Gnostic writers Ptolemaeus and Heracleon also attributed this Gospel, or at least the Prologue, to a disciple whom Ptolemaeus names as 'John' (Culpepper, 1994, pp. 114–19). Similar views are attested in the anti-Marcionite Prologue, and the Muratorian Canon (probably 2nd cent.). The traditional Gospel title 'According to John' may go back to this period (Hengel, 1989, pp. 74f.).

None of the above writers specifically names this 'John' as the son of Zebedee, though it is probable that he was intended. The situation is complicated by apparent references to another John, an elder (*presbyteros*), in a testimony attributed to Papias (*c.* 60–130 CE) by Eusebius (*HE*, III.39.4). This twice refers to a disciple of the Lord named John, once in the company of Andrew, Peter, and other apostles, and once as an 'elder' or 'presbyter', along with an otherwise unknown figure named Aristion. Some scholars have conjectured that John and 1–3 John were written by this second John, an idea receiving some support from the opening words of both 2 and 3 John ascribing authorship to an unnamed *presbyteros*.[3] But the passage is confused, and possibly textually corrupt; many doubt even the existence of 'John the Elder'. In any case it does not mention the authorship of any writing, nor does it link either 'John' with Ephesus (Culpepper, 1994, pp. 109–12). It therefore seems likely that when the early Fathers refer to 'John' they mean the well-known apostle, the son of Zebedee.[4]

There were, however, variant views. Those whom Epiphanius (*Pan.*

Haer. 51.3.1–6) calls the Alogoi[5] attributed John's Gospel to Cerinthus, the Apostle's traditional opponent (Eusebius *HE*, IV.14.6).[6] The presbyter Gaius also denied apostolic authorship, pointing out numerous differences between John and the Synoptics (*Dialogue with Proclus*; Culpepper, 1994, p. 121). He may have been partly motivated by his opposition to the Montanists, who made much of John, claiming direct inspiration from his Paraclete. The defence of apostolic authorship by Hippolytus of Rome (*c.* 204–5), and Irenaeus' insistence that John was written by a disciple intimate with Jesus, may have been in response to the scepticism of the Alogoi and Gaius (Gunther, 1980, pp. 414f.). Despite these doubts, by the time of Eusebius, in the later third century, the belief was firmly established that John was written by an eyewitness, John the Apostle, who was thought to have written Revelation and 1 John, the authorship of 2 and 3 John still being disputed. By around this time the Apostle John was believed to have left Jerusalem in the company of Jesus' mother. After a period of exile on Patmos (where he wrote Revelation), he was thought to have gone to Ephesus, where he wrote the Gospel and the first Johannine Epistle. He is said to have died there at a ripe old age in the reign of Trajan (98–117 CE).

In the light of this patristic witness a few conservative scholars still affirm the Apostle John as this Gospel's author (e.g. Morris, 1972; cf. Tasker, 1960). More commonly they defend the idea that he was the fountainhead of a tradition culminating in the Gospel (Carson, 1991), a view advocated also by Brown (1966) and Schnackenburg (1968) in their commentaries, though both later changed their minds. However, the majority of recent scholars reject even this possibility, for a variety of reasons. First, the traditions are not so clear-cut as our summary might suggest. (a) The New Testament itself is silent about any connection between the Apostle John and Asia Minor, though there are places where such a link might have been mentioned. (b) There is a curious absence of any reference to his presence at Ephesus in several early Fathers who might have been expected to allude to it. These include Papias, bishop of Hierapolis in Asia Minor, Polycarp, bishop of Smyrna in the same area, and Ignatius, bishop of Antioch, who wrote letters to the Ephesians and other Asian churches. (c) The idea that John lived into the reign of Trajan implies a very long life; but there is a variant tradition that John died young, being martyred with his brother James (Barrett, 1978, pp. 103f., citing various authorities including Papias).[7]

Second, the ancient views of the author as the Apostle John seem to depend on the identification of the 'beloved disciple' with the son of Zebedee. But how well-based is this? Those who support this identification argue that the 'beloved disciple' was present at the Last Supper (13.23) and must therefore be one of the Twelve. The description of him there as reclining in Jesus' bosom implies an intimate relationship, suggesting one of Jesus' close associates, i.e. Peter, James, or John. He clearly is not Peter, since Peter runs alongside the 'beloved disciple' in 20.1–10; he cannot be James, who was martyred early (Acts 12.2). The 'beloved disciple' is one of the seven fishermen to whom Jesus appears in 21.2, who include the two (unnamed) 'sons of Zebedee'. The Apostle John is never named in this Gospel, but Peter and John are associated together (13.23f.; 20.2; 21.20; possibly 18.15); they also occur as a pair in Acts (1.13; 3.1–11; 4.13–19; 8.14). It would all make sense if the 'beloved disciple' were John, the son of Zebedee.

Against this four arguments have been adduced. (i) There is no reason to assume that the 'beloved disciple' must be one of the Twelve. This group features rarely in John, and its author never states that only the Twelve were present at the Last Supper. The identification assumes that John tells exactly the same story as the Synoptics; in fact, as has already been seen, he shows considerable independence, not least in his handling of the disciples. (ii) John lacks all the special events witnessed by the Synoptic 'inner circle' – the raising of Jairus' daughter, the transfiguration, and the agony in the garden; this is odd if it rests on the testimony of the Apostle John. Once again the Gospels are being harmonized in an unscholarly way. (iii) If the 'beloved disciple' is one of the seven fishermen to whom the risen Jesus appears, he could be one of the two unnamed disciples. Some scholars also argue (iv) that John, the son of Zebedee, was an uneducated fisherman (Acts 4.13), incapable of writing this highly sophisticated Gospel with its use of Hellenistic philosophical ideas. Not all these arguments carry equal weight. To take the last point first, if the Apostle John led a long life, becoming a leader of the Church and mixing with educated people, he could have acquired sufficient knowledge of Hellenistic ideas to write this Gospel.[8] (In any case its 'Hellenistic' character has been exaggerated.) The Evangelist might have had reasons for omitting the special events witnessed by the 'inner circle': he had no need to relate the transfiguration since Jesus' divine glory shines throughout his Gospel; he has his own equivalent of Jesus' agony (12.27–36). The strongest points are probably (i) and (iii).

The chief ground for rejecting the identification of John the Apostle with the 'beloved disciple' (and hence with the implied author) is that there is no positive evidence in the text. Nothing in John 21 compels readers to understand the 'beloved disciple' as one of the 'sons of Zebedee'. Why, if 21.2 reveals the 'beloved disciple's' identity, should it be hidden again in 21.7? The author of John may have wished to remain anonymous (Marsh, 1968, p. 77). One can only speculate why: fear of persecution, though sometimes mentioned, is unlikely (the popular picture of early Christians as constantly under threat of persecution has

been greatly exaggerated). Possibly he felt no need to indicate his identity. Many Jewish and early Christian texts were originally anonymous
(e.g. 1 John, Hebrews), the question of authorship arising only when
their authority either became questioned or needed to be invoked.

Two puzzles remain: first, how did this Gospel become attributed to
the Apostle John? Possibly the attribution arose because John, 1 John,
and Revelation were already associated together by the second century
and linked with Asia Minor, especially Ephesus (where more than one
tomb purporting to be the Apostle's was shown). Revelation claims to be
by 'John' (1.1, 4, 9; 22.8); in the course of Montanist controversies, this
John (probably originally an Asian prophet) was identified as the
Apostle, the son of Zebedee. In due course all the Johannine writings
became ascribed to him.[9] Second, why does John mention the 'beloved
disciple' at all? The idea that 'the disciple whom Jesus loved' is a modest
self-designation simply fails to win conviction. One possibility is that he
was included originally as a role model for readers, and that a later editor
identified him with the Gospel's author (cf. 21.24). This does not exclude
the possibility that the 'beloved disciple' may still be based on a real
person. The fact that he is not named is no problem. Early Jewish texts
quite often refer obliquely to historical personages under enigmatic sobri-
quets, recognizable to insiders but obscure to those outside.[10] In the New
Testament one might mention 'the Elder' of 2 and 3 John, 'the beast' of
Revelation 13.11–18 (virtually certainly Nero), and 'the Elect Lady' (2 Jn
1) – if indeed this refers to a real woman. Such anonymous figures,
though based on real people, may also have a representative role.

Among scholars a popular hypothesis is that behind the figure of the
'beloved disciple' lies a well-loved leader of a Johannine community who
had recently died (cf. above, p. 19). He did not designate himself 'the
disciple whom Jesus loved', but his followers did so. Those who support
such a view often argue that this anonymous leader was in some way
opposed to the Petrine or 'apostolic' church (cf. his alleged rivalry with
Peter). They believe that the dialogue in 21.9–19 was added to the main
Gospel to rehabilitate Peter (whose earlier denials had been reported in
detail), and to resolve the tensions between these two figures (cf. Quast,
1989). Bauckham is unusual in taking John 21 as an integral part of the
Gospel, and in seeing the 'beloved disciple' as a personal disciple of Jesus
and eyewitness (1993b, esp. pp. 27, 31f.); he does, however, attribute
21.24f. to a redactor.

A Female 'Beloved Disciple' and a Woman Author?

Very recently Schneiders (1999, pp. 213–32) has suggested that the
'beloved disciple' might be understood as a woman. She claims that in

the scene at the cross when Jesus addresses his mother and the disciple whom he loved (19.26f.), the natural reading of the text is that the 'beloved disciple' is one of the named women with Jesus' mother, either Mary (wife) of Klopas or Mary Magdalene. The evident choice, she says, is Mary Magdalene (1999, p. 221). This idea can be shown to be highly improbable on several grounds. (a) In ancient Jewish society, women were put in the care of *men*, not other women. (b) Greek grammar precludes the interpretation of the 'beloved disciple' as a woman.[11] If an individual woman disciple had been intended, the form *mathētria* could have been used (cf. Acts 9.36, of Dorcas), with the corresponding feminine article, adjectives, etc. (c) The idea of a female disciple lying on Jesus' breast at the Last Supper (which would follow if the 'beloved disciple' were a woman) is culturally inappropriate. For all these reasons any identification of the 'beloved disciple' with Mary Magdalene must be rejected.

Schneiders further argues that if there were an eyewitness source this would correspond to Mary Magdalene, but she does not attribute authorship directly to her. In a complex, opaquely argued hypothesis, she sees the 'beloved disciple' as 'a kind of textual paradigm who concretely embodies the corporate authority of the Johannine school', being based on a whole series of disciples with whom the author is in sympathy. These include the Samaritan woman, whom she describes as 'the evangelist's textual alter ego', i.e. 'second self' (1999, pp. 229f.). She also hints strongly at the possibility of a female author, referring to John's sympathetic portrayals of women and their prominent roles:

> What *man* [italics mine] would have had so at heart the highlighting of women's roles in the community as to have assigned to women the apostolically significant roles and scenes assigned to the Twelve in the Synoptics, be so finely attuned to women's psychological and spiritual experience as to be able to create such scenes as the Samaritan woman and Mary Magdalene episodes, and be so concerned to defend women's autonomous relationship with Jesus as to have written these passages? (1999, p. 216)

Other scholars, too, use John's sensitive portrayals of women to support the possibility of a female author, including Scott (1992), who also makes much of John's 'sophia' christology,[12] and Fiorenza (1983). Scott argues that John's 'openness' to women reflects their leadership roles, and asks, 'Could it not also reflect something even more radical, namely that the Fourth Gospel was written by a woman?' (1992, pp. 239f.). Fiorenza regularly refers to the author of John as 's/he' and finds it astonishing that John should give such prominence to women. However, it is a fallacy that only women authors can depict women in leading roles or portray female characters sensitively (cf. Kraemer, 1991; Lefkowitz, 1991). The search for 'lost' women authors is a deliberate strategy for feminist scholars (cf. Fiorenza, 1992, pp. 28f.), and is in itself praiseworthy (as is the search for forgotten female artists, musicians, theologians, and the like); but the desire to give women their just due must not cloud academic judgement. Women authors were extremely rare in the ancient world.[13] If John had been written by a woman, this would have been such an unusual event that it would surely have left some mark on the tradition. The idea of a female author for John is about as likely as Samuel Butler's romantic conjecture that a woman composed Homer's *Odyssey* because of its sympathetic treatment of women.

Conclusions

The 'beloved disciple' cannot be convincingly identified with any specific individual from early Christianity. Probably based on a real person, whose identity may have been known to at least some of John's readers, he is deliberately left anonymous. He is not the Gospel's author, but the person whom the author (or at least whoever wrote John 21) wants readers to see as a reliable authority lying behind the Gospel. There is no reason to suppose that the actual author was female, or that John intended the 'beloved disciple' to be understood as a woman. If these conclusions seem disappointing, it must be stressed that a book's value does not depend on knowing who wrote it, but on its intrinsic worth. It will also be apparent that 'authorship' of an ancient text like John is not a straightforward question: the author may have incorporated old oral traditions, including the 'beloved disciple's' memories (if he was a historical person), or he may have had access to written sources. There were probably additions to the original Gospel, the most obvious being John 21 (though others have also been postulated). In a text used in worshipping communities, there is a distinct possibility of editing and redaction. These possibilities will be the theme of our next chapter, which concentrates on the composition and character of John's text.

4

Traditions, Sources, and the Nature of John's Writing

How did John compose his text? Did he have oral or written sources? Did he have access to any of the Synoptic Gospels? What are the origins of the materials where he differs from them? In the past, when this Gospel was attributed quite simply to the Apostle John, it was often assumed that the primary source was the author's own memory. Vivid details such as the plentiful grass at the time of the feeding miracle (6.10), or Martha's blunt exclamation, 'Lord, he's already stinking' (11.39), were thought to derive from the Evangelist's personal recollection. So too were the precise notes of time (e.g. 1.39: 'It was about four o'clock'), and the names of individuals who are anonymous in the Synoptics (e.g. 18.10, where the slave whose ear was cut off is said to have been called Malchus). Today it is generally recognized that these are the sort of details that are often added to orally transmitted, or even written, stories to bring them to life, as can be seen in later retellings of biblical stories and parallels from other literature (e.g. Greek legends). This means that one cannot assume that where John differs from the other Gospels he necessarily has a fresh source (though he may do so sometimes). The potential historical value of each unique detail needs to be assessed on its own merit.

Nor should it be assumed that the Gospel as a whole claims to be eyewitness testimony. It is true that the Prologue twice uses the first person plural: 'We have beheld his glory', and 'from his fulness we have all received grace' (1.14, 16). But these statements could express the faith of a group who witnessed Christ's glory at a spiritual level, and who have a sense of having received blessing through him (cf. 1 Jn 1.1–4). This would not preclude the possibility that some of John's circle had known Jesus personally, or that John might have interviewed people about their memories and community traditions. One passage in particular (besides 21.24, discussed earlier) claims to be eyewitness testimony. It comes in John's account of the crucifixion, when he comments in a peculiarly emphatic way on the blood and water that flowed from Jesus' side: 'He who saw this has borne witness, and his witness is reliable. He knows that he speaks the truth, so that you too may believe' (19.35). It is hard to imagine that such an explicit claim is mere literary fiction. But it refers directly to only one incident, and the possibility cannot be totally excluded of a *bona fide* addition to the text by an editor seeking to encourage trust in the narrative (Dodd, 1963, p. 14).

Possible Written Sources

The Synoptics

What written sources might have been available to John? The obvious possibility is one or more of the Synoptics. The Church Fathers seem to have assumed that John wrote last and in awareness of them. This is explicitly stated by Clement of Alexandria (*c.* 150–*c.* 215): 'John, last of all, realizing that the physical facts [*ta sōmatika*] had been made clear by the Gospels, urged by his friends and divinely moved by the Spirit, composed a spiritual Gospel' (in Eusebius, *HE*, VI.14). The word used for 'spiritual' (*pneumatikon*) can also mean 'mystical' or 'symbolic'. Patristic authors often supposed that when John supplied fresh details (like the time of day or the number of fish caught) it was for symbolic reasons, though they also believed that he corrected the other Gospels when he had additional information.

Early historical-critical scholars likewise assumed that John knew the Synoptics. Many of them were less sanguine about the possibility of fresh historical data, assuming that John's distinctive material arose mostly from his profound meditation on their stories, influenced by 'Hellenistic' ideas and developments. These views were strongly challenged by Gardner-Smith (1938). He worked right through John pointing out weaknesses in the arguments of scholars like Streeter (1924), who had postulated literary dependence on both Mark and Luke. Gardner-Smith put up a good case for believing that John preserves reliable information, probably from oral sources, about John the Baptist's ministry, and for the independence of John's healing of the official's son (sometimes thought to be dependent on the Synoptic story of the centurion's servant). But his arguments were marred by the repeated assertion that John is independent, when all he showed was that dependence had not been proved.

Gardner-Smith assumed that if John had known the Synoptics he would have had too much reverence for them to alter them in the ways commonly postulated. Thus he argued that had John known Mark, he could not have introduced the episode of Nicodemus and his spices because it contradicts Mark's account of the women coming to anoint the body on Easter morning (1938, pp. 71f.). This argument seems fallacious. In the first century CE the Synoptics were not yet regarded as canonical Gospels, verbally inspired and unalterable, and in any case parallels from Jewish historiography show that even texts regarded as divinely inspired were often rewritten to serve new purposes. Modern Synoptic scholarship demonstrates that where Matthew and Luke used Mark (and their postulated common source, usually designated 'Q') they did so with creative freedom. John would not have been thought irreverent for altering Mark any more than the Hebrew author(s) of Chronicles would be deemed disrespectful for reinterpreting 1 and 2 Kings, or the non-canonical book *Jubilees* for condensing and recasting Genesis and part of Exodus. It is striking that the author of *Jubilees* (probably a second-century CE Palestinian Jew) had no compunction about representing his text as direct revelation from God, through 'the Angel of the Presence', to Moses. He included fresh conversations, prayers, explanations, and legal ordinances, from a wide variety of sources, working up the whole into an edifying quasi-historical narrative.[1] The Jewish historian Josephus (*c.* 37–*c.* 100 CE) also rewrote biblical history with much imaginative material in his *Jewish Antiquities*. Greek and Roman biography and historiography equally support the idea that it was widely acceptable for authors to use sources very creatively.

What then are the principal reasons for assuming that John knew one or more of the Synoptics? The strongest case can made out for familiarity with Mark. John adopts the same literary genre of 'Gospel' (which Mark may have developed out of Graeco-Roman biography).[2] He follows the same basic order of events, beginning with the Baptist's witness, describing miracles and conflicts with the Jewish authorities, and culminating in a detailed Passion Narrative, and the empty tomb. Both Gospels include an anointing at Bethany and a 'triumphal entry' to Jerusalem (though they place them in a different chronological relationship). Both narrate a final meal with the disciples, Judas' betrayal, Jesus' arrest, an investigation by Jewish authorities, Peter's threefold denial, and Pilate's condemnation of Jesus. Both also include Jesus' mockery, scourging, crucifixion between two others, the drink of sour wine, women witnesses to the crucifixion, and a woman or women at the empty tomb (Mk 11.1–10; 14.1—16.8; Jn 12f.; 18—20). In both, the feeding miracle and the walking on the water are closely associated (Mk 6.30–52; Jn 6.1–21). John and Mark have Pilate ask the same question, 'Do you want me to release the King of the Jews?' (Mk 15.9; Jn 18.39). There are also some striking verbal agreements: 'Rise, take up your bed and walk' (Mk 2.11; Jn 5.8); 'loaves costing two hundred denarii' (Mk 6.37; Jn 6.7); 'expensive ointment of pure nard', worth at least 'three hundred denarii' (Mk 14.3, 5; Jn 12.3, 5). Some of these agreements involve unusual or rare words (*krabbatos*, a colloquial word for bed; *pistikos*, apparently meaning 'pure', of nard).

Some of this common material is also found in Matthew and Luke. However, it is striking that John agrees with them where they agree with

Mark, but rarely where they differ (Streeter, 1924, p. 399). John seems to show no knowledge of Q, though one Q passage has often been seen as very 'Johannine' (Mt. 11.25–7; Lk.10.21f.; note the references to 'the Son', a favourite title in John). There is little evidence to support the idea that John knew Matthew's special material ('M'), but he does have characters and incidents uniquely in common with Luke. These include the figures of Martha and Mary, with Martha's serving at supper (Jn 12.2), the name Lazarus, a visit by Peter to the empty tomb (only in some manuscripts of Luke), and an appearance of the risen Jesus to the assembled disciples in Jerusalem (Lk. 24.36–49; Jn 20.19–23).[3] John also shares with Luke the miraculous catch of fish, placed by Luke at the start of Jesus' ministry, and by John after the resurrection (Lk. 5.4–11; Jn 21.4–11), and several coincidences of wording, including Pilate's threefold proclamation of Jesus' innocence (Lk. 23.4, 14, 22; Jn 18.38; 19.4, 6), the double cry, 'Crucify him' (Lk. 23.21; Jn 19.6), the anointing of Jesus' *feet* (rather than his head, as in Mark and Matthew; Lk. 7.38; Jn 12.3), and the details that it was the right ear of the High Priest's servant that was cut off (Lk. 22.51; Jn 18.10) and that two angels were seen at the tomb (Lk. 24.4; Jn 20.12).

None of this *proves* that John used these Gospels in the form we now have them. Some of the shared materials must have been common knowledge among Christians; some may derive from common sources, or (hypothetical) earlier versions of Mark and Luke; some details might have been introduced into John's text by editors after its main composition, in the interests of harmonization. Nevertheless the precise coincidences of wording are impressive, as are the places where John appears to follow Mark's ordering of events. Taken as a whole, the evidence supports the idea that John was familiar with Mark and with some parts of Luke.[4] This does not necessarily imply that he had copies of their Gospels before him when he wrote. He may have heard stories from them through others; he may have heard them read liturgically; he may have become so familiar with them that phrases from them came unconsciously to his mind.

Did John write for an audience who might be presumed familiar at least in outline with the Synoptic stories? His account of the Baptist's witness to the descent of the Spirit on Jesus (1.32–4) presupposes that his audience knew the story of Jesus' baptism. His characterization of Thomas as 'one of the Twelve' (20.24; cf. 6.67) similarly assumes the importance of the Twelve, even though he has never described their appointment or listed their names. His reference, after the feeding miracle, to eating Jesus' flesh and drinking his blood (6.51c–8) presupposes familiarity with Jesus' interpretation of the bread and the cup at the Last Supper ('institution of the Eucharist'), not otherwise described in John (see further Bauckham, 1998a, pp. 147–71). If John did know Mark and Luke, he must have re-expressed their stories in his own style and omitted much that he did not find relevant to his special themes.

Other Potential Sources

The idea that John knew at least some of the Synoptics cannot account for all his unique materials. What other sources could he have used? Some scholars suppose that he had access to an independent, continuous Passion Narrative, which included some resurrection appearances (cf. Bultmann, 1959, 1971). There is no doubt that Jesus' passion and resurrection were extremely important for early Christians, and that they reflected on these events in the light of the Jewish Scriptures (Christian Old Testament), which they saw as foreshadowing or even foretelling them. It is certainly possible that early Christian story-telling instincts produced continuous accounts of the Passion that have not survived. The problem is one of methodology: no such independent narratives exist, and they have to be reconstructed from the Gospels. Some have attempted to do this with John by 'peeling off' what is distinctively 'Johannine' to see what remains. But this is a perilous procedure. Stylistically and theologically John's Passion and Resurrection Narratives (13, 18—20) cannot be separated from the rest of the Gospel. We simply do not have adequate tools to reconstruct any continuous written source (cf. Brown, 1994, p. 84).

One prime area where John differs from the Synoptics is in his attribution to Jesus of long speeches in a distinctive style (e.g. the Supper Discourses), differing sharply from his speech patterns in the other Gospels. Some have sought to explain this by suggesting that Jesus, when talking intimately with his disciples, used a different style from his public teaching. But this will not work. In John, Jesus speaks in the same style when confronting 'the Jews', teaching in the synagogue and Temple, conversing with individuals, or teaching the disciples privately. This style is quite different from that of the longer Synoptic discourses (e.g. Mk 13; Mt. 5—7). The *content* of these Johannine speeches and sayings also is often different, focusing on knowledge of God, and on Jesus' role as redeemer and the one sent to make God known (e.g. 17.3, 6–8); they also reveal a 'dualistic' outlook on the world.

Bultmann (e.g. 1955, pp. 10f., 1971) proposed that John used a collection of Gnostic *Offenbarungsreden*, 'revelation speeches', for his discourses. This hypothetical source, which Bultmann believed to have been originally composed in Aramaic (or Syriac), is also known as the *Redenquelle*, 'Discourse Source' (cf. Smalley, 1978, p. 104). It should be made clear that Bultmann did not picture it as a single document, and that by *Reden* he intended also conversations, since he sees John as drawing on this source for quite short sayings (as well as for the Prologue). In support of his hypothesis Bultmann cited many examples of Semitic-style poetic parallelism in John's sayings and discourses, and numerous parallels to their thought in the Mandaean writings, *Hermetica*, *Odes of Solomon*, and other 'Gnostic' literature. The problem is that the sayings cannot readily be disentangled from their narrative context (e.g. in Jn 3 and 6). Bultmann achieves continuity for his 'revelation speeches' only by postulating disruptions and transpositions in the text. There are also problems over the dating of the supposed 'Gnostic' sources. Sometimes closer parallels can be found in the Qumran texts (dated to before 70 CE), which are also dualistic in thought and contain references to 'messianic' or redeemer figures. One feature of John's discourse material that Bultmann especially stressed is the idea that Jesus came down from heaven and ascended to his Father (cf. 3.13; 6.38, 62). This descent–ascent theme is sometimes considered one of the strongest arguments for John's dependence on 'Gnostic' mythology (so Meeks, 1967, p. 297). Yet parallels are far from lacking in Jewish sources[5] (see further Smith, 1987, 40–53; Ashton, 1991, 45–50).

The upshot of all this is that direct dependence on written 'Gnostic' sources for John's discourses seems unlikely. Yet the question remains: whence did he derive the speeches that he puts on Jesus' lips where there are no Synoptic parallels? The most likely hypothesis is that he composed the bulk of them himself, seeing them as a valid means of communicating his understanding of Jesus, in the firm belief that he was guided by the Holy Spirit who Jesus had promised would lead his followers into all truth (Jn 14.16f., 26; 15.26; 16.13). Such a procedure is amply paralleled in Greek and Roman literature, in Jewish authors like Josephus, and in Christian writers like Luke in Acts. This is not to suggest that everything in John's discourses is invented. Conscientious writers, like Thucydides (1.22), attempted to include anything known (or believed) to have been said on the occasions in question, or at least to express ideas consistent with the views of the person to whom the speeches were attributed. We may presume John did the same.

In fact, the speeches and dialogues which John puts on the lips of Jesus quite often contain sayings which cohere with the Synoptic presentation of his teaching and which some scholars see as having an authentic ring. These include sayings about his 'works', e.g. 4.34; 5.17; 9.3b–4 (see Ensor, 1996, applying criteria similar to those used to test authenticity in Synoptic scholarship), parabolic sayings, e.g. 13.16 (cf. Mt. 10.24f.) and 5.19, sometimes called 'the parable of the apprenticed son', and other Synoptic-type sayings recast into Johannine form.[6] Christologically such sayings are important for expressing Jesus' belief he was sent by God, and that his mission was to do God's will (cf. Dodd, 1963, pp. 315–17; 1967).

Did John have a separate written source for Jesus' miracles? He certainly handles these distinctively: though only eight in number, they include several without Synoptic parallels. Moreover, they are presented as 'signs' (*sēmeia*), a term occurring 16 times in John 2—12 (the so-called 'Book of Signs'). These signs reveal Jesus' identity (2.11), and induce faith in him (e.g. 2.23; 4.53) – or occasionally unbelief (e.g. 9.18, 34 beside 9.35–8). They are not presented as arising from compassion (contrast Mk 1.41), nor are they specifically linked with the dawn of the Kingdom (contrast Lk.11.20); nor yet are they primarily demonstrations of power, as implied by *dynamis*, a Synoptic term for miracle (Mk 6.2, 5; Mt. 7.22; Lk. 10.13; etc.). Bultmann and many others have therefore argued that John had a distinctive 'Signs Source' (*Sēmeiaquelle*).[7]

The first point to be noted is that there is nothing particularly unusual about the designation of the miracles as 'signs'. *Sēmeia* is widely used in the New Testament for Jesus' miracles (e.g. Acts 2.22; 4.16; Rom. 15.19; 2 Cor. 12.12); it is also the regular term for 'miracle' in the Septuagint, appearing no fewer than 100 times. In the Hebrew Bible miracles often induce faith (or unbelief), as can be seen most obviously in Exodus (e.g. 4.8f.). Indeed, in recounting his 'signs' John may well have been influenced by biblical miracle traditions, especially the Moses, Elijah, and Elisha cycles (cf. Boismard, 1993). In addition, it must be observed that *sēmeion* is not John's only term for 'miracle': he also calls them collectively *erga* or 'works' (e.g. 5.36; 7.3).

Some have argued that stylistically John's miracle narratives may be distinguished from the rest of the Gospel. This claim is extremely difficult to prove, partly because it is hard to define where a miracle narrative begins and ends, and partly because of the general homogeneity of John's style. Some miracles are described in short, readily defined units, e.g. the wine miracle (2.1–11), the healing of the official's son (4.46–54), and the walking on the water (6.16–21). Others are harder to delimit. The raising of Lazarus is part of a long, elaborately constructed narrative (11.1—12.11) in which the miracle itself is integrated with episodes involving the disciples, Lazarus' sisters Martha and Mary, and 'the Jews'. Are we to suppose that all of this came from the 'Signs Source'?[8] Another awkwardness is that three of the miracles are not termed *sēmeia* in the course of the miracle account, but only in the ensuing interpretative dialogues – 6.14 (feeding miracle); 9.16 (lame man); 11.47; 12.18 (Lazarus). Another three – the blind man's healing, the water-walking, and the miraculous catch of fish – are not directly called 'signs' at all. Only in two – the wine miracle and the official's son – is the term *sēmeion* used in close connection with the miracle, occurring in editorial-style comments involving a numbering of the sign (2.11; 4.54). All this must weaken the case for the term *sēmeion* being derived from a special source for all eight miracles.

What about style? Even in English translation it can be observed that some parts of John (e.g. 13.31—17.26) are written in a leisurely, rather repetitive style, while others are more succinct and fast-moving. However, skilled authors often vary the pace of their works. Attempts to isolate distinctive 'Johannine' stylistic traits, and to separate off passages displaying these and attribute them to specific sources, have not met with success.[9] Reconstructed sources vary enormously in their contents: for some, the 'Signs Source' recounted only miracles; for others, it contained most of John 1—12 (see Fortna, 1970, app.). Scholars also differ as to whether the conclusion in 20.30f., which includes the word 'signs', is John's own composition or stems from this source.

There are also theological arguments. Some suggest that the 'Signs Source' depicted Jesus as a wonder-worker or *theios anēr*,[10] which they see as inconsistent with the rest of the Gospel's 'high' christology. But the striking thing about John's miracle narratives is how *little* the element of wonder occurs. It has also been argued that miracles in the 'Signs Source' induce faith, whereas elsewhere faith that depends on physical signs is disparaged.[11] But no tidy line can be drawn between places where 'signs faith' is acceptable and places where it is not. The official is reproached by Jesus for expecting 'signs and wonders' (4.48) right in the middle of a passage attributed to the 'Signs Source' allegedly promoting this sort of faith. In fact, John has a sophisticated under-standing of faith, which involves more than the 'signs'. The disciples' faith at Cana was just a first step: it needed to be deepened through long association with Jesus before they were ready to be sent out in mission. In any case, if the theology of the supposed source differed from John's own views, why did he make so much use of it (cf. Lindars, 1971, p. 37)?

Sometimes literary arguments are added for the 'Signs Source'. John's narrative is not fully consistent at story level. For example, after the Temple 'cleansing' John says that many believed when they saw 'the signs' (2.23); but up to this point only one sign has been related. Similarly Nicodemus refers to 'the signs' (plural: 3.2), when no further miracles have taken place. Then the healing of the official's son is described as 'the second sign' (4.54), despite these earlier references to plural 'signs'. Some argue that such anomalies arise from source mate-rials not being properly integrated. But the Gospel writers, like classical dramatists and poets, did not compose their works anticipating the minutely detailed scrutiny to which their texts have been subjected. They had far fewer opportunities for revision than modern authors using word-processors, or even writing long-hand; writing materials were expensive and not lightly wasted. Minor inconsistencies were bound to remain.[12] In any case readers can readily supply in imagination many details not narrated in the text.

The oddest feature about John's 'signs' is the explicit numbering of the first two – water into wine and the official's son – but none of the others. A case can be made for these two miracles as coming from a distinct 'short Signs Source', originating in Galilee. Both miracles are located there, being linked by a cross-reference (4.46a); neither can plausibly be derived from any Synoptic narrative. Stylistically they contain the fewest peculiarly 'Johannine' characteristics (listed in van Belle, 1994, app. 2). Sometimes the fishing miracle (21.1–8), also located in Galilee, has been seen as coming from this source; but this is not a numbered sign,[13] and it is hard to understand why John should have separated it so far from the first two if it was originally connected to them (van Belle, 1994, pp. 251–71). This story more likely came either from Luke, or a source in common with Luke.

As for the remaining miracles, John probably derived the feeding miracle and the walking on the water from Mark. He may have had a separate 'Jerusalem' source for the miracles there (the lame man, the blind man, and Lazarus), though there are some parallels to the first two in the Synoptics. Lazarus' raising is different in tone and detail from Synoptic resurrection miracles (Mk 5.22–43 par.; Lk. 7.11–15). John could have had a special source, or he may have created this magnificent episode for theological reasons (cf. Lindars, 1972, pp. 382–6). We conclude, with van Belle (1994, esp. p. 376), that the case for a 'Signs Source', in the sense of a single document describing all eight of John's miracles, has not been made.

This does not mean that John had no written sources, merely that they cannot be identified with confidence. Even dependence on Mark and Luke remains conjectural. John has evidently remodelled whatever oral or written sources he had in the interests of his theology, transposing them into his own distinctive style. If this search for sources has proved inconclusive, at least it may have led to a better understanding of his Gospel.

The Nature of John's Writing

The conclusion just reached has implications for attempts to recover 'the historical Jesus'. Ever since the 'new look' (cf. above, Ch. 2) some scholars have scoured John for factual information about Jesus additional to that derived from the Synoptics. It must be frankly recognized that this task is well-nigh impossible. Even the Synoptic portrayals are not factual reporting. They, too, offer 'portraits' of Jesus rather than 'photographs', influenced by the available traditions, the Evangelists' own perceptions, and their theological and pastoral purposes. Modern scholarship has gone some way towards establishing Synoptic interrelationships (using verbal repetitions and apparent redaction) and in setting up criteria for the 'authenticity' of Jesus' words, but there are still many disputed issues. A basic problem is the absence of independent documentary sources to confirm, in any detail, the Synoptic data.

With John the problems of recovering historical information (other than that already in the Synoptics) is fraught with problems, because no independent written sources have been convincingly identified. This means that one has to rely to a considerable extent on general probability. There are features which look historically plausible, such as the idea that some of Jesus' first disciples were followers of the Baptist; the overlap of their ministries; and the spread of Jesus' ministry over several years. There are topographical details which may derive from personal memory (discussed in Ch. 5), and one passage claiming eyewitness testimony (19.35); but John's supposed use of independent oral traditions is notoriously hard to demonstrate. Possibilities for genuinely historical elements are Jesus' appearance before Annas (which has no obvious theological or literary function), some details of Jesus' Roman trial which fit in with what is known of Roman judicial procedure, and John's dating of the crucifixion. But there are also many details which John may have introduced for symbolic reasons (e.g. Jesus' carrying his own cross; his seamless robe), and episodes where he seems to have dramatized historical events, reinterpreted them to find Scripture fulfilment, or created dialogues, as an effective means of conveying his theology. Jesus' conversations with Nicodemus and the Samaritan woman may possibly come into this last category,[14] as well as some of his confrontations with 'the Jews'.

This does not mean that John lacks all historical foundation, far less that it consists of deliberate untruths; but only that one cannot expect to recover data of the sort recorded in Hansard or in city archives. John must be seen as an *interpretation* of history, not as a historical record. Its primary purpose seems to have been theological and evangelistic rather than historical.

5

Purpose, Audience, Place and Date of Composition

The previous chapter suggested that John's primary purpose was theological and evangelistic. This raises further important questions. What motives prompted him to write and for whom did he intend his Gospel? Where and when was it composed? In contemporary literary criticism attempts to identify an author's purpose are viewed with suspicion. People speak of 'the intentional fallacy' (e.g. Malbon, 2000, p. 21). But nobody would attempt a work with such sustained narrative and theological content as John without having an aim. In fact, John states his purpose in 20.31: 'These things are written that you may believe that Jesus is the Anointed, the Son of God, and that believing you may have life in his Name'. This suggests that his main purpose was to encourage life-giving faith in Jesus as 'messiah'.[1] It is left ambiguous whether the aim is to induce this faith in new converts or those already committed to Christianity, or both.[2]

The titles chosen in 20.31 are significant: John does not say, 'that you may believe that Jesus is the Word' (*logos*), or 'that Jesus is God' (*theos*), but 'that Jesus is the *christos*', i.e. 'Anointed'. This expression would be readily intelligible to Jews, who would naturally be interested in the identity of the Lord's Anointed (i.e. God's authoritative agent, and Israel's 'end-time' deliverer). They would also have immediate meaning for Christians familiar with the idea of Jesus as the long-awaited 'Christ' (Mk 1.1; Mt. 16.16; 26.63; Rom. 1.1–3; etc.). But for Gentiles *christos* would be puzzling, since in secular Greek it means 'rubbed in' of oil (e.g. as applied to wounds).[3] Possibly John added 'Son of God' as an explanation for them, though this phrase is capable of a range of interpretations. Readers would, however, be guided by John's earlier presentation of Jesus (including the Prologue). For authors' intentions are revealed not just by specific statements of purpose, but perhaps even more by the ways they present events, or depict characters, and through their choice of language. This means we, too, need to look at the broader picture.

A Gospel for Hellenism?

A once popular theory was that John wrote primarily to commend Christianity to devout and thoughtful people in cosmopolitan

Hellenistic society (Dodd, 1953, p. 9; further references in Smalley, 1998, pp. 160f.). Educated pagans and Hellenized Jews would be interested in the presentation of Jesus as the *logos*, a term with special meaning in Stoic philosophy (Scott, 1906, esp. pp. 6f., 145–8). John's dualistic concepts and his theme of an ascending–descending redeemer would appeal to Gentiles familiar with oriental 'Gnosticism'. His emphasis on Jesus as the 'true light', 'true vine', etc. could be related to the Platonic concept that visible objects and perceptible qualities are shadows of eternal realities. Today this theory is generally discounted. John's *logos* image seems to owe more to Jewish religious thought than Greek philosophy; his dualism can be paralleled at Qumran, while the ascent–descent theme is at home in Judaism. The application of the epithet 'true' (or 'real') to Jesus probably implies a contrast with Judaism rather than familiarity with Plato's theory of forms (Smalley, 1998, pp. 46–64).

Another argument against the idea that John's primary purpose was to convert pagans is its lack of explicit references to them. Unlike other New Testament authors, John never uses *ta ethnē* in the sense of 'Gentiles' (Robinson, 1962, pp. 109f.), nor does he use pagans as models of discipleship. Very few Gentiles feature, and those who do – notably Pilate and the Roman soldiers – are hardly examples to be imitated. Jesus never visits the Hellenized areas of the Decapolis, Syro-Phoenicia, or the region of Caesarea Philippi, as he does in the Synoptics. No Syro-Phoenician woman puts her faith in him; no demon-possessed man is set free in the Gentile territory of Gerasa; no Roman soldier confesses Jesus at the cross; there is no great commission to the nations. All this strongly suggests that John had little interest in mission to pagans. The only external mission is to Samaritans (4.1–42),[4] whom Jews would have seen as heretical fellow-Jews rather than Gentiles. The strongest pieces of evidence for pagans (or Gentile Christians) being among the intended audience are John's use of the term *Ioudaioi*, since Jews normally spoke of themselves to fellow-Jews as 'Israelites' or 'Hebrews', and the explanations of Jewish terms, customs, and feasts (e.g. 1.41f.; 2.6; 7.2; 19.40).

A Gospel for Jews?

The idea that Jews formed a major element in the target audience is suggested already in the Proem, when John the Baptist says that he came baptizing with water so that Jesus might be revealed to *Israel* (1.31). It is strongly supported by John's use of Jewish Scripture in ways that would make sense only to those already familiar with it. This Gospel is steeped in allusions to themes from the Hebrew Bible, including Law, Sabbath, and Temple; sin, forgiveness, holiness, and 'election'; Passover, manna, and the bronze serpent; images of shepherd, living water, word, and lamb; the patriarchs Abraham, Moses, Jacob, and the Deuteronomic prophet; Spirit and 'Anointed'. Some of the references are direct and clear, and might be intelligible to educated non-Jews, but many are indirect. Would anyone unfamiliar with the Hebrew Scriptures detect the probable allusions in the Prologue to the *shekinah* and the revelation of God's glory on Mount Sinai, or its background in Jacob's vision of a stairway to heaven in 1.47–51? How many non-Jewish readers could pick up the subtle scriptural 'fulfilments' of the Passion Narrative?

Furthermore, the audience is evidently expected to be familiar with contemporary Jewish controversies. These include the questions of whether God 'worked' on the Sabbath (5.17), and whether anyone has ascended to heaven to 'see' God (cf. 1.18; 3.13; 6.46). The whole theme of Jesus as revealer relates to Jewish debate about whether God still discloses himself after the apparent cessation of prophecy. Jesus' pre-existence as *logos*, and the *logos*' role in creation, are illuminated by Jewish wisdom ideas. John also assumes that readers can grasp rabbinical methods of exegesis, including the argument about Abraham 'rejoicing' to see Jesus' day (8.56), and the application of the Isaianic text, 'You are gods' (10.34). All this suggests that some or most of the intended audience were biblically literate, educated Jews.

Were these Jews still practising their faith within the Synagogue, or were they already separated from it? This question has greatly vexed scholars. On the one hand John often portrays 'the Jews' negatively. He sometimes appears to distance himself from Judaism, representing Jesus as speaking as if Jews were outsiders (e.g. 13.33), and saying '*your* Law', rather than '*our* Law', when addressing fellow-Jews (8.17; 10.34; cf. 7.22: 'Moses gave *you* [not us] circumcision'). This has led to the belief that, for all its Jewish flavour, John was written for those who perceived themselves as Gentiles (so Casey, 1991, 1996, esp. pp. 111–33). On the other hand there may have been special reasons for these second-person pronouns (see below, Ch. 12), and John's sharp criticisms of 'the Jews' seem to fall within what was acceptable in ancient literary polemic. Judaism in the first century CE was not monolithic, but included groups with varied beliefs and practices, so that John could have been operating within the context of an 'intra-Jewish factional dispute' (Dunn, 1991, p. 160; cf. 2001, p. 59). Others who support the idea that John wrote for Jews, including proselytes, are Carson (1987; 1991, p. 91) and Motyer (1997, esp. pp. 6f.).

Motyer offers a plausible scenario for John's ambivalent attitude to Judaism, at times positive, at others negative. He sets the Gospel's composition in the context of the upheavals following the destruction of the Jerusalem Temple in 70 CE, interpreting it as an appeal for a new start. The Roman action under Titus had effectively ended the Jewish priesthood and sacrificial system. One group of Jewish religious leaders, based at the rabbinic academy at Jamnia (Yavne) in Palestine, sought to rebuild Judaism by minutely detailed study of Torah, 'Law', and by applying the rules of Temple purity to the home. The synagogue had already become a focus of worship and piety for many, especially in the Dispersion. According to Motyer, John offers an alternative to extreme Torah devotion by setting out Jesus as the fulfilment of Temple rites and festivals, and as providing atonement for sin, replacing animal sacrifices. There is also the possibility that some Jews for whom John wrote might have considered themselves as still belonging to the Synagogue, but were not so regarded by their fellow-Jews (cf. John's references to people being made *aposynagōgoi*, discussed below). Paul's letters and Acts amply affirm the existence of Christians who still kept Jewish food-laws and other ritual observances, a situation persisting into the second century.

To sum up the position so far: some of John's intended audience must have been pagans, for whom he included his explanations of Jewish customs; but many were Jews or Jewish Christians. These might have been still within the Synagogue or outside it. Were such Jews living within Palestine, or in the Dispersion? Van Unnik (1959) and Robinson (1962, pp. 107–25) argued that John was intended as a missionary document to Diaspora Jews. They noted the explicit reference to Jews of the Greek Dispersion (7.35), using the correct rabbinic phrase for this group, and the coming to Jesus of *Hellēnes* (12.20–2), plausibly interpreted as Greek-speaking Jews.[5] They also pointed to Caiaphas' prophecy that Jesus would gather in 'the scattered children of God' (11.51f.); on the lips of the High Priest, this might readily mean Diaspora Jews rather than Gentiles. John's interpretations of Aramaic words (e.g. 1.38, 42; 20.16), usually seen as for the benefit of Gentiles, could also help Greek-speaking Jews unfamiliar with that language. John's emphasis on Jesus as messiah ('anointed') and God's Son (1.34, 41; 7.41; 20.31, etc.) would be of special interest to Jews generally.

Van Unnik and Robinson put up a good case for Greek-speaking Diaspora Jews as *part* of John's target audience; what they did not demonstrate was that they were its sole intended readers. These must surely have included Palestinian Jews, and possibly Jews from the Eastern Diaspora. Did it also include Christians (whether of Jewish or Gentile origin)?

A Gospel for Christians?

Barrett (1975) was surprisingly critical of van Unnik's and Robinson's thesis, believing that John was written primarily for Christians. Jewish concepts and images, he argued, are used in characteristically *Christian* ways. Thus 'messiah', which in Hebrew simply means 'anointed', appears as a title, sometimes almost as a proper name (1.17; 17.3; cf. Mk 1.1; Rom.1.1; etc.). The description of Jesus as 'God's lamb, who takes away the sin of the world' (1.29, 36) goes beyond Jewish sacrificial imagery, reflecting specifically Christian thought (cf. 1 Cor. 5.7; 1 Pet. 1.19). John's picture of Jesus' intimate relationship with the Father also presupposes Christian understanding. Other arguments in favour of an intended Christian audience include the assumption that readers will be familiar with incidents in the Synoptics, John's apparent distancing from Judaism, probable allusions to the Eucharist (6.51c–8), and interest in Petrine ministry (21.15–19).

All this certainly shows that John wrote from a Christian perspective, but it does not prove an *exclusively* Christian audience. The hypothesis that best suits the complex pattern of evidence is that John intended his book for a wide readership. This would have included Jews still within the Synagogue whom he hoped to win over, Jewish Christians whose faith he wished to strengthen, and at least some Gentiles, either already converted to Christianity, or even still pagan. Granted the overwhelmingly 'Jewish' tone of his Gospel, it is likely that Christians of Jewish origin were the prime target. This conclusion of a wide intended audience runs counter to much recent Johannine scholarship which sees John as written for a small, inward-looking community – a hypothesis which must now demand attention.

The Johannine Writings and the Johannine 'Community'

For many centuries it was believed that one man wrote John, 1–3 John, and Revelation. These writings share important features: uniquely in the New Testament, they refer to Jesus as the *logos* (though they use this term differently).[6] All three have a dualistic outlook, but they express this in different ways: Revelation makes use of apocalyptic imagery (beasts with horns, angels with trumpets, etc.), while John and 1–3 John use polarized opposites, such as light and darkness, truth and falsehood. John, like Revelation (Rev. 1.17; 22.16, etc.), has distinctive 'I am' sayings (though none is the same in the two writings). All the Johannine writings are composed in a 'Semitizing' style of Greek, John and 1 John being stylistically very close.[7]

John and 1 John are also close theologically, with an emphasis on truth, witness, judgement, eternal life, and God's love (some of these themes recur in the very short letters of 2 and 3 John). Both John and 1 John stress the need for faith in Jesus as 'the Christ' and God's Son, and both bid believers love one another. They share other striking concepts, including being born of God; abiding in God (or Christ); the Spirit of Truth; the world's hatred; conquering the world; water and blood, symbolically as a pair; the contrast between God's children and those belonging to the devil; and the term 'Paraclete' (used, however, differently). Some therefore attribute John and 1–3 John to the same author (e.g. Marshall, 1982, pp. 1096f.). On the other hand there are differences in style and theology, which have led to the widespread view that John and 1–3 John stem rather from a common 'community' (e.g. Brown, 1979). Some (e.g. Smalley, 1994) believe that Revelation originated in this community; others think it belongs to a separate group. The main arguments for the latter view are that Revelation lacks key concepts and expressions of John and 1–3 John, and uses others differently (Fiorenza, 1977, pp. 410–18). Thus Revelation emphasizes future eschatology, whereas John and 1 John work mostly with 'realized' concepts (e.g. Jn 3.36; 1 Jn 3.14).[8] Stylistically, too, Revelation stands apart in that it contains numerous solecisms (breaches of grammar), whereas the Greek of John and 1–3 John is usually grammatically correct (though not free from ambiguity). These linguistic errors were noted already by Dionysius, 'the great bishop of the Alexandrians', who described Revelation's Greek as barbarous (Eusebius, *HE*, VII.1, 25.26). Revelation also has a much bigger vocabulary than John and 1–3 John, though this is hardly surprising in view of its length and subject matter. Some see it as more 'Hebraic'.[9]

On balance, it seems most likely that John originated in the same Christian milieu as 1–3 John, rather than by the same hand; this does not mean that all these writings were destined for the same recipients. 2 and 3 John were clearly written for small groups, possibly house-churches, under the authority of 'the elder'.[10] 1 John's audience is uncertain, as it lacks addressees: it may be a summary of a master's teaching for quite a wide readership (Edwards, 1996a, p. 45). Revelation is probably the work of a Christian prophet; addressed to seven churches, i.e. congregations, in 'Asia' (modern western Turkey), it may stem from a separate circle from that of John and 1–3 John, with access to both Johannine and Pauline traditions (Fiorenza, 1977, pp. 425–7).

In what sort of circle did John and 1–3 John come to birth? Culpepper (1975) argued for a Johannine 'school', like the Greek philosophical academies of Plato and Epicurus. Grayston (1984, p. 9) found in the 'we' references of John 21.24 (cf. 1.14, 16) and 1 John 1.1–4 evidence that leaders of this school served as an 'authorizing group' for both John and 1 John. It has further been suggested that the author of 1 John may have been responsible for editing John, possibly adding the Supper Discourses (stylistically especially close to 1 John). Others find the 'school' idea unhelpful.[11] A more popular hypothesis is of a 'community', though this is rarely defined. The term might suggest a monastic-style group who shared worship and a common life, and such communities are indeed attested within Judaism of this period. But there is no evidence in the Johannine writings for elaborate disciplinary rules of the type that feature so prominently in the Qumran texts such as the *Community Rule* (1QS) and the *Damascus Document* (CD). If there was a 'community' it must have been of a much looser nature, perhaps a number of Christian congregations in touch with one another (like the Pauline churches), and sharing common emphases in their faith.

Those who favour the 'community' hypothesis often rely on social-scientific understandings of religious sects, arguing on the basis of internal indications for a 'sectarian' character of John and 1–3 John.[12] In support of their views they cite John's negative use of 'the world' (e.g. Jn 17.16; 1 Jn 2.15–17), and references to the disciples being hated (Jn 15.18f.; 16.2; 17.14; cf. 1 Jn 3.13), suggesting alienation from outsiders. Further evidence is found in John's ethical dualism, and in his frequent and emphatic use of personal pronouns. His 'community' is therefore seen as small and isolated, struggling from the margins against the powerful Jewish Synagogue (Rensberger, 1999, esp. p. 151, and many others). John's christology is even seen as a 'legitimating' defence against Synagogue opposition (McGrath, 2001; cf. Meeks, 1972). This 'community' is allegedly preoccupied with salvation, using its own 'antilanguage' not readily intelligible to outsiders (Malina and Rohrbaugh, 1998, pp. 7–19). Jesus' commands to his disciples to love one another (Jn 13.34f.; 15.12f.; 1 Jn 3.23; 4.7–12; 2 Jn 5) or their 'brothers' (1 Jn 3.14, 16–18; 4.21) are interpreted as narrowing the Synoptic injunctions to love one's neighbour (Mk 12.31 par.) and one's enemies (Mt. 5.44; Lk. 6.27, 35). Johannine ethics are considered weak and 'morally bankrupt': J. T. Sanders claims that if a Johannine Christian saw a wounded traveller on the road, instead of giving aid he would ask, 'Are you saved, brother?' (1986, p. 100).

Such interpretations seem to parody Johannine Christianity. The basic problem, as often, is methodological. Those who rely on social-scientific analysis do so by a process of 'mirror reading', i.e. studying texts not for what they relate, but for social conditions and conflicts which they purportedly reflect. But as Barclay (1987) and Motyer (1997, pp. 18–31) point out, this is a hazardous process, readily leading to over-interpretation. Some studies of the Johannine 'community' draw heavily on only parts of John (e.g. Martyn, 1979; Woll, 1981). Many stress negative uses of 'the world' and 'the Jews' at the expense of positive concepts, resulting in lack of balance. Others fail to set John's teaching on love in its fuller context of the mutual love of the Father and Jesus, God's love for the world, and Jesus' laying down his life for his friends (cf. Edwards, 1996a, ch. 7). John's characters are often read implausibly as standing anachronistically for specific later groups. The peculiarities of John's language are exaggerated (as noted by Carson, 1991, p. 89, criticizing Malina's sociolinguistics). Sociological models of 'sectarianism' are simplistically applied without external verification (Motyer, 1997, pp. 30f., with criticisms of Meeks, 1972).

The isolation of John's 'community' also seems greatly exaggerated. There is abundant evidence for travel in the ancient world and for communication between early Christian communities (Thompson, 1998). John shows himself familiar with elements from the Synoptic tradition, and may have known both Mark and Luke (see above Ch. 4). It is unlikely that his understanding of Jesus' pre-existence, role in creation, and divinity originated in complete isolation from similar developments in the Pauline corpus and Hebrews (e.g. Col. 1.15–19; Heb. 1.2).[13] If Revelation originated in a separate milieu from John and 1–3 John (as often maintained), its points of similarity with John could indicate contact with another stream of Christian tradition. All this is quite apart from broader 'Hellenistic' thought, which many believe to have influenced John.

The scholarly construct of John writing from, and for, a small and isolated community with narrow sectarian views should therefore be rejected. The Gospel would have been produced in the context of a believing community, but there is no need to suppose that it was written exclusively for this group (cf. Bauckham, 1998b, on the Gospels' audiences, esp. ch. 6 by S. C. Barton). The evidence reviewed here suggests that John intended his Gospel for a wide audience, including Jews, Jewish Christians, Gentiles, Gentile Christians, and, conceivably, Samaritans.

Place of Composition

It is impossible to determine *where* John was written. Unlike Revelation, which claims (1.9) to have been written on Patmos (a Greek island in the east Aegean), John makes no reference to its place of composition. This has to be deduced from internal hints (topography, language, climate of thought) and later external testimonies. With regard to topography, in addition to knowledge of Galilee (in common with the Synoptists), John seems familiar with localities in pre-70 CE Jerusalem. These include 'the Sheep Gate' and the Bethesda pool with its five porticoes (5.2), the pool of Siloam (9.7), Solomon's Portico (10.22f.), and Pilate's Praetorium (18.28, 33), with the place called Lithostratos, 'stone-paved', in Greek and Gabbatha (probably 'ridge' or 'elevated place') in Aramaic (19.13). He mentions Palestinian localities not otherwise known from Jewish sources with apparent precision (Westcott, 1919, p. xi). Names like

Cana of Galilee, Bethany beyond Jordan, and Aenon near Salim sound authentic and have good Semitic derivations. He is also familiar with aspects of Samaritan topography – Jacob's well and 'this mountain' (Mount Gerizim) as a cult centre (4.5f., 20f.). All this material is unique to John in the New Testament. John reveals no comparable details of localities in Asia Minor, Syria, Egypt, or any area outside Palestine. Such topographical knowledge could suggest careful research by outsiders who had visited Palestine (Casey, 1996, p. 173), access to reliable old traditions (Albright, 1956; Robinson, 1976; and others), or a phase of composition in Palestine. Very few scholars argue for the main composition there, though this possibility cannot be excluded.

Language could also be an indicator of origin. John writes in *Koinē* Greek, the simple 'vernacular' (popular language) throughout the Graeco-Roman world. John's Greek does, however, display one striking characteristic. It has a 'Semitic' ring about it, both in syntax (grammatical constructions) and vocabulary;[14] there are also traces of Semitic poetic forms. These 'Semitisms' (i.e. linguistic uses rare – or unknown – in Greek, but common in Semitic languages) occur throughout the Gospel, and seem unlikely to derive merely from literary imitation of Hebrew style via the Septuagint. Many seem to reflect Aramaic rather than Hebrew usage (though this can be hard to determine). Several explanations are possible: (a) John might have used Aramaic sources; (b) his Gospel might be a translation from the Aramaic; (c) John could have been a native Aramaic speaker, fluent in Greek, but with his language unconsciously influenced by Aramaic idiom. These explanations are not mutually exclusive.

Bultmann believed that all three of his postulated written sources were composed in Aramaic; but, as was seen earlier (Ch. 4), their very existence is problematic. Other, shorter Aramaic sources remain a possibility, especially for Jesus' sayings (cf. Black, 1967, pp. 273f.; Ensor, 1996). Burney (1922) argued that John was translated from Aramaic, a hypothesis recently supported on a more scientific basis by Martin (1989, esp. pp. 5–94; cf. 1974), who considers all but a few short sections to be a translation. However, other experts argue that John's style does not have the characteristics of 'translation Greek'. They claim that it betrays the mindset of someone whose second language was Greek, but who still thought in Semitic language patterns (e.g. Barrett, 1978, pp. 8–11; Casey, 1996, with some criticisms of Martin). On balance, composition by a bilingual author and native Aramaic speaker seems most likely – or rather a trilingual author, since John appears to have known Hebrew. This hypothesis does not preclude the use of Aramaic sources.

It is sometimes assumed that knowledge of Aramaic must point to Palestine as the place of composition, since it was the language of ordinary people there (though the better-educated also knew Greek and Hebrew). But even at this date Aramaic was still spoken quite widely in the Near East, where it had once been the *lingua franca*, especially among Jews. John's Aramaisms are therefore compatible also with composition in some part of the Dispersion where unassimilated Jews still used Aramaic, or with the idea of a Palestinian Jewish author who had moved abroad (as many Jews did after the fall of Jerusalem). Jewish communities are attested in Asia Minor (including Acmonia, Apamea, Aphrodisias, Laodicea, and Sardis, to mention just a few cities), Greece, Syria, Mesopotamia, Cyrenaica (North Africa), Rome, and other areas. There were especially large numbers of Jews at Alexandria in Egypt. Some of these Jewish communities were so heavily acculturated to Hellenistic ways that knowledge of Aramaic (and Hebrew) was largely lost (Trebilco, 1991; Barclay, 1996); in others it survived, as evidenced by inscriptions, papyri, and literary sources (cf. Reynolds and Tannenbaum, 1987; Mitchell, 1993, vol. 2, pp. 8f., 31–7). Very few Aramaic inscriptions have been found at Ephesus, but there is literary evidence for Jews there, probably mostly Greek-speaking (Horsley, 1992). All this means that no firm conclusions can be drawn about place of composition from language (which offers no special support to those who argue for Ephesus).

John's occasional distancing from things Jewish and his negative portrayals of the Jerusalem religious leaders are often seen as pointing to final composition in an environment estranged from 'official' Judaism; this need not be in the Diaspora. Many scholars assume that John must have been published in a cosmopolitan city because of its use of 'Hellenistic' ideas, but by the first century CE much of Palestine was Hellenized. Three cities, in particular, have been favoured as likely places for composition: Alexandria (cf. possible links with Philo's thought, and the early papyrus fragments from Egypt); Syrian Antioch, where John appears to have been known early (cf. Ignatius' apparent citations); and Ephesus, traditionally associated with the Apostle John. However, the case for Ephesus weakens if apostolic authorship is rejected, and even more if John is no longer closely linked with Revelation.[15] Traditions placing composition in Ephesus are no earlier than the second century CE. Leaving these aside, there is nothing to prove that the whole Gospel was not written in Palestine, or in any other Jewish-Christian community in Asia Minor, Syria (or elsewhere) where both Greek and Aramaic were spoken.

Date of Composition

Most scholars suppose that John was composed over a long period, incorporating both old oral traditions, cast into Johannine form, and newer materials resulting from personal reflection, contact with a wider world of ideas, and possibly additional sources. Most also believe that it was edited, probably more than once. Editorial additions might be minor explanatory glosses (e.g. 4.2), 'ecclesiastical' alterations (e.g. possibly 6.51c–8), or more substantial modifications (e.g. the addition of chapter 21). The Prologue has often been seen as belonging to a late phase of writing, as have chapter 6, the section on Lazarus, the second Farewell Discourse, and the High-Priestly Prayer (cf. Lindars, 1972, pp. 50f.; see further Brown, 1966, pp. xxxiv–xxxix; Schnackenburg, 1968, pp. 100–4). None of this composition history can be demonstrated beyond doubt, though different phases of writing are highly probable. In discussing date, it may therefore be more helpful to talk about the time of *publication* rather than composition, i.e. when the Gospel was issued in something like its present form.

Papyrus fragments from Egypt, together with patristic citations, show that John was circulating by the early to mid-second century CE – how soon before this is debatable. A few scholars support a pre-70 date (notably Robinson, 1976, pp. 254–311; 1985), arguing from the difficulty of proving allusions to circumstances after 70 CE, the possible presence of old Palestinian traditions, and the failure to mention the Temple destruction as a past event. These arguments have failed to convince many. Old traditions (if such they be) might belong to an early edition or have been incorporated from fresh sources after 70 CE. The destruction of the Temple may be indirectly alluded to (2.19f.). Most scholars therefore support publication after 70 CE. Arguments include the lack of references to the Sadducees (a Jewish group active before 70 CE), the prominence given to the Pharisees, who seem to have become ascendant at Jamnia, and John's use of *rabbi* in the sense of 'teacher' (but see below, Ch. 7, n. 2). His emphasis on Jesus as fulfilling, or possibly replacing, the Temple and its rites would also fit this period.

John's apparently hostile use of 'the Jews' and expressions like 'your law' distancing Jesus from the Jewish leadership could also plausibly be set in the context of the stress on Torah observance by the Jamnian rabbis (though this is not the only possible explanation). Sometimes it is said that it must have taken time for John's advanced christology to develop; but this is a weak argument. Some of Paul's almost certainly authentic letters (e.g. Philippians) display a 'high' christology, as does Hebrews (possibly composed before 70 CE). Some consider that belief in Jesus' divinity could hardly have developed when Christians were still members of the Synagogue (so Casey, 1996), but others disagree. Not much can be learnt from John's relationship to the Synoptics, as it is uncertain how far he used them. If he knew only Mark, a date soon after 70 would be possible; if he was dependent on the final versions of Luke or Matthew (which many would not accept), then a date in the late 80s or even 90s would be more plausible.

Publication after *c.* 85 CE is often postulated because of John's refer-ences to people being made *aposynagōgoi*, 'separated from the Synagogue' (9.22; 12.42; 16.2). These are widely held to relate to the introduction of a new clause to the Synagogue prayers, reputedly by the Jamnian authorities, around this date (e.g. Brown, 1979; Martyn, 1979). This is known as the Twelfth Benediction or *birkat ha-minim*, 'blessing of the heretics'. The relevant section begins by calling on God to destroy speedily the apostates and insolent government, continuing: 'and let the Christians [*noşĕrim*] and the heretics [*minim*] perish in a moment, let them be blotted out of the book of life, and let them not be written with the righteous. Blessed art thou, O Lord, who humblest the insolent'.[16] Thus, although technically a blessing (*birkat*), this was effec-tively a curse. Often this text is believed to refer to the same event as the 'cursing' of Christians in synagogues mentioned by Justin Martyr in the second century (*Dial.* 16; 96).

There are, however, serious problems with using the *birkat* to date John. First, in its earliest form it did not include the word *noşĕrim* (inter-preted as 'Nazoraeans', i.e. Christians); the *noşĕrim* could, conceivably, be included with the *minim* ('heretics') – which does occur in early versions – but *minim* normally refers to unorthodox Jews rather than Christians. Secondly, the dating of the *birkat* to *c.* 85 CE has been strongly challenged: the rabbinic sources (*b. Ber. Bar.*28b–29a; *y. Ber.* IV, 3.8a) linking it with Samuel the Small (85–100 CE) and/or the Jamnian academy are late and possibly unreliable (Lincoln, 2000, p. 270). Nor is it evident that Justin's accusation that Jews cursed Christians in the synagogues necessarily refers to this clause.[17] It is also questionable whether the Palestinian rabbis had authority to impose such prayers throughout the Jewish world, including Ephesus, where most scholars locate John's 'community'. For all these reasons the evidence of this *birkat* must be rejected for dating purposes.[18]

Nor can any help be derived from John's relationship to Revelation or 1–3 John. It is not clear whether Revelation was written before or after the Gospel, and in any case it cannot be securely dated – it is generally assigned to the reign of Domitian (81–96 CE), though some support a date in Nero's reign (54–68 CE). The letters of 1–3 John are generally placed after the Gospel (Edwards, 1996a, pp. 53–5) and usually dated before *c.* 100 CE (Grayston, 1984, is exceptional in placing 1–3 John before John); but this only slightly reduces the *ante quem* provided by papyri. To conclude: a date before 70 CE seems unlikely on various grounds; publication after *c.* 100 CE is improbable. Therefore *c.* 75–*c.* 95 CE seems the most plausible time for John's publication in something close to its present form.

Conclusion

There can be no certainty about either the place or date of publication of John. Its association with Ephesus rests on the strength of patristic testimony (and possible links with Revelation) rather than on internal evidence. John must have worked in the context of a Christian environment, but attempts to use social-scientific analysis to delineate the character of his 'community' have proved unsuccessful. He probably wrote for a broad audience, including Jews and Jewish Christians, to whom he was eager to demonstrate Jesus' messiahship. But his aim extended beyond this: he also wanted to set out his own understanding of Jesus' actions and person, offering to readers salvation and new life through him.

6

Jesus' Miracles
as Narrative Theology

The heart of John's Gospel is its christology or presentation of Christ. Jesus dominates its narrative from start to finish, hardly ever being 'off-stage'. All the rest of John's theology – ethics, eschatology, ecclesiology, doctrine of God, the Spirit, and the Church – is so intimately bound up with his christology that any attempt to cover these aspects separately is likely to distort his thought (cf. Barrett, 1978, p. 67; Carson, 1991, p. 95). Yet John's understanding is far from straightforward. Parts of his narrative presuppose a 'higher' christology than others, and there are tensions in his portrayal of Jesus as fully human and yet divine.

One reason for these tensions may be John's reuse of traditional materials, not always fully integrated with his own more sophisticated ideas. Another is the nature of biblical theology, which is not propositional, but rather experiential and often 'narrative'. Instead of presenting systematic, logical propositions, with a firm philosophical base, the Gospel authors write narratives embodying their experience of God in Jesus. John communicates his theology in different ways: through the shape of his Gospel as a whole; through significant actions of Jesus; through dialogues (including 'confessions of faith'); and through Jesus' statements about himself. He also presents it through interpretative asides and longer reflections like the Prologue.

Chapters 6–9 examine these varied ways in which John conveys his christology, beginning with Jesus' miracles. The possibility that all of these came from a special 'Signs Source' has already been discussed (and rejected); we concentrate here on their theological content. John calls the miracles either *erga*, 'works',[1] usually on the lips of Jesus, or *sēmeia*, 'signs', mostly in comments by other characters or by the narrator. John stresses that Jesus' fine deeds are performed in accordance with God's will (5.36; 10.32); they are God's 'works' as well as Jesus' (9.3; 10.37f.); they bear witness to him (10.25). *Sēmeion*, probably derived from the Septuagint (though occurring in secular Greek), suggests that the miracles point to something beyond themselves. Just as God revealed his character through 'signs and wonders', so Jesus, through his signs, reveals God's glory (11.40) and his own (2.11; cf. 11.4). Apart from the incarnation and resurrection, eight miracles are recounted; but John knows of many more (20.30). Sometimes John makes his understanding plain through specific comments; sometimes it is brought out by interpretative dialogues; sometimes it has to be deduced from context, or from pointers in language and imagery. As well as revealing Jesus' character, the miracles serve as a catalyst to faith (or unbelief). Each miracle needs to be studied separately.

(1) The 'Sign' at Cana (2.1–11)

This story, unique to John, is told with vividness but restraint. The wine runs out at a wedding, and Jesus' mother tells him, 'They have no wine'; Jesus apparently rebukes her. Nevertheless she tells the servants, 'Do whatever he bids you'. Jesus bids the servants fill six large stone jars with water, draw off some, and take it to the banquet master (Greek *architriklinos*). They do so, and when he has tasted the water, now become wine, he congratulates the bridegroom on its excellent quality (2.10).

Sometimes this episode is criticized as a 'luxury' miracle. Although honour was involved for the village family who faced humiliation in running out of wine, it can hardly be said to meet an extreme need. Jesus apparently produces over 100 gallons of wine (the six jars each contain 'two or three measures', i.e. 18–24 gallons: Barrett, 1978, p. 192). Why should Jesus create so much wine, especially when the guests have already drunk freely (2.10)? Is he encouraging alcoholic indulgence? To ask such questions is to misunderstand the nature of John's narrative. This is no ordinary miracle, but a 'sign', revealing Jesus' glory (2.11). 'Glory' (Greek *doxa*) can mean reputation or ordinary human honour (cf. 12.43), but here it denotes divine splendour, majesty, and transcendence. The disciples have glimpsed this through Jesus' action.

The miraculous production of top-quality wine in large quantity would suggest varying symbolism to different readers. Those with a Jewish background would recall how wine in the Hebrew Bible symbolizes joy: it gladdens the human heart (Ps. 104.15) and cheers both God and mortals (Jdg. 9.13). Created to make people rejoice, when drunk in moderation it is 'equal to life for humans' (Ecclus 31.27). Abundance of wine portends the end-time, when God was expected to intervene dramatically in history. Isaiah promised that 'on that day' the Lord would prepare on the mountain a rich feast with mature wines; he would wipe away tears, and bring salvation to his people (25.6–9). Amos (9.13) and Joel (3.18) similarly speak of the mountains dripping sweet wine on 'the day of the Lord'. 2 Baruch 29[2] foretells that when the 'Anointed One' (messiah) begins to be revealed vines will produce supernaturally large quantities of grapes. Targums and rabbinic sources associate abundance of fine wine with the messianic age (Aus, 1988, pp. 8f.). The Pirke Aboth, probably the earliest text of the Mishnah (c. 2nd cent. CE), uses 'the banquet' to describe enjoyment of life with God (cf. the Synoptic banquet or wedding feast symbolizing the Kingdom[3]). Some Hellenized Jews might recall Philo's interpretation of the priest-king Melchizedek (Gen. 14.18) as the logos who offered wine instead of water, so that souls might be 'possessed by divine intoxication, more sober than sobriety itself' (Leg. All., III.79–82); note his image of the logos as God's 'wine-pourer', himself the drink which he pours, filling sacred goblets with pure joy (Somn., II.249). For Philo, the wine produced by the logos stands for grace, joy, virtue, and wisdom.

Christian readers would probably see the quantity and quality of the Cana wine as illustrating God's generosity, and Jesus as God's promised agent of salvation, bringing eschatological joy. John's placing of this miracle at the start of Jesus' ministry would be taken as a sign of the dawn of a new age, and as a pointer to what is to follow. For these readers, 'the third day' (2.1) might suggest Jesus' resurrection (cf., e.g. Mt. 16.21; 17.23; Lk. 9.22; 24.7; Acts 10.40; 1 Cor. 15.4).[4] Jesus' mention of his hour (2.4) could be seen as pointing forward to John's characteristic use of 'hour' to refer to Jesus' Passion (e.g. 12.23, 27; 13.1; cf. Brown, 1966, pp. 517f.). Those for whom the Eucharist formed an important element in their lives would undoubtedly also interpret the wine as foreshadowing this sacrament, as did many of the Church Fathers (Cullmann, 1953, p. 69; Brown, 1966, p. 110).

How would pagan readers (or Christians converted from Hellenism) understand this story? Many would be reminded of the miracles of Dionysos, the Greek god of wine and irrepressible new life. A well-known legend tells how Dionysos once caused his ship's mast to turn into a grape-laden vine and the ship to flow with fragrant sweet wine (*h.Hom.*, VII.34–40), a scene depicted in Greek art. According to Pausanias (VI.26.1f.), on the eve of Dionysos' feast empty jars placed in his temple at Elis were miraculously filled overnight with wine. At his festival on Andros and Teos, the temple springs miraculously flowed with wine instead of water (Pliny, *NH*, II.231, XXXI.16; Diod. Sic., III.66.2). Hellenized readers, familiar with such stories, might suppose John's message to be that Jesus is greater than Dionysos. But it is doubtful how far John deliberately draws on Dionysiac imagery (Dodd, 1963, pp. 224f.; Morris, 1972, pp. 175f.). Although the miracle has some 'Hellenistic' colouring (including the presence of a banquet master), Jewish symbolism seems to be paramount; compare the miraculous production of water, oil, and barley-meal in the Moses, Elijah, and Elisha stories.

The possibility of another symbolic meaning must also be discussed. The stone water-jars are described as being there 'according to the *katharismos* [literally, purification] of the Jews' (2.6). Some commentators have suggested that a deliberate contrast is intended between the insipidness, or imperfection, of Judaism (symbolized by the water) and the exhilarating 'wine' of Christianity (e.g. Barclay, 1956, vol. 1, pp. 89f.; Hunter, 1965, p. 31). Thus the miracle has been seen as symbolizing the supersession of Judaism in the glory of Jesus (Barrett, 1978, p. 189). But it is far from obvious that this is John's intention. The reference to Jewish *katharismos* may be simply to explain the presence of so many large water-jars; it also points forward to the debate over purificatory rites in 3.25.

The 'sign' at Cana illustrates both the joys and the problems of studying John. A simple narrative is packed with potential symbolism with seemingly endless interpretative possibilities. There is no sure way of determining how many of these were intended by the Evangelist. All we can say is that he deliberately chose this 'sign' to open his account of Jesus' active ministry. Its most important message is probably that Jesus is God's eschatological agent in dispensing good gifts in the form of wine, a symbol of joy and of the 'messianic' age.

(2) The Official's Son (4.46–54)

This story forms a pair with the wine miracle. The narrative is quite straightforward: an official begs Jesus to heal his son who is dying of a fever. At first Jesus demurs (4.48; cf. 2.4), but the man persists; so Jesus tells him, 'Go; your son lives' (4.50). He trusts Jesus' word and returns home to find that the fever left his son at the exact time that Jesus spoke. The official 'believes' with all his household (cf. Acts 10.2; 11.14; 16.15). This healing at a distance is paralleled in the Synoptic (Q) healing of the centurion's servant (Mt. 8.5–13; Lk. 7.1–10), with many details in common with John, and the Syro-Phoenician woman's daughter (Mk 7.24–30). But John's episode appears to be independent of both, though possibly deriving from a common oral source with the Q story (Dodd, 1963, pp. 188–95; Davies and Allison, 1991, pp. 17f.).

Non-Jewish readers, including Gentile Christians, might be reminded of Greek and Roman tales of divine healers, including many seers and heroes. Some scholars see John as presenting Jesus as a *theios anēr* (cf. above, p. 34), like Apollonius of Tyana, an itinerant Neo-Pythagorean philosopher, whose supposed miracles are described by Philostratus (3rd cent. CE). But there is no need to look as late as this for parallels. From Homer onwards, miraculous cures were attributed to Asklepios and his sons, whose cults continued into the Graeco-Roman period when Asklepios is said to have cured fevers, paralysis, leprosy, and many other diseases (Blackburn, 1991, pp. 24–8, 188–91). Jewish readers (and Christians converted from Judaism) might be more inclined to interpret Jesus' actions in the light of Jewish charismatic healers. Many scholars quote an anecdote from the Babylonian Talmud (*b. Ber. Bar.* 43b): Rabbi Hanina ben Dosa, after praying for a colleague's sick son, told those who came to him for aid, 'Go, for the fever has left him'; they found that the boy had been healed at the exact same hour. The parallel with John 4.42 is striking, but the text is very late and so might have been influenced by John.[5]

More importantly, readers familiar with the Hebrew Bible would recall miracles attributed to Elijah and Elisha. 2 Kings 5 describes how Elisha cured Naaman of leprosy by an authoritative command to wash in the Jordan. Both Elijah and Elisha reputedly raised the dead (1 Kgs 17.17–24; 2 Kgs 4.18–37). The parallel with Elijah's restoration of the widow of Zarephath's son is particularly remarkable. Elijah says to the mother, 'See, your son *lives*', almost exactly the same words in the Septuagint (3 Kgms [1 Kgs] 17.23) as Jesus uses to the official, 'Go; your son *lives*' (Jn 4.50). The choice of the Hebraic-sounding term 'lives' (Greek *zaō*, cognate with *zōē*, 'life') rather than the idiomatic Greek 'is better' or 'has recovered' is striking. The miracle follows immediately after Jesus' encounter with the Samaritan woman, to whom Jesus has offered *living* water (4.10), 'welling up to eternal *life*' (4.14). This can hardly be coincidence. In restoring life to the dying boy Jesus acts out his life-giving powers, of which he has spoken to the Samaritan woman under the image of 'living water'. The gift of life to the boy echoes the Prologue's theme of life (1.4), and points forward to other passages featuring Jesus as life-giver (e.g. 5.26; 6.33), a prerogative shared with God. This second 'sign', then, shows Jesus as much more than a Hellenistic miracle worker (or *theios anēr*). It reveals him as closely associated with God, and as following in the steps of the Hebrew prophets.

(3) The Lame Man (5.1–47)

The healing of the lame man (5.1–9) follows a pattern of Hellenistic miracle story of a type often found in the Synoptics. A realistic setting is given – a pool in Jerusalem where disabled people gather in the hope of healing (5.2f.). The man's illness is described, including its length (38 years); Jesus' authoritative command is recorded, 'Rise, take up your bed, and walk' (5.8; cf. Mk 2.11). The man demonstrates the reality of his cure by doing precisely this. Similar features occur in the healings of Peter's mother-in-law (Mk 1.29–31 par.), of the woman bent double (Lk. 13.11–13), and in the raising of Jairus' daughter (Mk 5.22–4, 35–43). There are also parallels in Acts (3.1–10; 14.8–11). The most similar Synoptic miracle is the healing of the paralysed man at Capernaum (Mk 2.1–12 par.), to which John may be indebted.

In both John and Mark the lame man's healing is more than a simple miracle: it is also a controversy story. In Mark, the issue is Jesus' authority to forgive sins; in John, it is working on the Sabbath – an issue raised in other Synoptic miracle stories (e.g. Mk 3.1–6; Mt. 12.9–14; Lk. 13.10–17; 14.1–6), as well as in the grain controversy (Mk 2.23–8 par.). It is illuminating to compare Jesus' defence in the different Gospels. In the Synoptics, Jesus meets criticisms with rabbinical-style arguments, especially that known as *qal waḥomer* (literally 'light and heavy'), an argument from the lesser to the greater (e.g. Lk. 13.15f.; 14.5f.): if you would untie an animal so that it can drink, or rescue one from a pit on the sabbath, how much more should you free a suffering human being? In John, Jesus counters accusations of Sabbath-breaking by claiming that his Father is still working, and he is too (5.17). It was a matter of debate among learned Jews whether God could rest on the Sabbath without ceasing his creative activity. Jesus' response presupposes that God never ceases to be creative on the Sabbath; Jesus, as his Son, must be the same. This is a more radical defence than the Synoptic *qal waḥomer* arguments, or the clever repartee that 'the Sabbath was made for humankind, not humankind for the Sabbath' (Mk 2.27 par.).[6]

'The Jews' accuse Jesus of making himself 'equal with God', but he does not claim this. He rather stresses his subordination as a dutiful son: he does only what he 'sees' the Father doing (5.19); he can do nothing independently, and seeks the Father's will, not his own (5.30). But he acts with the full authority of the Father, who has granted him to have life 'within himself' and to execute judgement (5.22, 26f.). The Father himself bears witness to him (5.37), as do John the Baptist and his own deeds (*erga*). He reproaches his accusers for not believing in him, the one whom God has sent, and for not believing in Moses, who wrote of him (5.38, 45–7). In the face of these claims, the original healing which sparked off the criticisms is almost forgotten. While further symbolism has sometimes been read into this miracle,[7] its main purpose (besides depicting Jesus as a healer) is to serve as a peg on which to hang this christological discourse.

(4) The Feeding of the Multitude and (5) the Walking on the Water (6.1–71)

These two miracles are closely associated (cf. Mk 6.32–52) and may be discussed together. The scene is set in Galilee near Passover time.[8] First, the feeding miracle is related with its immediate consequences (6.1–15). Then, when it was dark and a strong wind blowing, Jesus walks on the water (6.16–21); he reassures the frightened disciples, who take him into the boat; it immediately arrives at the shore (cf. Ps. 107.30). Finally (6.22–71), the feeding is interpreted through a lengthy dialogue between Jesus, the crowd, 'the Jews', and the disciples, ending with some of them withdrawing. The feeding miracle is specifically called a 'sign' (6.14).

John's account is christologically rich and resonant with symbolism. Jews and Jewish Christian readers would, once again, be aware of precedents in the Elijah and Elisha stories, both prophets miraculously producing food at a time of need (1 Kgs 17.8–16; 2 Kgs 4.1–7, 42–4). Even closer is the parallel between Jesus' production of food in the desert at Passover-time and Moses' giving of manna to the Israelites, to which John specifically draws attention (6.31f., 49). The walking on the water suggests other familiar Scripture stories, including Elijah's and Elisha's crossing of the Jordan dry-shod (2 Kgs 2.8, 14), and, especially, Israel's crossing of the Red Sea under Moses after the first Passover (Ex. 14.19–25). All this leads readily to the crowd's identification of Jesus as 'the prophet who is to come into the world' (6.14). Their words allude to a specific text – Moses' promise that God will raise up a prophet like him (Dt. 18.15–18). Immediately after this the crowd attempt to make Jesus king (discussed below, Ch. 7). One gets a strong impression that for John the feeding miracle, like the wine miracle of Cana, symbolizes the advent of the end-time or 'messianic' age.[9]

John offers no interpretation of the walking on the water. Educated Greek readers, and Christians converted from Hellenism, might well recall tales of heroes like Euphemos, the companion of Jason, who walked on water without even wetting his feet (Apol. Rhod., 1.179–84), and of ships which miraculously sped their way under divine guidance (*h.Hom.*, III.418–21). Readers from a Jewish background would be more

likely to see parallels with God's actions in the Hebrew Bible, where
YHWH controls the unruly waters and makes his path in the sea (cf. Isa.
51.10; Ps. 77.19f.). This impression would be enhanced by Jesus' use of
the phrase *egō eimi* (6.20). While this might be simply a formula of recognition, 'It is I', it could also be understood absolutely in the sense of 'I
am', recalling YHWH's self-revelation to Moses at the burning bush (Ex.
3.14) and various Isaianic texts (discussed below, Ch. 12).

However, the ensuing dialogue does not focus on Jesus' divinity, but on
his giving food that endures to eternal life (6.27). The people refer to the
bread which their fathers ate in the desert (6.31; cf. Ex. 16.15). Jesus
corrects them: it was not Moses who *gave* the bread, but his Father who
gives the true bread from heaven (note the tenses, and John's characteristic
use of 'true' in the sense of 'real'). The people ask for this bread, and Jesus
identifies himself with the 'bread of life'. He has come down from heaven
to do the will of him who sent him. It is his Father's will that everyone who
sees the Son and puts faith in him may have eternal life, and be raised on
the last day (6.25–40). Thus Jesus is revealed as 'the prophet like Moses',
as fulfilling typologically[10] Moses' actions, and as superior to Moses.

'The Jews' complain, 'Isn't this the son of Joseph whose father and
mother we know?' (ironical words for readers familiar with the story of
the Virgin Birth). Jesus speaks of his mission from the Father (6.44f.),
citing 'and they shall all be taught by God' (Isa. 54.13). The inference
seems plain: Jesus' 'bread' is his life-bringing teaching. Yet somehow
Jesus also is the bread itself (6.35, 48). Those who ate manna in the
wilderness died, but those who eat the living bread will not die. Many
scholars assume that Jesus is now identified with personified Wisdom,
who summons people to her banquet (Prov. 9.5; Ecclus 24.19), feeding
those who keep Torah with 'the bread of understanding' and 'the water
of wisdom' (Ecclus 15.3). There are even more striking parallels in
Philo, who speaks of the divine *logos* distributing wisdom, the heavenly
food (*ourania trophē*) of the soul, which Moses calls 'manna' (*Quis
Rer.*, 191); the phrase 'true bread from heaven' (6.32) also recalls a
fragment of a possibly pre-Christian Sibylline oracle (preserved in
Theophilus of Antioch) which says that those who worship the true and
eternal God will receive life, and dwell in the Garden of Paradise, eating
'the sweet bread from the starry heaven' (Fr. 3, 46–9; Charlesworth,
1983, p. 471). It is striking that Jesus both *provides* food (6.27) and *is*
the food (6.33, 35).

Jesus goes on to say that the bread which he will give for the life of
the world is his 'flesh' (6.51c). 'The Jews' not unnaturally question how
this can be. He replies, 'Unless you eat the flesh of the Son of Man and
drink his blood, you have no life in you' (6.53); after repeating that he
is the bread come down from heaven, he says, 'Those who eat this bread

will live for ever' (6.58). The original miracle has faded into the background, as the thought has moved through themes of Jesus and Moses, Jesus and Wisdom, to Jesus' giving his 'flesh'. The section 6.51c–58 is most plausibly understood as alluding to the Eucharist, whose 'institution' is omitted from John's account of the Last Supper.[11] It is remarkable for interpreting this sacrament not primarily as a memorial (or bringing to remembrance) of Jesus' death (cf. 1 Cor. 11.24f.; Lk. 22.19), but rather as spiritual food, enabling the mutual indwelling of believers and Jesus and leading to everlasting life (6.56–8); compare Ignatius' description of the one eucharistic bread as 'the medicine of immortality, an antidote that we should not die, but live for ever with Jesus Christ' (*Eph.*, 20.2). However, it is unlikely that John intended 6.51c–58 to be understood exclusively of the Eucharist (Edwards, 2000). For him, the 'bread from heaven' is simultaneously Jesus' life-bringing teaching (cf. 6.63), the eucharistic bread, and Jesus' giving of his life for the world. The 'Bread of Life discourse' (6.26–59) has many resonances with the dialogue about the 'living water' (4.4–16); both may ultimately draw on Jewish traditions which interpreted the manna and the 'well' (i.e. the rock from which Moses struck water) as Torah.[12]

(6) The Blind Man, (9.1–41)

This story forms a pair with (3), the lame man's healing (5.1–47). Both stories are set in Jerusalem, where Jesus comes into conflict with the Jewish authorities. But whereas the cured lame man apparently does not come to faith, the newly sighted man becomes a model disciple. There are Synoptic parallels, but these are general rather than specific (Mk 8.22–6; Mt. 9.27–31; Mk 10.46–52 par.). In John the magnitude of the miracle is enhanced by the fact that the man was born blind. The miracle is depicted as one of Jesus' 'works', the man's blindness happening 'so that God's works may be disclosed in him' (9.3f.). The manner of healing is striking. Jesus makes 'clay' (a creative act) with his spittle, anoints the man, and bids him wash in the pool of Siloam (interpreted as 'Sent'); the injunction recalls Elisha's command to Naaman to wash in the Jordan (2 Kgs 5.10); for the use of spittle compare Mark 8.23.[13]

As with the lame man, the miracle leads to a dialogue, in this case quite dramatic. First his neighbours question the man, wondering whether he is indeed the person they knew. He is well aware that it is Jesus who healed him (9.8–12; contrast the lame man, 5.13). Then the Pharisees interrogate him, and readers discover that it was a Sabbath when his sight was restored (9.13–17). Next 'the Jews' establish the man's identity from his parents (9.18–23). The man is interrogated a second time, and 'cast out' (9.24–34). Jesus finds him and asks, 'Do you believe in the Son of Man?' He replies with faith (9.35–8). Finally Jesus confronts the Pharisees, describing them as 'blind', which they resent; their sin remains because they claim to be able to see (9.39–41).

Recurrent motifs are light and darkness, and blindness and sight. At the start Jesus proclaims, 'I am the light of the world' (9.5), picking up the Prologue's image of the *logos* as 'the true light' (1.9; cf. 3.19–21; 8.12; etc.). By calling Jesus 'light', John brings out his role as life-giver, revealer of God's true nature, and as judge (for the light shows up the darkness of evil). The miracle is a practical demonstration of Jesus' role in bringing 'light' – not just physical sight, but also spiritual insight. It further illustrates his call to decide between good and evil, knowledge of God or its opposite. There are repeated ironical contrasts between the man born blind, who moves from darkness to light, acknowledging Jesus first as 'a prophet' (9.17), then as sent from God (9.33), and finally as 'Son of Man' (9.35–8),[14] and the Jewish leaders, who move from apparent enlightenment to darkness or spiritual blindness. This use of 'blindness' to symbolize unbelief and sin can have been written only by a sighted person, as pointed out by John Hull (himself blind), who draws attention to the problems raised by such imagery for blind people (2001, pp. 49f., 87).

The drama of John 9 forms the main plank of the hypothesis that John should be read at two levels, that of the historical Jesus and that of the Johannine community (Martyn, 1979, esp. pp. 24–62; cf. Brown, 1979, esp. pp. 17–20). Martyn sees the newly sighted man as standing for Jewish Christians who, following the introduction of the *birkat ha-minim*, came out openly with their new faith despite risk of expulsion from the Synagogue (see above, pp. 48f.). It must be said that this is by no means the only context in which John 9 can be understood. Historically Jesus did come into conflict with the Jewish authorities, and some of his followers may have suffered already during his lifetime for their loyalty to him. As Christianity emerged as a distinct movement within Judaism, and then as a separate religious grouping, conflict intensified. Paul's letters often mention his sufferings as a Christian (e.g. 1 Thess. 2.14–16; 2 Cor. 11.24f.), a picture supported by Acts.[15] Josephus describes how the High Priest Ananus (the son of the Annas mentioned in John) had Jesus' brother James killed after condemnation by the Sanhedrin (*Ant.*, 20.200). In the Synoptics Jesus predicts that his followers will be persecuted (Mk 13.9; cf. Mt. 5.11f.; Lk. 6.22), including being flogged in synagogues – prophecies often seen as *post eventum*. John's references to synagogue expulsion (9.22; 12.42), and Jesus' warning that the disciples will be cast out of synagogues or killed (16.2), can readily be understood as foreshadowing the suffering that would come to some Christians. The newly sighted man functions as a shining example of faith, courage, and pertinacity.

(7) The Raising of Lazarus and its Consequences (11.1–53)

Lazarus' raising forms the climax of Jesus' miraculous signs. The story is elaborately constructed, with some detailed characterization, and is unique to John. Some scholars believe that it was freely created from Luke's story of Martha and Mary (10.38–42) and his tale of the rich man and Lazarus (16.19–31), which mentions the possibility of someone returning from the dead. Others see this suggestion as far-fetched. The episode is sometimes seen as a later element in John (see above, p. 47), but it plays a significant role in his story-line since it (rather than the Temple cleansing, as in the Synoptics) precipitates the Jewish leaders' plot to kill Jesus.

The Synoptics relate two stories of restoration from death – those of Jairus' daughter (Mk 5.22–43 par.) and the widow of Nain's son (Lk. 7.11–17) – an action seen as a messianic sign (cf. Mt. 11.5; Lk. 7.22). There are also parallels in Acts (9.36–42; 20.7–12), the Elijah–Elisha cycle, and other Jewish and Hellenistic sources. In the Synoptic stories (and those of Acts) the person restored to life has only just died, so that the possibility of resuscitation cannot be ruled out, whereas in John's story, Lazarus has been dead for four days, and his corpse is decaying. No convincing rationalization is possible: most commentators concentrate on possible symbolism.

As far as christology is concerned, Lazarus' raising forcefully demonstrates Jesus' power to give life. After healing the lame man, Jesus foretold that the dead would hear the voice of God's Son and live, and that those in the tombs would hear it and come forth (5.25, 28). Now a dead man is portrayed as physically coming out of a tomb at Jesus' command (11.43f.). Lazarus' resurrection brings glory to God, so that his Son may also be glorified (11.4). It provides a perfect setting for teaching on resurrection, including Jesus' famous saying, 'I am the resurrection and the life' (11.25). He is depicted both as the one who brings resurrection and the one who *is* the resurrection (just as he both gives and is the 'bread of life').

This episode also foreshadows Jesus' own resurrection. In both cases the dead man has been for some days in a cave-like tomb, sealed with a stone. In both he is swathed in bandages, with a separate head-cloth. But Lazarus comes out bound, whereas the risen Jesus emerges free, the graveclothes left behind. Lazarus comes back to life temporarily, for he will die again; Jesus rises to live eternally. Like his earlier miracles, this one causes division: some see and believe (11.45; cf. 12.11), while others report on Jesus to the Pharisees.

(8) The Miraculous Catch of Fish (21.1–14)

This last miracle occurs in John's Appendix. The risen Jesus reveals himself to seven disciples who have been fishing. He bids them lower their net on the right side, and it catches so many fish that they cannot haul it in. The miracle is paralleled in Luke 5.1–11. In both stories the men have been fishing all night without success. In both, Peter plays a prominent role: in Luke he falls down and 'worships' Jesus (in recognition of his uncanny powers, maybe even his divinity); in John he leaps out of the boat to go to him, but it is the 'beloved disciple' who first recognizes Jesus as 'the Lord'. In Luke, the catch is so heavy that the net breaks; in John, it remains intact. In Luke the miracle leads to the call of Peter to 'catch' people; in John it leads to Peter's pastoral commissioning, and the command 'Follow me' (21.15–19). The two stories must be related. Some suggest that Luke has used a miracle associated with Jesus' resurrection to enhance a call story – in the Marcan parallel (1.16–20) there is no miraculous catch. Others suppose that John has moved a miracle originally located at the start of Jesus' ministry to a post-resurrection context. Possibly the two stories draw on a common tradition, which the Evangelists use differently.

Like the feeding miracle of John 6, the miraculous draught of fish illustrates Jesus' care for his people in providing food (he has already cooked fish on a charcoal fire before they haul their catch in). John's description of its distribution, 'Jesus ... took the bread and gave it to them, and likewise the fish' (21.13), recalls both his earlier feeding miracle (6.11) and the breaking of bread in Luke's Emmaus meal (Lk. 24.30). For Christian readers all three meals would prefigure the Eucharist (cf. Mk 14.22), though it is uncertain whether this was John's intention. Many scholars interpret the miraculous catch as primarily a symbol for mission (cf. Mk 1.17 par.; also Matthew's parable of the drag-net, 13.47f.).[16] The significance of the 153 fish (21.11) is obscure: some interpret them as representing the nations of the world, but this is unlikely (Lindars, 1972, pp. 629f.). More probably the exceptionally large catch symbolizes God's generosity in response to obedience and faith (21.6f.); compare the abundant wine at Cana. The unbroken net may stand for the unity of the Church (Schnackenburg, 1982, p. 358). Certainly, for its author, this final appearance adds further proof of the reality of Jesus' resurrection, and illustrates his continuing concern for the disciples and by implication for the future Church.

Conclusions

Jesus' miracles most obviously depict him as a healer and wonder-worker: but it is clear that John intends more than this. Jesus is presented as a prophet, sent from God (cf. 3.2; 4.19). His actions recall those of Moses, Elijah, and Elisha; they could be seen as fulfilling Jewish expectations of the Deuteronomic 'prophet like Moses', or even of Elijah's return to prepare for 'the day of the Lord' (cf. Mal. 4.5; Mk 8.28; 9.11f.). The wine miracle and the feeding of the crowd would almost certainly be understood as symbolizing the inauguration of the new eschatological era. Jesus' restoration of mobility to the lame, sight to the blind, and life to the dead might also be seen as showing that God's salvation had drawn near (cf. Isa. 35.1–6; Mt. 11.5; Lk. 7.22). Thus the 'signs' point to Jesus as the expected 'messianic' deliverer, bringing vibrant new life, both physical and spiritual. They are the setting for three of his great 'I am' sayings: 'I am the bread of life' (6.35; cf. 6.48–51, 57f.), 'I am the light of the world' (9.5), and 'I am the resurrection and the life' (11.25).

The miracles reveal Jesus' special relationship with God. They are performed in the Father's name and show the Father's good works (*kala erga*, 10.32). They depict Jesus as God's emissary, who does what the Father does. They hint at Jesus' divinity, but do not make it explicit. They inspire faith (cf. 2.11; 4.53; 6.69; 9.37f.; 12.11); but some fail to believe (6.66–71; 9.39–41). They are indeed 'narrative christology'. Our next chapter will consider how 'confessions of faith' fill out this picture.

7

Christological Confessions and Titles for Jesus

The christology implied by Jesus' miracles is developed and made explicit by confessions of faith from those who encountered him. These acts of witness, often involving christological 'titles', begin already in the Prologue; they feature prominently in John's dramatic dialogues, and culminate in the acclamations of Mary Magdalene and Thomas in the Resurrection Narrative. They are complemented by what Jesus says about himself, by indirect statements about him, and by controversies, questions, and comments from Jesus' opponents, often used with dramatic irony (e.g. 7.41, 52; 9.29; 11.50; 19.3). The 'titles'[1] would convey different ideas to different readers. Most of them have a complex and controversial background in Judaism which can here be treated only in outline; most are also part of the common stock of Christian thinking about Jesus articulated in varying ways by the New Testament writers. This chapter concentrates on how the titles in John's christological confessions might have been understood by his first readers.

'Rabbi' or 'Teacher'

'Rabbi' is an Aramaic address of high respect for a religious teacher,[2] which John explains, presumably for Gentile readers (1.38), by translating it as *didaskale* (vocative of the Greek for 'teacher'). In the Synoptics, Jesus is twice addressed as 'Rabbi' in Matthew (both times by Judas), four or five times in Mark, but never in Luke. In John, he is called 'Rabbi' six times by disciples or would-be disciples (1.38, 49; 3.2; 4.31; 9.2; 11.8), and once by a crowd (6.25). The lengthened form 'Rabboni' (possibly more deferential or caritative) occurs once (20.16; cf. Mk 10.51, most manuscripts). John's comparatively frequent use of 'Rabbi' underlines both the Jewish flavour of his Gospel, and the importance for him of Jesus' role as teacher. In his programmatic 'Testimony' (1.19–51), the disciples are gathered following a rabbinic model whereby pupils seek out a teacher and find fellow-disciples, rather than by the Synoptic 'Follow me' (Philip in 1.43 is an exception); Jesus is here already twice addressed as 'Rabbi'. Later John stresses that Jesus taught publicly in synagogue and Temple (6.59; 7.14, 28; 8.20; 18.20). Teaching to individuals and disciples constitutes a high proportion of this Gospel.

Sometimes 'Rabbi' is seen as an inadequate faith-confession, since the address is also applied to other teachers (cf. 3.26). Barrett claims that it is put on the lips of 'imperfect or mistaken disciples' (1978, p. 180); Moloney thinks that it illustrates the 'poor quality' of the first disciples' initial understanding of Jesus (1998b, p. 60). While 'Rabbi' may occasionally be followed by a remark revealing an imperfect grasp of Jesus' mission (4.31; 11.8), too much should not be made of this. In 1.49 Nathanael follows it by acclaiming Jesus as 'Son of God', and 'King of Israel', both terms with very positive connotations. Nicodemus does not just call Jesus 'Rabbi' (3.2); he also acknowledges him as 'come from God' (an important theme for John). At the footwashing Jesus calls himself 'Teacher and Lord' (13.13), indicating a high understanding of the status of teacher, while giving an example of humble service.

Mary Magdalene's 'Rabboni' (20.16) is especially intriguing. Some scholars argue that to call the risen Jesus merely 'Teacher' must indicate limited faith. Brodie sees her as representing 'unbelieving Israel' (1993b, p. 567); Carson attempts a psychological explanation: 'It may not be the highest Christological confession ... but at this point Mary is enthralled by the restored relationship, not contemplating its theological implications' (1991, p. 641). By contrast others, seeking to find a nicely balanced parallel with Thomas' acclamation, 'My Lord and my God' (20.28), suggest that Mary's address implies divinity (so Hoskyns, 1947, p. 543; Marsh, 1968, p. 637). This idea is not supported by John's simple translation of 'Rabboni' as 'Teacher' (20.16).[3] In fact, Mary's 'Rabboni' is neither an 'inadequate' confession, nor a climactic acknowledgement of Jesus as God. It is a cry of recognition: she calls Jesus by the term by which she has always known him, 'Teacher!' Compare Martha's words to her sister: 'The Teacher is here and is calling you' (11.28). Jesus' role as teacher is of the profoundest significance for John's theology: his teaching is not his own, but that of God who sent him (3.31–4; 7.16; etc.). He is the Word of God, God's 'exegete' or interpreter (1.1, 18). To call him 'Rabbi' or 'Teacher' is not to belittle his status, but to express one of its most vital aspects.

'Prophet'

This term would be readily recognized by Gentile, Jewish, and Christian readers as denoting a spokesman for the gods or God. Already in the Synoptics, people speculate whether Jesus might be a prophet (Mk 8.28 par.); he is acclaimed as such after the 'triumphal entry' (Mt. 21.11), and after the raising of the widow of Nain's son (Lk. 7.16): 'A mighty prophet has arisen among us'. Jesus indirectly alludes to himself as a prophet when he wryly quotes a proverb about a prophet not having honour in his own country (Mk 6.4; Mt. 13.57; Lk. 4.24), a saying given a puzzling new twist by John (4.44). He is explicitly acknowledged as 'prophet' by the Samaritan woman (4.19)[4] after he has given her details of her life that no stranger could possibly have known (prophets were popularly supposed to have supernatural knowledge of events past and present, as well as future). She later speculates whether he is 'messiah', and helps bring others to faith in him (4.29). The newly sighted man also acknowledges Jesus as 'prophet' (9.17); Barrett sees this acknowledgement as merely revealing awareness 'of the presence of an unusual person, who excites wonder and respect' (1978, p. 360). But the context suggests much more: Jesus has just effected an incredibly difficult cure – restoration of sight to a man blind from birth, an action revealing that God is powerfully with him. The appellation 'prophet' would align him with the great prophets of old – Moses, famed for his wonders at the Exodus, and Elijah and Elisha, both workers of healing miracles (cf. above, Ch. 6).

The anarthrous (indefinite) use of 'prophet' should be distinguished from that with the definite article. Twice Jesus is unambiguously acclaimed as *'the* prophet': in Galilee after his feeding miracle, when the people say, 'This is truly the Prophet who is to come into the world' (6.14), and in Jerusalem after his call to the thirsty (7.37–40), echoing Isaiah 55.1 (cf. Rev. 22.17). In these two places the definite article implies a specific prophet,[5] most likely the 'prophet like Moses' predicted in the words: 'A prophet I will raise up for them from among their brethren, like you [Moses], and I will put my words in his mouth; and he shall speak to them everything I shall command him' (Dt. 18.18). This text may have referred originally to a succession of prophets who would teach the people faithfully, but it became understood as foretelling an eschatological (end-time) prophet. This belief is attested already at Qumran, where the *Community Rule* speaks of the coming of 'the Prophet and the Anointed Ones of Aaron and Israel' (1QS IX.11; Vermes, 1998, p. 110). Early Christians identified 'the Prophet' with Jesus (Acts 3.22; 7.37), an identification seemingly accepted by John, who has earlier referred to Jesus as the 'one of whom Moses wrote in the Law' (1.45; cf. 5.46). The theme is especially apposite in John 6 with its further reference to Moses and its echoes of Exodus themes (6.32). Just as the Deuteronomic prophet will speak what God tells him, so does Jesus (7.16f.; 14.24; cf. 17.14).

Immediately after acknowledging Jesus as 'the Prophet', the people try to take him by force to make him king (6.15). Many scholars assume that 'the Prophet' is here understood as a political 'royal messiah', and that Jesus withdraws to avoid a popular uprising. This may be John's intention, though contemporary Jewish evidence for a 'messianic' understanding of 'the Prophet' is lacking (in 1QS IX.11 'the Prophet' is clearly distinguished from 'the Anointed Ones').[6] But Josephus attests that some messianic claimants were called 'prophets' (*Ant.*, 20.97f., 169; cf. Acts 5.36; 21.38).[7] Perhaps we are to imagine the people's reaction in John 6.15 as a mistaken response to the proper recognition of Jesus as 'the Prophet' (Schnackenburg, 1980, p. 19).

'Messiah' or 'Christ'

'Messiah' (Hebrew *mashiah*; cf. *mashah*, 'anoint') would be unfamiliar to Gentiles; hence the usual Christian rendering *christos*, 'anointed' (cf. Greek *chriō*, 'anoint'), a term found already in the Septuagint. For Jews it would suggest somebody specially chosen by God, though some might be puzzled by its titular use by Christians. In the Hebrew Bible *mashiah* is an adjective rather than a title, being used of kings who were anointed as a sign of their divine appointment (e.g. 1 Sam. 15.1; 24.6). It is also applied to the High Priest and other priests (e.g. Ex. 28.41), occasionally to prophets (1 Kgs 19.16; cf. Isa. 61.1, where it is metaphorical).

Christian readers would be well familiar with the term, which is applied to Jesus in virtually every book of the New Testament. For them it would denote Jesus' role as saviour and redeemer, fulfilling a whole range of Scripture prophecies, including some where the word *mashiaḥ* is not used (e.g. Isa. 7.14; 9.2–7; 11.1–10; Mic. 5.2).

John is the only New Testament writer to use the transliterated Semitic form *messias*, explaining it both times (1.41; 4.25). He uses 'Christ' or 'the Christ' no fewer than 19 times (cf. Mk, 8 times; Mt., 17 times; Lk., 12 times), beginning in the Prologue with the formula 'Jesus Christ' – a solemn Christian usage where 'Christ' is almost a proper name (cf. 17.3). The phrase 'the Christ', presuming the identification of God's 'Anointed' with one particular individual, comes in debates about Jesus' identity (7.26, 27, 31, 41, twice, 42; 10.24; 12.34; cf. 9.22), in confessions of faith by individuals (1.41; 4.29; 11.27; cf. 4.25), in the Baptist's denials that he is 'the Christ' (1.20; 3.28; cf. 1.25), and in John's conclusion on the Gospel's purpose (20.31).

What sort of 'messiah' is Jesus in John? It may be helpful to consider some Jewish post-biblical developments, bearing in mind that beliefs varied, and that the dating, interpretation, and sometimes even the readings of texts are disputed, with the result that exact knowledge is hard to attain. It is clear that by the time John wrote many Jews expected a 'royal messiah', from the tribe of Judah, who would liberate his people from Roman rule and usher in a period of peace, justice, and prosperity. Creatively interpreting scriptural texts which spoke of God's blessings on David's royal successors (e.g. 2 Sam. 7.11–16; Ps. 89.3f., 33–7), a 'shoot' from the stump of Jesse (Isa. 11.1, 10), and 'a righteous Branch' (Jer. 23.5), they began to look for a specific figure descended from David who would liberate Israel. Like David he would be a 'shepherd', a prince who would feed and care for his united 'flock' (Ezk. 34.23f.). Important evidence comes from the Qumran texts (before 70 CE), which look for a triumphant, royal figure, called 'the Branch of David' and 'Anointed One of Israel'.[8] Other non-canonical Jewish texts fill out the picture. The *Psalms of Solomon* (also before 70 CE) describe the massacres and desecration perpetrated by 'the Lawless One' (Pompey), and give glowing descriptions of the 'Son of David', the 'Lord Messiah' (or 'Lord's Anointed'), who would purify Jerusalem and reign as king (17, esp. 11–32; cf. 18.5–9). A little later, *Fourth Ezra* (= 2 *Esdras*) tells how the Most High has kept the Anointed One from the posterity of David 'to the end of days'. Like a lion roused from the forest he will first reprove and then destroy the 'eagle' (symbolizing Rome) and deliver his people (4 *Ez.* 11—12, esp. 12.31–4).

Usually a purely human figure is expected; but some texts picture 'the

Anointed' (or 'Chosen One') as pre-existent, present before the Lord of the Spirits, and as sitting in glory on God's throne ready to judge (so *1 En.* 48—51[9]). Another expectation was for 'the Anointed of Aaron' (e.g. CD XII.22; Vermes, 1998, p. 141), a priestly figure of Aaronic descent, a teacher who would interpret Torah, bringing true enlightenment (CD VII.18; Vermes, 1998, p. 133; cf. *Test. Levi,* 18). One Qumran text describes this priestly 'Anointed One' as begotten (*yalad*) by God (1QSa II.11; Vermes, 1998, p. 159). The same text simultaneously looks forward to a royal 'Anointed One', while another (1QS IX.11, already cited) refers to the coming of 'the Prophet' as well as 'the Anointed Ones of Aaron and Israel'. Some Jews thought that the messiah's origin would remain unknown until his appearing (*1 En.* 48.6; *4 Ez.* 7.28f.; cf. Justin, *Dial.* 8; on Jewish messianic ideas, see further Hahn, 1969, ch. 3; Neusner, 1987; Charlesworth, 1992; Horbury, 1998a).

To return to John's presentation: unlike the Synoptics he never uses the title 'Son of David' of Jesus. This may be because he wishes to avoid depicting him as a political or national liberator; but he knows the belief that the Christ would be a descendant of David, born in Bethlehem (7.41f.; cf. Mt. 2.5, citing Mic. 5.2). He also shows himself familiar with the concept of a 'hidden messiah' when he depicts a crowd as saying, 'We know whence this man comes; but when the Christ comes nobody will know his origin' (7.27; cf. 9.29). He shows awareness of the idea that the 'messiah' will work miracles (7.31). In this he may have been influenced by Christian interpretations of passages like Isaiah 35.5f., 'Then shall the eyes of the blind be opened, and the ears of the deaf unstopped; then shall the lame leap like a hart, and the tongue of the dumb sing' (see further Brown, 1966, p. 313; Barrett, 1978, p. 323; Schnackenburg, 1980, pp. 39f.).

John recognizes Jesus as a royal figure (1.49; 12.13–16; 19.19–21), but stresses that his kingdom is 'not of this world' (18.33–7). Whether he also saw Jesus as a priestly 'messiah' is debatable. Jesus refers to his 'consecration' by the Father for his work (10.36, using *hagiazō*; cf. *hagios,* 'holy'), and in his 'High-Priestly Prayer' when he intercedes for the disciples and future believers (17.17, 19); John's unique description of Jesus' seamless robe (19.23) may also suggest a priestly role. In 6.68f., in a passage comparable to Mark's version of Peter's confession of Jesus as 'the Christ' (Mk 8.29), Peter confesses Jesus as 'God's Holy One', who has 'the words of life'.[10] The title 'Holy One' is not specifically associated with the 'messiah' in first-century Judaism, but was given to Aaron, the archetypal High Priest (Ps. 106.16); holiness was also seen as characteristic of priests generally and of prophets (2 Kgs 4.9 Septuagint; Jer. 1.5; Wisd. 11.1). John's use of this term would suit an understanding of Jesus either as a prophet, acting as spokesman for God, or as a priestly teacher of the type envisaged at Qumran. Jesus' action in 'cleansing' the Temple (Jn 2.13–22) could also readily be interpreted as the deed of a priestly (or royal) 'messiah' (cf. Mal. 3.1–4; Zech. 14.20f.; Ps. Sol. 17.26–30); an eschatological purification of the Temple cult was also expected at Qumran.

'Son of God'

This designation is used in apposition to 'Christ' in both 11.27 and 20.31, and may be intended to help explain that term for Gentiles. But it would again suggest different things to different readers. Few living in the Graeco-Roman world could be unfamiliar with the claims of Hellenistic monarchs and Roman emperors to be 'sons of God'; those with a Greek education would also be aware of numerous mythological figures like Herakles and the Dioskouroi (literally 'sons of Zeus') to whom divine paternity was ascribed. However, for traditional Jews (and Christians familiar with the Jewish Scriptures) 'Son of God' would have rather different overtones. In Semitic languages 'son of x' is often used to indicate character, an idiom imitated in semitizing Greek, e.g. 'son of Gehenna' (Mt. 23.15), 'sons of light' (Jn 12.36; cf. Eph. 5.8). In the Hebrew Bible (including the Septuagint) 'sons of God' is used for angels as God-like beings (Job 38.7; Dan. 3.25), and for righteous people as sharing God's character (Ecclus 4.10; Wisd. 2.17f.; cf. Mt. 5.9). Additionally, the Davidic king was pictured as God's son (cf. Ps. 2.7), an idea extended to his royal 'messianic' descendant (2 Sam. 7.11–14; cf. Ps. 89.19–37). By the first century CE God's son seems to be directly equated with 'messiah' (4 Ez. 7.28f., etc.; cf. 4Q 174; 1QSa II.11). Christians familiar with Paul's writings, or the Letter to the Hebrews, or the birth narratives of Matthew and Luke, would find still more significance in the designation 'Son of God'.

John calls Jesus 'Son of God' c. nine times and 'the Son' – a usage probably derived from this – c. 18 times. 'The Son' occurs exclusively on the lips of Jesus (3.17; 'his only Son' may be either Jesus' words or the narrator's reflection). It conveys Jesus' sense of familial relationship and unity with God, his subordination to God, and his authority to act in God's name. 'Son of God' is used with the same connotations on Jesus' lips (5.25; 10.36; 11.4; 12.23; cf. 3.18). It is also used quasi-messiani-cally in faith-confessions, as when Nathanael acknowledges him as 'Son of God, the King of Israel' (1.49). A similar meaning is probable when the Baptist testifies to him as the one on whom the Spirit descended and remained, the 'Son of God' (1.33f.);[11] the messiah was often seen as the bearer of God's Spirit.

In 11.27 Martha confesses Jesus as 'the Christ, the Son of God, the one coming into the world'. While 'the coming one' could denote Elijah (cf. Mal. 3.1; 4.5) or the Deuteronomic prophet (cf. Jn 6.14), its juxta-position with 'Christ' and 'Son of God' strongly suggests that it is intended here messianically (cf. Mt. 11.2f.; Lk. 7.19). The idea of Jesus as 'the coming one' occurs also in the Baptist's testimony (1.15, 27, 30), in speculations about the Christ (7.27, 31, 41, 42), and in the crowd's shout as Jesus enters Jerusalem: 'Blessed is he that comes in the Name of the Lord, even the King of Israel' (12.13). To some, at least, it would suggest Jesus' identification with a 'royal messiah'. But for John it prob-ably has deeper meaning: he has Jesus refer regularly to himself as 'coming' or 'coming into the world' (5.43; 9.39; 10.10; 12.46f.), hinting at both his mission and his pre-existence. Moloney argues that Martha's confession, reflecting as it does contemporary messianic expectation, falls short of true Johannine faith, being at best partial (1996, p. 162; 1998b, p. 339). But no single formula can express the full profundity of Christian understanding of Jesus' person and it is hard to see what more could be expected of her. John's own Conclusion refers to Jesus as 'the Christ, the Son of God' (20.31). Martha's words, then, should be seen as representing a real insight into his identity.

'Saviour of the World'

In 4.42 the Samaritans confess Jesus as *ho sōtēr tou kosmou*, 'the Saviour of the World' (1 Jn 4.14 is the only other New Testament occurrence). This title also would have different connotations for different readers. Gentiles familiar with Graeco-Roman cults would be reminded of pagan 'saviour gods', like Asklepios, the god of healing, Isis, or Zeus, all worshipped under the title 'Saviour'. They (and others) would know that 'Saviour' was also applied to Hellenistic rulers such as Ptolemy Soter and Roman emperors for their exploits in saving people from their enemies and establishing peace (both Nero and later Hadrian were acclaimed 'Saviour of the World'). In using this title John may be seeking to elucidate his idea of Jesus as 'messiah' for non-Jews by showing that Jesus deserves this appellation far better than political and military leaders. Readers knowing the Jewish Scriptures might also recall God's role as Saviour (Septuagint *sōtēr*) in texts like Isaiah 45.15, 21 and Psalms 25.5; 27.9. Christians acquainted with Luke's Gospel would remember his calling both God (1.47) and Jesus 'Saviour' (2.11). Others might recall Matthew's picture of Jesus as the one who would save his people from their sins (1.21), or Paul's understanding of Jesus as Saviour (e.g. Phil. 3.20).

Some have claimed that *sōtēr* in John 4.42 and the Samaritan woman's earlier faith-confessions reflect contemporary Samaritan theology; but this is very doubtful.[12] John seems to use these dialogues to express his own ideas. For him Jesus is not just 'Saviour', but 'Saviour *of the World*', adding a universal dimension to Jewish messianic hopes. And for him the primary meaning of salvation is not physical security, but eternal life and preservation from judgement: 'God sent the Son into the world, not to condemn the world, but that the world might be saved through him' (3.17; cf. 5.34; 12.47).

'Lamb of God'

This designation occurs only on the lips of John the Baptist: 'Behold, the Lamb of God, who takes away the sin of the world' (1.29; cf. 1.34). O'Neill (1997) sees it as a 'messianic' title, citing the *Testament of Joseph* 19.8, where a virgin from the tribe of Judah gives birth to a lamb, which overcomes warring animals by trampling them underfoot (cf. also *Test. Benj.* 3.8). This idea is also viewed with favour by Beasley-Murray (1987, pp. 24f.). But such animal imagery, though at home in Revelation (e.g. 17.14), seems alien to John's Gospel. There are suspicions of Christian interpolations into the *Testaments* and no evidence that an apocalyptic lamb was expected to remove sin. Other scholars have suggested that 'Lamb of God' echoes Isaiah's 'Servant', led like a lamb to the slaughter, who is said to have borne the sins of many (Isa. 53.7, 12). This text was certainly interpreted messianically by early Christians (e.g. Acts 8.32–5), though not, at this date, by Jews. One should, however, note that the same passage also compares Isaiah's 'Servant' to a sheep which did not open its mouth before its shearers (53.7), whereas John's Jesus is hardly silent before his accusers.

While some learned readers in John's day might have detected allusions to an apocalyptic lamb or Isaiah's Servant, more would probably understand the Baptist's words as referring to the Paschal lamb as a symbol of deliverance (cf. the 'slain lamb' of Rev. 5.6; 7.14; etc.; 1 Cor. 5.7f.; 1 Pet. 1.19).[13] Jewish and Jewish-Christian readers might also recall the *tamid*, a perpetual daily offering of two lambs in the Temple (Ex. 29.38–42), or the female lamb prescribed as a sin-offering (Lev. 4.32).[14] These lambs were, however, killed to atone for the sin of Israel (or of individual Jews), whereas Jesus is said to take away the sin *of the world*, with universal reference (cf. 1 Jn 2.1f.; also Jn 4.42, cited above). The Evangelist presents Christian theology rather than the historical words of John the Baptist.

'Son of Man'

'One of the greatest puzzles of New Testament theology and criticism' (Barrett, 1978, p. 72), this title (*ho huios tou anthrōpou*) appears in all four Gospels exclusively on Jesus' lips (except Jn 12.34, where a crowd echoes Jesus' words, asking 'Who is this Son of Man?'). The phrase is not normal Greek, but corresponds to the Hebrew *ben 'adam*, literally 'son of humankind', i.e. a human being or man, or its Aramaic equivalent, *bar (e)nash(a)*, used idiomatically to mean 'a man like myself'. One would expect it to emphasize a person's humanity, or mortality, just as 'son of God' implies God-like qualities. In the Hebrew Bible it is not a title, but is normally used, in either the singular or plural without the definite article, as a general term for 'man' (i.e. 'humanity'), often in poetic parallelism with *'adam* or *'ĕnosh*, with similar meaning (e.g. Num. 23.19; Ps. 144.3; Job 25.6). It occurs some 70 times in Ezekiel (e.g. 2.1), when God addresses the prophet as '(you) son of man'. In a striking passage of Daniel (7.13f.), the prophet sees 'one like a son of man' coming with the clouds and being presented to the 'Ancient of Days'; he is given glory and an everlasting kingdom. Probably an angelic being is intended, though he later seems to be identified with 'the saints of the Most High' (7.18, 22, 27).

In the New Testament 'son of man' occurs for humanity collectively (e.g. Heb. 2.6, quoting Ps. 8.4; Mk 3.28, plural), once for Jesus standing at God's right hand in glory (Acts 7.56, with definite article), and twice in Revelation (1.13; 14.14), describing the glorified Christ as 'one like a son of man', with echoes of Daniel's vision. It also occurs 82 times in the Gospels as a self-designation of Jesus (Aune, 1988), a usage which many scholars believe may reflect the historical Jesus' own speech patterns (e.g. Mk 8.31: 'the Son of Man must suffer many things'). In the Gospels the phrase occurs with the definite article, and is often titular. There has been extensive scholarly debate about the origin, authenticity, and meaning of these 'Son of Man' sayings. Traditionally the Synoptic examples are divided into three groups, where Jesus refers to (a) his earthly activities (e.g. Mt. 8.20), (b) his forthcoming passion and resurrection (e.g. Mk 9.31 par.), and (c) his future coming in glory (e.g. Mk 13.26 par.). Some examples in the first two groups may reflect Aramaic idiom and have a wider reference than Jesus alone (Lindars, 1983, esp. ch. 2); those of the third group may reflect Daniel 7.13f.

John uses '(the) Son of Man' 13 times (details in Schnackenburg, 1968, p. 530), with little trace of the colloquial Aramaic idiom, except where he is dependent on the Synoptics (Lindars, 1983, p. 145; Casey, 1996, pp. 59f., denies any traces). These occur where Jesus refers to his heavenly descent and ascent (3.13; cf. 6.62), his 'lifting up', or 'glorification', on the cross (3.14, etc.), and his roles as heavenly revealer (1.51; cf. 3.12f.) and judge (5.27).[15] Many of John's first readers would find the term puzzling, though they would soon grasp that it was being used as a self-designation of Jesus. Some might imagine that John intended it in similar ways to Gnostic writings. Here phrases like 'Man', 'First

Man', 'Perfect Man', and 'Son of Man' are used for a primordial human being made in God's image, or a divine being in the 'Pleroma' (fulness of heavenly beings). But it is uncertain how far these ideas were current when John wrote; many of the texts are so abstruse that, even if known to John's readers, they would offer little illumination.[16] The Church Fathers assumed that 'Son of Man' referred to Jesus' human nature in contrast to 'Son of God', denoting his divinity (Lampe, 1961, p. 1428); but John does not use the terms in this way. Rather he seems to draw on an understanding of 'the Son of Man' as a heavenly being, as illustrated in *1 Enoch* (46–53, 61f., etc.), where this figure is pre-existent, and identified with both 'the Elect One' and 'the Messiah' (and in some way with Enoch), and is invited to sit on God's throne;[17] comparable ideas are also found in *4 Ezra* (esp. 11—13). Readers familiar with such texts might well perceive John as depicting Jesus as a similar being.

John's usage is complex and varied, but it seems fair to say that he uses 'the Son of Man' to denote both Jesus' role as a representative human being who is 'lifted up', i.e. crucified, for the sake of humanity (3.14; 8.28; 12.23, 34c; cf. 13.31f.), and as revealer of heavenly things, because he was with God before creation and is in constant communion with God (3.12f.; cf. 1.18, etc.). Like Jacob's ladder, he links heaven and earth (1.51). It is precisely because he is the Son of Man that Jesus can act as judge (5.27), not merely as representative 'man', but as 'humanity restored and vindicated by God' (Barrett, 1978, p. 262). (See further Marshall, 1990, pp. 63–82; Moloney, 1978; Pazdan, 1991, pp. 21–9 with résumé of scholarship; Davies, 1992, pp. 182–96.)

Sometimes Jesus is called simply *ho anthrōpos*, 'the man', without any special theological connotations, except perhaps in 19.5. Here Pilate displays Jesus, bleeding from his scourging, and wearing his purple robe and crown of thorns, and says, 'Behold, the man'. Scholars debate whether the words are uttered to mock or excite pity; they are probably a *double entendre*, meaning 'poor fellow' (a regular use of *anthrōpos*) and hinting at Jesus' role as 'Son of Man', John having substituted a normal Greek expression for the Semitizing 'Son of Man', which would have sounded odd on Pilate's lips.[18]

Kyrios ('Sir', 'Master', 'Lord')

This is probably the most ambiguous of the designations applied to Jesus. It can serve as a polite address for male persons, like the English 'Sir' (e.g. Jn 12.21), or as the equivalent of the Aramaic *mari*, 'My Lord', in deferential address to kings, teachers, or social superiors. It was a title for the Roman emperor (cf. *kyrios Kaisar*, 'Caesar is Lord') and for pagan gods (e.g. 'the Lord Serapis'); also a Greek rendering for *'adonai*, standing for YHWH, in both Septuagint and New Testament (cf. Jn 1.23; 12.13). It is also a Christian title given to Jesus to express his exaltation and universal authority (e.g. Phil. 2.11). Its meaning must be determined by context, and different readers would obviously understand the term in varying ways.

John uses *kyrios* some 46 to 50 times of Jesus (depending on manuscript readings, and the interpretation of ambiguous phrases). Some 30 examples are in the vocative, *kyrie*, usually translated as 'Sir': these are generally discounted in christological discussions. Moule (1977, p. 35) goes so far as to say that to include them is like counting a schoolboy's 'O Sir' as evidence that the schoolmaster has been knighted! The comparison, though amusing, is misleading. John shows himself familiar with the standard Christian term *ho kyrios* ('the Lord') for Jesus (e.g. 6.23; 11.2; 20.2; 21.7, twice; 21.12). In dialogues he sometimes uses *kyrie* quite subtly to indicate a transition from politeness to faith, e.g. the newly sighted man's address of Jesus in 9.36 and 38 (where the RSV quite properly translates *kyrie* first as 'Sir', and then as 'Lord'). Martha twice addresses Jesus as *kyrie* in the context of faith-professions (11.21, 27; rendered 'Lord' both times in the RSV, but only the second time in the NEB). Sometimes there is irony, as when Mary Magdalene addresses the risen Jesus as *kyrie* in the sense of 'Sir', presuming him to be the gardener, having just used the same word for him as 'Master' or 'Lord' (20.15; cf. 20.13). In 21.7 the 'beloved disciple's' joyful cry, 'It is the Lord', represents his recognition of the mysterious lakeside figure as his beloved teacher or 'master' (cf. Dalman, 1902, pp. 327–31). It would also be understood by many as an acknowledgement of Jesus as 'Lord'.[19]

'My Lord and My God'

With this acclamation of Thomas (20.28: *ho kyrios mou kai ho theos mou*) we reach 'the supreme christological pronouncement of the Fourth Gospel' (so Brown, 1966, p. 1047). Naturally the phrase would not have identical connotations for all readers. There is good evidence that the emperor Domitian demanded to be called 'Lord and God.', a form of address unacceptable to many Romans (Suetonius, *Dom.*, 13; Martial, *Epigr.*, V.8.1, X.72.3; discussion in Aune, 1997–8, pp. 310f.). One can imagine how some readers might react to finding the same titles applied to Jesus! Some might, of course, interpret John's use of the phrase as polemic against the emperor cult, as has often been suggested for Revelation, which uses the same phrase in its account of the heavenly worship (4.11).

Others might see John's use of this phrase as bestowing on Jesus the same titles as the Hebrew Bible ascribes to YHWH (cf. Pss 30.2f.; 35.23;

88.1; Zech. 13.9 Septuagint). This does not, however, mean that John should be seen as simply equating Jesus with God, still less subscribing to the later doctrines of the creeds. This is one disciple's faith-confession, its individual character being heightened by the repetition of the personal pronoun, '*My* Lord and *my* God' (see further below, Ch. 12).

Conclusions

The titles accorded to Jesus in confessions of faith contribute, each in its own way, to John's overall presentation of christology. Jesus is acknowledged in turn as Israel's 'messiah' and king, as God's Son and Holy One, as Saviour of the World, and as sacrificial 'Lamb'. He comes as a teacher and prophet, in fulfilment of Moses' promises, revealing God's nature in life-bringing words and actions. He is 'the Son of Man' who came down from heaven and returns to the Father through the way of the cross, an example of love and conformity to God's will. He is 'Master' and 'Lord', demanding obedience and loyalty, but also acts as a slave in washing his disciples' feet. While several of the faith-confessions effectively acknowledge Jesus' character as like God's, only Thomas's acclamation actually calls him 'God'. Thus John's faith-confessions themselves serve as 'narrative theology', reinforcing and developing the message of the 'signs'. The next chapter will consider how John uses other actions, and especially Jesus' passion and resurrection, to express his christology.

8

Jesus' Passion
and Resurrection

What light does John's depiction of Jesus' death and resurrection shed on his understanding of Jesus' person and mission? Perhaps the most striking point is his perception of Jesus' passion as something that Jesus actively undertakes rather than as something he passively endures. A basic theme in the Synoptics is that Jesus is a *suffering* messiah. In Mark he teaches his disciples that the Son of Man must suffer grievously, be rejected by the elders, High Priests, and scribes, and be killed, and rise again three days later (8.31; cf. 9.12, 31; 10.33f.). Matthew and Luke have similar predictions, and Luke has the risen Jesus specifically explain that this suffering was foretold by the prophets (24.26f.). But although John presents Jesus as rejected by his own people (1.11; 12.37; 18.40; etc.), he never once uses *paschō*, 'suffer', of Jesus. Rather he depicts him as giving his life voluntarily, in obedience to the Father, knowing that he will rise again: as he says, 'I have power to lay [my life] down, and I have power to take it up again. No one takes it from me, but I lay it down of my own accord' (10.17f.; cf. 10.11, 15). In describing Jesus' passion John stresses his autonomy: he knows before-hand who will betray him, and tells Judas to do quickly what he has to do (13.11, 18, 26f.; cf. 6.70f.). When the soldiers come to arrest Jesus, Judas does not need to identify him with a kiss, for he identifies himself with the words 'I am [he]' (18.5f.) – possibly a divine 'epiphany' (discussed below, Ch. 12). Jesus takes the initiative in bidding them let his disciples go (18.8f.), fulfilling words from his Farewell Prayer, 'I have guarded them, and none of them perished, except the son of perdition, that Scripture might be fulfilled' (17.12).

Trial and 'Glorification'

When brought before Pilate, Jesus questions the governor in a way that would be impertinent for an ordinary prisoner (18.34–7), speaking of truth, and of his own kingship, 'not of this world' – hardly the conduct of someone on trial for his life. He even tells Pilate that he would have no authority over him if it had not been given him 'from above' (19.11). This contrasts with his silence in the Synoptics before both the High Priest and Pilate (Mk 14.60f.; 15.4f.; Mt. 26.62f.; 27.14; Lk. 23.9; cf. 1 Pet. 2.23). In John, Jesus carries his own cross (19.17); contrast Mark (15.21 par.), where it is carried by Simon of Cyrene. John's trial and crucifixion narratives are full of symbolic allusions to Jesus' kingship, including his crowning with thorns, being arrayed in purple, and mock-ingly acclaimed king (19.1–3). His dying cry, 'It is accomplished' (*tete-lestai*), echoes words from his Farewell Prayer, when he spoke prolepti-cally of having completed (*teleiōsas*) the work God gave him to do (17.4); cf. 13.1: 'he loved them to the end' (*eis telos*). Then 'he bowed his head and handed over his spirit' (19.30), words bringing out the voluntary nature of his death.[1] The purpose of all this is to show that, far from being passive, Jesus consents to and controls what happens to him: he dies so that God may be glorified, and so doing is himself glori-fied (17.1–5). He willingly drinks the cup that the Father has given him (18.11), and reigns from the cross (19.19–22). This is John's solution to the problem of a crucified messiah, 'a stumbling-block to Jews and fool-ishness to Gentiles' (1 Cor. 1.23; cf. Gal. 5.11; Heb. 12.2).[2]

This image of the passion as Jesus' triumph rather than humiliation is borne out by earlier references which carefully prepare the way for John's presentation of Jesus' death. In his passion predictions Jesus speaks of being 'lifted up' or 'exalted' (Greek *hypsoō*) rather than of suffering (e.g. 3.14; 8.28; 12.32f.). He repeatedly refers to his 'hour' (e.g. 7.30; 8.20), when he will be 'glorified' (*doxazō*: 12.23f.; 17.1; cf. 12.16; 13.31f.), a theme already obliquely heralded by the references to his 'glory' in the Prologue (1.14) and the wine miracle (2.11). In this understanding John was probably influenced by Isaiah's picture of the Lord's despised and rejected Servant (52.13—53.12), who bore his people's iniquities and was vindicated by God. The coincidences of language are striking: in Isaiah (52.13, Hebrew text) God promises: 'My servant ... shall be high [*yarum*], and lifted up [*niśśa'*], and exceedingly exalted [*gabah*]' (Septuagint, *hypsōthēsetai kai doxasthēsetai sphodra*); in John (12.23, 32), Jesus is 'lifted up' (*hypsoomai*) and 'glorified' (*doxazomai*). In Isaiah the Servant 'pours out his soul to death' (53.12, Hebrew text); in John, Jesus 'hands over' his spirit, using *paradidōmi* (cf. Isa. 53.12 Septuagint, with the same verb in the passive).[3] John's knowledge of this part of Isaiah is shown by his direct quotation in 12.38 of Isaiah 53.1. He also refers to Isaiah's call vision (12.40f., citing Isa. 6.10); he says that Isaiah 'saw' Jesus' glory and spoke of him. Presumably he understood Isaiah as seeing the pre-existent Word, identified with YHWH's glorious presence.[4]

But Jesus' 'glorification' in John does not just encompass his death; it also involves his resurrection, seen as part of one movement with his exaltation. At the 'triumphal entry' when the crowds acclaim Jesus as 'King of Israel', John quotes Zechariah (9.9), 'Do not be afraid, daughter of Zion; behold, your king comes, seated on the foal of an ass'. He explains that the disciples did not understand at first, 'but *when Jesus was glorified*, then they remembered that this had been written of him' (12.16). The phrase italicized corresponds to 'when he was raised [*ēgerthē*] from the dead' in a parallel passage in 2.22, where the disciples understand Jesus' enigmatic Temple saying only after his resurrection.[5] 'Glorify' is also used in 7.39 when it is explained that the Spirit had not yet been given 'because he was not yet glorified'.

Departure, Ascent and Return

John also has Jesus regularly speak of his death as his 'departure' to the Father.[6] In 7.33 he warns officers sent to arrest him, 'For yet a little while I am with you, and [then] I depart to him who sent me'. 'The Jews' misunderstand him, and wonder whether he is going to teach the Greeks; but Jesus is speaking of his going to God when he has fulfilled his mission. In 8.21f. Jesus again speaks to 'the Jews' of his departure, and this time they think that he may be intending to kill himself. In the Farewell Discourses 'departure' is a prominent theme: Jesus tells the disciples that he goes to prepare a place for them (14.2f.). Because he is going to the Father, they will be able to do even greater works than he has (14.12). He promises not to leave them desolate, but to come again and take them to him (14.3, 18). The climax comes in his 'High-Priestly Prayer', when he says to his Father, God: 'Now I am coming to you' (17.13).

There is an ambiguity in Jesus' promise to 'come again': is he speaking of his *parousia*, '[second] coming', as predicted in the Synoptics and in John's Appendix (21.22), or the resurrection appearances? In general, the hope of an imminent apocalyptic *parousia* has faded in John, in favour of what is now called 'realized' eschatology. John presents the 'last days' or 'messianic age' as already present in Jesus' ministry, and judgement as happening here and now as people make decisions for or against him (3.18, 36; 8.24; etc.). Many scholars therefore see Jesus' promised 'coming' as his resurrection, with his gift of Spirit as a continuation of his presence, fulfilling his promises to send the Paraclete (16.7) to guide the disciples and remind them of his teaching (14.26; 15.26; 16.13). However, John's eschatology is not entirely 'realized': he refers repeatedly to 'the last day' (6.39, 40, 44, 54; 11.24; 12.48) and to the future resurrection of believers (5.25, 28f.). It is therefore likely that in passages like 14.3 there is at least an indirect allusion to the *parousia* (cf. 1 Jn 2.28).[7] In other words, present and future eschatology are held together in creative tension: cf. 4.23, 'The hour is coming and now is …'.

As well as speaking of Jesus' 'lifting up' and 'departure', John uses the language of 'ascent', referring, for example, to 'the Son of Man ascending to where he was before' (6.62). This raises the question of how he understood the ascension, pictured traditionally in the Church as a physical return to heaven forty days after the resurrection (cf. Acts 1.1–11).[8] John never describes Jesus' ascent as an event, but sees it as an integral part of his 'glorification', the process by which he returns to the Father through death and resurrection. He regularly uses spatial, 'up/down' language in talking of Jesus' earthly life and his presence with God. Thus in the Nicodemus episode, immediately before mentioning his 'lifting up', Jesus says, 'Nobody has ascended into heaven, but he who descended from heaven, the Son of Man' (3.13).[9] Jesus 'comes down' from heaven to fulfil God's will (6.38) and bring life to the world (6.33; cf. 6.41, 50f., 58); when this is accomplished he goes back to God. He also speaks of himself as being 'from above' and 'not of this world', in contrast to those who are 'from below' and 'of this world' (8.23; cf. 17.11, 14). And he refers to his 'coming' or being 'sent' into the world (3.17, 19; 10.36; 12.46; 17.18; etc.) like 'an embassage from without' (Bultmann, 1955, p. 33).

Passion and Death

Because John understands Jesus' teaching as life-giving, and speaks of the disciples being 'clean' through his word (15.3), some scholars have suggested that Jesus' death has no soteriological significance for him. In a much quoted passage Bultmann wrote, 'In John, Jesus' death has no pre-eminent importance for salvation, but is the accomplishment of the "work" which began with the incarnation: the last demonstration of the obedience (14.31) which governs the whole life of Jesus' (1955, p. 52). Käsemann similarly argued that Jesus' glory so thoroughly determines John's whole presentation that his Passion Narrative becomes problematic. He is tempted to regard it as 'a mere postscript which had to be included because John could not ignore this tradition nor yet could he fit it organically into his work' (1968, p. 7).

Such remarks underestimate the significance of Jesus' passion and death in John, and the degree to which they are integrated into the Gospel's structure. If the passion was only a 'postscript', why did John spend so long describing Jesus' last days on earth (Jn 12—19)? Why did John prepare so carefully for his death? Jesus' 'hour' and his 'glory' are already mentioned in the Cana narrative (2.4, 11), and John's Temple 'cleansing' story contains more than one allusion to his death. When Jesus bids the pigeon-sellers, 'Take these things away', the disciples remember Psalm 69.9, 'Zeal for your house shall consume me' (2.17). The verb translated 'consume' means to eat up in the sense of 'destroy'; in its original context it described, in a past tense, the pains, anguish, and insults which the Psalmist had to bear because of his loyalty to Israel's God. But John cites it in the future tense as a prophecy of how Jesus' loyalty to his Father will lead to his own destruction. His resurrection, as well as his death, is predicted in his words, 'Destroy this Temple and in three days I will raise it' (2.19, 22). This saying must relate in some way to the Synoptic accusations at Jesus' trial (Mk 14.57f.; Mt. 26.61), and the taunts of the bystanders at the crucifixion: 'Ah! You that destroy the Temple and rebuild it in three days, save yourself and come down from the cross' (Mk 15.29; Mt. 27.40; cf. Acts 6.14). To anyone who knew these texts, John's Temple saying would certainly point forward to the passion.

There are also references to Jesus' death in the reflections following the Nicodemus dialogue (3.12–21), in the sequel to the feeding miracle (6.51c; cf. 6.70–1), and at numerous points in John 7 and 8. References forward are prominent in the Good Shepherd Discourse (Jn 10) and in the aftermath of the raising of Lazarus, when the Jewish authorities resolve that Jesus must die (11.50–3). Merely as part of John's story-line, Jesus' death is necessary as the climax to the machinations attributed to 'the Jews' to arrest or destroy him (7.30f.; 8.59; 10.31, 39; 11.53).

John 12 is particularly important as a preparation for Jesus' passion. It begins with his anointing at Bethany by Mary, Martha's sister (12.1–8). In Mark's and Matthew's parallel a woman anoints Jesus' head, possibly a royal 'messianic' anointing (Hooker, 1991, p. 328); but that is not John's emphasis. He has Mary anoint Jesus' *feet* (cf. Lk. 7.38), and she is told to keep the ointment for his *burial*. The mention of Judas' betrayal (12.4) strengthens the sense that Mary's act points forward to his death. Jesus' glorification is mentioned in John's comment on the 'triumphal entry' (12.16); his death is further interpreted in the saying about a grain of wheat needing to 'die' before it can bear fruit (12.24). Thereupon Jesus is troubled in his soul, and wonders whether he should ask God to save him from 'this hour', but concludes that God's Name must be glorified (12.27f.). This is the nearest one gets to the Synoptic agony at Gethsemane (Mk 14.32–42 par.), with which John seems to be familiar (cf. 18.11), but the scene is much less poignant. Jesus is vindicated by a voice from heaven saying, 'I have glorified [my Name] and I will glorify [it] again' (12.28), and he goes on to speak of his 'lifting up', explicitly explained as his death (12.32f.). John's account of the foot-washing is marked by a clear reference to Jesus' forthcoming betrayal (13.18–30) and allusions to his death (13.1, 31–3). While performed as an example of humble service, his laying aside and resumption of his garments also symbolize his laying down his life and taking it up again (exactly the same, unusual Greek verbs are used as in the Good Shepherd Discourse: Edwards, 1994).

The Farewell Discourses are replete with allusions to his death and resurrection under the scarcely veiled terminology of 'departure', 'going to the Father', 'being glorified', and 'coming again'. The High-Priestly (or Consecration) Prayer, occupying the whole of John 17, is rightly treasured by Christians. John Knox asked his wife to read it to him on his death-bed (Bruce, 1983, p. 328); William Temple believed it to be, perhaps, 'the most sacred passage even in the four Gospels' (1940, p. 307). It complements John's version of Jesus' agony by expressing his total dedication to God's will. It also balances the Prologue by giving, in prayer form, a summary of how he has glorified God through manifesting God's Name on earth. Käsemann (1968) calls it 'the Testament of Jesus' because it expresses his last wishes. Jesus' continuing care for the disciples is demonstrated by his prayer that they may be one, as he and God are one, and that they may be preserved from the Evil One and made holy. He also looks to the future Church, by interceding for those who will believe through the disciples, and prays that they too may be one. The prayer is both a reflection on Jesus' life and relation to God, and a powerful interpretation of the events that are to follow.

Jesus' passion and death, then, are no mere 'postscript', but an essential part of John's story and theological message. Apart from depicting Jesus' kingship and autonomy, they demonstrate his obedience to his Father, who loved the world so much that he gave his only Son so that those who have faith in him may have eternal life (3.16). Thus Jesus' passion and death, like his teaching, are life-giving: they reveal not just God's love, but also Jesus' own love expressed through the ultimate gift of his life: 'Having loved his own who were in the world, he loved them to the end' (13.1).

Atonement and Salvation

But did John see Jesus' death as atonement for sin? Bultmann's words about it having 'no pre-eminent importance for salvation' have triggered considerable scholarly controversy (e.g. Forestell, 1974; Turner, 1990). The problem is that for many centuries Christian scholars have sought to harmonize the various New Testament writings in an attempt to discover a consistent theology of sin and redemption. All too often it has been assumed that John must have the same message as other Scripture writers. There is no doubt that Paul's writings, Hebrews, 1 Peter, 1 John, and Revelation all interpret Jesus' death as a sacrifice for sin. This is illustrated by their use of such terms as *hilastērion* and *hilasmos* ('propitiation' or 'expiation'), *lutroō* and *lutrōsis* ('redeem', 'redemption'), and the image of Jesus as a slain lamb. The same is probably true of the Synoptics though their theology in this respect is less developed and less explicit.[10] In interpreting Jesus' death in this way the New Testament writers were applying to the Christian faith the idea common to Judaism and many ancient religions that blood-sacrifice is necessary as a means of reconciling humanity to God (see the sensitive discussion in Bradley, 1995, chs. 3–4).

John's Gospel does not use the language of 'redemption' or expiation/propitiation (though 1 Jn does: 1.7, 9; 2.2); it is, however, beyond doubt that its author is familiar with such ideas. Jesus is 'the Lamb of God that takes away the sin of the world' (1.29); he dies on the day of preparation for Passover (19.14). During the crucifixion he is given a drink 'on hyssop' (19.29), recalling the original Passover ritual when hyssop (a leafy plant) was used to sprinkle blood on the Hebrews' doorposts (Ex. 12.22). Furthermore, when the soldiers refrain from breaking Jesus' legs (because he is already dead), John refers explicitly to the Scripture that no bone of the Passover lamb should be broken (19.33–6; cf. Ex. 12.46; Num. 9.12).

He also tells of blood and water flowing from the spear-wound in Jesus' side (19.34). While many different interpretations of this have been offered, the most probable is that the blood represents Jesus' atoning sacrifice, and the water new life (cf. Lindars, 1972, p. 587). All this strongly argues for a sacrificial understanding of Jesus' death.

This idea is supported by a series of texts involving the preposition *hyper* ('for' or 'on behalf of') where Jesus speaks of giving his flesh for the life of the world (6.51), of laying down his life for the sheep (10.11, 15) or for his friends (15.13), of consecrating himself for the disciples (17.19); cf. Caiaphas' reference to his dying for the nation (11.50f.; 18.14). Although the word 'sin' is not mentioned, such texts seem to suggest that Jesus' death somehow enabled the forgiveness of sins, not only of his friends, but also of the whole world (cf. 1.29; 1 Jn 2.2). To say this is not to insist that John's theology must be harmonized with that of the rest of the New Testament; it is merely to point out that such an explanation would make sense. The idea that Jesus' death is merely an example of obedience or only a demonstration of love seems inadequate to explain both the '*hyper*' texts, and the underlying paschal symbolism of the Passion Narrative.

Jesus' death in John is also seen as attracting humanity to Jesus: 'When I am lifted up, I will draw all people to me' (12.32). It will enable people to know who Jesus truly is (8.28), and through knowing him, and God who sent him, they will be able to attain eternal life (17.3; cf. 3.14f.). His passion and death, as well as his teaching, are the means of conquering evil: immediately after his agony over his 'hour', he says (in anticipation of his death), 'Now is the judgement of this world; now the ruler of this world will be cast out' (12.31). Similarly at the end of his second Supper Discourse he says, 'Take courage; I have overcome the world' (16.33). Though couched in a perfect tense these words again look forward to his victory on the cross, where he is both priest and victim (so Bruce, 1983, p. 328).

Yet, for John, the interpretation of Jesus' death cannot be separated from that of his life. Jesus comes as a light shining in the darkness (3.19; 9.5; etc.). Through his life and his death he is indeed 'the Saviour of the World' (4.42). In everything he says and does he opposes evil, falsehood, and hypocrisy. His words convey life (6.68) – they *are* 'spirit and life' (6.63) – precisely because they reveal the true nature of God. In his own person he has revealed the character of God (14.9), because he came from him and lived his whole earthly life in unity with his will (cf. 10.30; 14.10; 15.10; etc.). Seen this way, there is no conflict between the concept of Jesus bringing salvation through his words, and that of his bringing it through his death.

Resurrection and Commissioning

Nor can the understanding of Jesus' death be separated from that of his resurrection. Bultmann suggested that if Jesus' death on the cross is already his exaltation, his resurrection cannot have special significance: 'No resurrection is needed to destroy the triumph which death might be supposed to have gained in the crucifixion. For the cross itself was already triumph over the world and its ruler' (1955, p. 56). There is a logic about this comment; but an even stronger logic required John to include the resurrection. If Jesus embodies the divine Word that existed from eternity, if he is the source of life for others, if he can claim to be 'the Resurrection and the Life' (11.25), then it is incomprehensible that his own life could be ended by human actions. As the Prologue states, 'The light shines on in the darkness, and the darkness has not extinguished it' (1.5). The resurrection is part of 'exaltation' and glorification as much as the cross.

Stories of the empty tomb and of resurrection appearances were already part of the Christian tradition when John wrote, and could not be ignored. If the resurrection 'cannot be an event of special significance' and the Easter stories are 'not indispensable' for John's theology, as Bultmann claims, one might expect him to relate them briefly and sketchily. In fact, John narrates *more* resurrection appearances than the other Evangelists, and does so with exceptional skill. He describes Jesus' appearance to Mary Magdalene (20.1f., 11–18) so vividly that many think he must be drawing on eyewitness experience (cf. Dodd's comment, 1963, p. 148, that there is something 'indefinably first-hand' about the account). He also tells of Peter and the 'beloved disciple' at the tomb (20.2–10), of an appearance in Jerusalem on the same day (20.19–23), and of a third appearance a week later to the disciples with Thomas (20.24–9). Then there is the meeting with seven disciples by the lake and the final conversations with Peter and the 'beloved disciple' (Jn 21). The sheer amount of space and care devoted to the resurrection demonstrates its importance for John.

Much scholarly energy has been expended on comparing the various resurrection accounts with a view to harmonizing them, or in an attempt to trace the development and interrelationship of the traditions. John shares key elements with the Synoptics (see Appendix 2): Jesus' body is laid in a new/rock-cut tomb; very early on Easter morning it is found empty by a woman or group of women, who see angelic figure(s) and tell the disciples (except in Mark). That evening Jesus appears to the assembled disciples in Jerusalem, and commissions them (John; Luke). He later appears in Galilee (John; Matthew). At the same time the accounts reveal substantial differences. John has Jesus' body buried with a large quantity of scented oils and spices, while in Mark's account the women go to the tomb on Easter day 'to anoint the body' (as if it had not been done previously). In all the Synoptics Jesus' body is wrapped in a shroud (*sindōn*);[11] in John, it is bound with bandage-like cloths (*othonia*) with a separate head napkin, as was Lazarus' body (11.44, *keiriai* – another word for bandages).

The other Evangelists all have three women (including Mary Magdalene and another Mary) go to the tomb; John has only Mary Magdalene. He may be adapting tradition here so that he can focus on her personal encounter with her Lord. Only John describes Peter and the 'beloved disciple' as going to the tomb. Paul knows a tradition of Peter as the first resurrection witness (1 Cor. 15.5; cf. Lk. 24.34, where 'Simon' may be Peter), but it is not clear whether John draws on this; he describes Peter seeing the tomb empty, but not seeing the risen Jesus. Some regard John's episode of Peter and the 'beloved disciple' as created by him for theological purposes.

In both Matthew and John the risen Jesus meets the women/Mary. Matthew's narrative (28.9f.) is very brief, with Jesus giving the same message as the angel; some consider this secondary to the women's encounter with the angel. By contrast, John's account of Jesus and Mary Magdalene is full and detailed, and includes her moving recognition of Jesus as she utters the word 'Rabboni' (cf. above, pp. 62f.). Interestingly, in Matthew the women grasp Jesus' feet, but in John Mary is told not to touch him (*haptomai*), 'for I have not yet ascended to the Father' (20.17). Most scholars believe that *haptomai* is used here in the sense of 'cling to'. There is a strange contrast with 20.27, where Jesus bids Thomas put his fingers into his wounds.

Both Luke and John describe an appearance to disciples in Jerusalem on Easter Day (cf. his appearance to 'the Twelve' in 1 Cor. 15.5). In Luke it follows the Emmaus episode, not found in the other Gospels (see Appendix 2); John alone says that the doors were shut 'for fear of the Jews'. In both, Jesus shows his wounds as a means of identification – his hands and feet in Luke (24.39); in John his hands and side (20.27; cf. 19.34). Luke stresses the physicality of the resurrection: Jesus explicitly says that he is not a ghost, and eats in front of the disciples (Lk. 24.39, 43; cf. Acts 1.4; 10.41). In John Jesus apparently passes through locked doors (suggesting a non-physical body),[12] but his breathing into the disciples (20.22) and his invitation to Thomas to touch him (20.27) – both unique to John – imply a physical body. The insufflation (breathing) is the gift of the Paraclete, equipping the disciples for their future work. Some also see it as a symbol of a new creation: the verb used for 'breathe into' (or 'on'), *emphysaō*, is comparatively rare, being found only here in the New Testament. But it occurs in Genesis 2.7

(Septuagint), for the Lord's breathing into Adam's nostrils the breath of life, so that he becomes a living being (cf. Wisd. 15.11), and in Ezekiel's vision, when the wind/spirit brings life to the dry bones (37.9f.). The new creation would be the Church, brought to life by Jesus' symbolic action and his 'sending' of the disciples. This is surely John's equivalent of Luke's Pentecost (Acts 2).

All the Gospels conclude with a commissioning of the disciples (except Mark's, where the end may be lost).[13] In Luke and John the commission takes place in Jerusalem on Easter day, but in Matthew it occurs, at an unspecified time, on a mountain in Galilee (28.16–20). The accounts differ in the manner of Jesus' final leaving. In Luke (24.50–2) he leads the disciples out to Bethany, blesses them, and is carried up to heaven; but in Acts (1.2–11) he presents himself alive to them over a period of forty days before ascending, and the Spirit is given ten days later (contrast Jn 20.19–22). John nowhere describes any physical departure: Jesus simply bids Mary tell 'his brothers' (presumably the male disciples), 'I am ascending to my Father and your Father, and my God and your God' (20.17). Does he picture Jesus as ascending immediately? If he does, the subsequent appearances to disciples would presumably be of a different character, perhaps comparable to Paul's vision on the Damascus road – well after the ascension on Luke's chronology – which Paul describes as if it were on a par with the others (1 Cor. 15.8). But we cannot be sure of this point.

The differences between the Gospel accounts, and the problems of reconciling their testimony with 1 Corinthians, make one doubt the wisdom of trying to reconstruct precisely what happened (as in Wenham, 1984). There are similar problems in reconciling the various trial narratives, but the situation is especially acute with the resurrection, which is not the sort of happening that can be recovered by painstaking source-analysis or other tools of historical enquiry.[14] Each Evangelist presents his own understanding in a way that he thinks will convince readers. Other New Testament writers add their conviction that the same Jesus who died on the cross is alive and has returned to be with God (cf. Heb. 1.3; 2.9; 13.20; 1 Pet. 3.18–22; 1 Tim. 3.16; Eph. 4.10). This is the historic faith of the Church. Yet the resurrection is beyond normal human experience – to be apprehended by living faith (or not at all). A fascinating aspect of John's presentation is the stress placed not on physical viewing and touching (which Thomas demanded), but on the need to be 'believing' (*pistos*: 20.27). The climax of this episode is Jesus' beatitude: 'Blessed are those who do not see, and [yet] believe' (20.29), leading beautifully into John's conclusion on the Gospel's purpose (20.30f.). The Appendix (Jn 21) offers further evidence for the resurrection and deals with other issues (discussed above, pp. 19f.; 60).[15]

Conclusion

Thus John's achievement in his Passion and Resurrection Narratives is his presentation of the cross not as a humiliation inflicted on Jesus, but as something voluntarily undertaken and the means of his 'glorification', through which he returned to the Father having brought life to the world. His resurrection appearances reassure the disciples that he is alive, demonstrate his continuing care for them, and make possible their commissioning to act by his authority; but they are not essential for faith.

9

Jesus: Word Incarnate and Father's Son

John's Prologue (1.1–18) has been called 'the pearl' of his Gospel (Brown, 1966, p. 18). Venerated since antiquity, it is generally seen as the Evangelist's maturest reflection and the high point of his theology, being responsible above all else for the traditional image of John as an eagle soaring to heaven. Yet few texts have caused such problems to commentators or given rise to so much scholarly literature. Haenchen, who worked on John almost daily for twenty years, described it quite simply as 'difficult to understand' (1984, vol. 1, p. 101). The problems arise partly through disputed manuscript readings, partly through controversies over a hypothetical pre-Johannine hymn, and perhaps most of all because the Prologue's grand ideas, open-ended images, and abstract terminology defy precise definition. Scholars dispute even its structure and basic shape.

The Form and Origin of the Prologue

Barrett (1978, pp. 149f.) saw it as composed of four sections, which together prepare readers for John's main narrative:

1 1.1–5. *Cosmological.* The eternal divine Word, God's agent in creation, is the source of light and life for humanity.
2 1.6–8. *The Witness of the Baptist.* Following early Christian tradi-

tion, John introduces the Baptist, carefully distinguishing him from 'the true light'.

3 1.9–13. *The Coming of the Light.* Neither 'the world' nor 'his own' recognize and receive the light; but those who do so constitute the Church.

4 1.14–18. *The Economy of Salvation.* The Word is made flesh, displaying the glory and mercy of God; the Baptist's role is clarified.

This analysis offers a useful way of looking at the Prologue, but makes too little of the new birth of believers in 1.12f. (substituting the concept of 'the Church'), and does less than justice to the theological wealth of 1.16–18, with the idea of Jesus as the only Son (or God) in the bosom of the Father, who makes God known.

Talbert (1992, p. 66), following Culpepper (1980), detects a more elaborate 'concentric' or 'chiastic' structure:

A (1.1–5): The relation of the Word to God, creation, humanity
  B (1.6–8): The witness of the Baptist
    C (1.9–11): The coming and rejection of the Light/Word
      D (1.12f.): Benefits of belief in the Word
    C′ (1.14): The coming and reception of the Word
  B′ (1.15): The witness of the Baptist
A′ (1.16–18): The relation of the Word to humanity, re-creation, God.

This brings out nicely the symmetry of the Baptist references; it recognizes the importance of 1.18 on Jesus as revealer of God to humanity. However, the idea of 're-creation' there seems forced, and the reading 'God' (of Jesus) in 1.18 is uncertain. This analysis still fails to deal adequately with the complex interweaving of theological ideas in 1.16–18, including 'fulness', 'law', 'grace', 'truth', and 'seeing God', and, while it rightly recognizes the importance of the birth of 'God's children' in 1.12f., one must query whether this is really the Prologue's pivot, rather than the incarnation (1.14).

Moloney (1998b, pp. 34f.) finds three main sections:

  I   (1.1–5)   The Word in God becomes the Light of the World
  II (1.6–14) The Incarnation of the Word
  III (1.15–18) The Revealer: the only Son turned toward the Father.[1]

In a further complex analysis he detects, within these sections, four repeated themes that are stated and restated in a movement like waves on a shore. The Baptist references fit poorly into his scheme. Other scholars produce different analyses of greater or lesser complexity: e.g.

Brown (1966, pp. 3f.) finds four poetic strophes, plus four prose sections including the two Baptist references (1.6–9, 15), which he brackets as interrupting the thread. Hooker (1969), on the other hand, sees them as essential in linking the Prologue's metaphysical truths with later historical statements.

The difficulty of finding a clear structure for the Prologue highlights the basic problem of determining precisely what John intends by his picturesque and powerful, yet obscure, language. At what point does he first allude to the incarnation? The earliest possible point is 1.5, when 'the light' shines in the darkness; but 'light' in the Prologue could refer to God's revelation through creation, or his self-disclosure to the Hebrew people. Possibly both pre-Christian revelation and the revelation in Jesus are presupposed. Some see the incarnation as first alluded to in 1.9: 'The true light which enlightens everyone was coming into the world' (NRSV). But the Greek is ambiguous, and the sentence could also be translated, 'This was the true light that enlightens everyone who comes into the world' (cf. AV). The reference to the *logos* coming to 'his own', and 'his own' not receiving him (1.11), is also ambiguous. It may refer to Israel's refusal of God's word through the prophets (Dodd, 1953, p. 270), or conceivably a 'wisdom myth', whereby Wisdom is unable to find a home among mortals (discussed below, p. 88); but most probably it anticipates the incarnation. Perhaps John deliberately left Jesus' entry on the scene ambiguous, using 1.5, 9, 11 as pointers to it before proclaiming it unequivocally in 1.14.

Scholars who postulate a pre-existing hymn differ as to its length, structure, and source. Brown (1966, p. 22) tabulates eight different theories: these agree in omitting the references to the Baptist (1.6–8, 13, 15) from the hypothetical original, and in attributing to it 1.1, 3f., 10f.; they disagree in almost all other details. The problem is that, though elevated in tone and in places rhythmic, the Prologue is not formally poetry, either in classical Greek form (which depends on syllable length), or of Semitic type, with metrical units displaying clear-cut parallelism. Proponents of an underlying 'poem' or 'hymn' have to take scissors to the text, excising a verse here and a phrase there (e.g. Schnackenburg, 1968, p. 226). While parts of the Prologue do follow Semitic verse-patterns (including 'step' or 'stair' parallelism), others do not.[2] In any case this feature is not unique to the Prologue, rhythmic and poetic sections being found also in John's discourses.

Another difficulty is determining the potential source of the 'hymn'. Bultmann thought that 'the whole Prologue has been adopted from a Baptist document', with 1.6–8, 15 as later additions reducing the Baptist's role by making him only a witness to the light (1986, p. 33; cf. 1971, p. 18). But evidence for a pre-Johannine Gnostic-Baptist sect is weak, and there are no grounds for supposing that John the Baptist was ever called 'the Word' or was envisaged as being incarnate. More commonly John is thought to draw on a *Christian* hymn (e.g. Brown, 1966, pp. 20f.; Haenchen, 1984, vol. 1, p. 101). But it is still not easy to find a good literary parallel: the Prologue lacks the praise and thanksgiving characteristic of Jewish and Christian hymns of around this period,[3] and nowhere addresses God in the second person. It is also longer and structurally different from other New Testament christological 'hymns' (Sanders, 1971, pp. 20–4); contrast Phil. 2.6–11; Col. 1.15–20; 1 Tim. 3.16; 2 Tim. 2.11–13. Stylistically the Prologue cannot be separated from the rest of the Gospel: Johannine language and ideas appear in the supposedly pre-Johannine 'hymn', while untypical terminology occurs in parts of the Prologue attributed to the Evangelist. The Prologue fits its present context admirably, and heralds major themes to be developed in the Gospel. For all these reasons it is best regarded as composed by John, either before or after the main text.[4]

Leading Ideas

The Logos *in Creation and Revelation*

Foremost in any discussion must be the concept of Jesus as *logos*, found only here in the New Testament (though note Rev. 19.11–13; 1 Jn 1.1). The noun *logos*, conventionally translated 'word' (cf. Greek *legō*, 'say'), has a wide semantic field, including ideas of reason and thought, as well as rational spoken utterance. Ironically it never means one single word, as its English translation might imply. In what sense(s) did John use the term? He states that the *logos* existed *en archē(i)*, 'in the beginning' (1.1), words evoking 'In the beginning God created the heavens and the earth' (Gen. 1.1); he also says that the *logos* was 'with God', and 'was God'. It/he is further described as the agent of creation, in which/whom was 'life, the light of humanity'.[5]

Educated pagan readers, and Jews familiar with Greek philosophy, might recall Stoic concepts of the *logos* as a kind of divine essence, or underlying principle of natural order, pervading the universe (cf. Barrett, 1987, pp. 65–72). The Church Fathers certainly read John this way, as have many earlier exegetes. Yet it remains doubtful whether this is what John intended; it is certainly not *all* that he intended. Readers familiar with the Jewish Scriptures could not fail to remember the rich and diverse ways in which 'word' is used there. *Logos* would be seen as corresponding to *dabar*, occurring no fewer than 1,430 times in the Hebrew Bible in the sense of 'matter', 'thing', or 'spoken' or 'written word' (Edwards, 1988a, pp. 1101f.). Along with *rhēma*, 'spoken word', 'saying' (an alternative translation for *dabar*), *logos* expresses God's action in creation: 'By the word of the Lord the heavens were made' (Ps. 33.6; cf. Ps. 148.5; Gen. 1.3, 6, etc.). Ever reliable and effective, God's word sustains the universe through what we call natural phenomena (cf. Ps. 147. 16–18), and acts in history for healing and salvation (cf. Ps. 107.20; Isa. 55.10f.). It also serves as God's agent for judgement, as in Wisdom 18.15f., where God's all-powerful *logos* leaps down from heaven like a stern warrior, bearing his decree for the Egyptians' death.[6]

Other readers might perceive allusions to the concept of wisdom as God's agent in creation. In Jewish wisdom literature Hebrew *hohmah* and Greek *sophia* (both feminine nouns) are regularly personified as a woman. In Proverbs 8.22–31 Wisdom speaks in the first person, saying that God created her before the world was made: she was at his side when he established the heavens, and created the sea and earth. In Ecclesiasticus 24.1–11, Wisdom says that she came forth from God's mouth, and she alone created the circuit of heaven's vault, and walked in the depths of the abyss. She sought a dwelling-place (*skēnē*) to rest in, and God bade her dwell (*kataskēnoō*) in Jacob/Israel (cf. Bar. 3.36f.). The use of *kataskēnoō*, meaning both 'pitch a tent' and 'dwell', and *skēnē*, 'tent' or 'dwelling-place', recalls the idea of the tabernacle as the symbol of God's presence (e.g. Ex. 29.43–6; 40.34–8); Wisdom is specifically said to have ministered there (Ecclus 24.10). John may have had this image in mind when he wrote (1.14) 'the Word became flesh and dwelt among us' (*eskēnōsen*, using the related verb *skēnoō*). There may also be an allusion to Aramaic *shekinah*, 'residence' or 'presence', a periphrasis for God in the Targums and among rabbis (note the coincidence of the consonants *skn* with *skēnē*).

Sometimes Wisdom fails to find a resting-place on earth. In *1 Enoch* 42 she goes to live with the 'children of the people' but finds no dwelling-place, and so returns to the heavens, while iniquity goes to live with them instead. From this some scholars have inferred the existence of a 'wisdom myth' lying behind John's statement (1.11) that 'the *logos* came to his own, and his own did not receive him' (so Bultmann, 1971, p. 22; cf. 1986, p. 23). But it is doubtful how developed or widespread this 'myth' was when John was writing. Many of the passages cited in its support are quite general references to sinful human beings searching for Wisdom or rejecting her (e.g. Ecclus 15.7; Bar. 3.12, 29–31). And although John says the *logos* was not received, he immediately follows this statement by saying that those who did so were given authority to become children of God (1.12f.).

Another point to be noted is that wisdom in Jewish literature is always pictured as created by God, rather than existing before creation (like John's *logos*). Moreover, although 'wisdom' occasionally occurs in parallel with 'word', wisdom is never directly called 'the word of God' (cf. Brown,

1966, p. 522). If Jewish wisdom ideas were as important for John as some scholars claim, why did he choose *logos* rather than *sophia* to describe Christ, and never use the word 'wisdom' in his entire Gospel? The usual answer is that it would have been too awkward to use *sophia*, since Jesus was male and wisdom was regularly personified as a woman (Scott, 1992, pp. 170f.). This did not, however, stop Paul from calling Jesus the 'wisdom of God' (1 Cor. 1.24; cf. 1.30). Perhaps there were other reasons why John equated Jesus with 'word' rather than 'wisdom', and other connotations he might expect his *logos* image to have for readers.

In the Hebrew Bible (including the Septuagint) 'word' is also used for God's revelation to the prophets, especially in the formula, 'the word of the Lord came to *X*' (cf. 1 Kgs 12.22; Hos. 1.1; etc.) – a formula used by John himself (10.35, on Jesus' lips). In poetry 'word' often appears in parallel with *torah*, conventionally translated 'law' (e.g. Isa. 2.3; Ps. 119.17f., 43f.). The Ten Commandments – the 'ten words' in Hebrew – were seen as bringing life and light, as was the Law generally (Dt. 32.46f.; Prov. 6.23; cf. Jn 12.50). This usage fits in beautifully with the Prologue's statement that in the *logos* was life, 'the light of men' (1.3 AV), and its description of Jesus as the one who makes God known (1.18). It raises the question whether John is identifying Jesus with Torah, just as Wisdom became identified with it (Ecclus 24.23; Bar. 4.1). In rabbinic theology Torah (feminine in Hebrew) was one of the seven things created before the world. Rabbi Eliezer ben Jose (*c.* 150 CE) reportedly said, 'Before the world was made Torah was written, and lay in God's bosom' (Dodd, 1953, p. 85, citing *Pesaḥim* 54a Bar.). It has been doubted whether Jewish personification of Torah was sufficiently strong, or attested early enough, to serve as a source for John's *logos*. But ancient readers familiar with the concept of Torah's pre-existence would certainly have no problem in grasping John's idea of the *logos* as existing from the beginning.

There are also fascinating parallels in Philo's writings: he used *logos* over 1,300 times, mostly in the sense of 'spoken word' or 'reason', but also in a special religious sense for God's expressed thought and his power active in the world. Thus the *logos* is said to be God's *eikōn* or image (e.g. *Somn.*, II.45); it is identified with wisdom, with *archē* ('beginning' or 'first principle') and with archetypal light; it is God's chief messenger, eternal, not created as a human being (*Quis Rer.*, 206), though 'the eldest of created things' (*Leg. All.*, III.175). It feeds and guides human beings, serving as a mediator between them and God. It implants its 'seed' in them so that they become like it (cf. the Stoic *logos spermatikos*), bringing them to repentance and salvation; it is the mysterious 'bread of heaven' (cf. Ex. 16.15). Sometimes Philo's *logos* is described as God's first-born (*Conf. Ling.*, 146), and even as *ho deuteros theos*, 'the second God' (*Quaest. in Gen.*, II.62). Occasionally it is identified with specific human beings – Moses, called 'the law-giving *logos*' (*Migr.*, 23) and even the High Priest (*Fug.*, 108) (further details in Williamson, 1989, pp. 103–43). Philo does not have a consistent '*logos* doctrine', and recent commentators have been wary of postulating his influence on John; but older scholars took the possibility very seriously (e.g. Dodd, 1953; Barrett, 1978). Some of the parallels with John's thought are impressive, especially Philo's calling the *logos* 'God', and using the same term for human beings. Readers who knew his works would perceive similarities between Philo's ideas and John's.

Philo lived in Alexandria and wrote in Greek. It is not clear how widely disseminated his writings were, but it is likely that only learned Jews with exegetical and philosophical interests would have known his works. But many Jews in Palestine, the Eastern Diaspora, and other Aramaic-speaking communities would have been familiar with the Targums, biblical paraphrases which were read regularly in synagogues for the benefit of Jews who found Hebrew difficult. In these the term *memra*, 'word', frequently appears in reverential idioms designed to prevent the uttering of the divine Name (YHWH), and to 'protect' God's transcendence by avoiding references to people – even Moses or Isaiah – 'seeing God' or 'talking with God'.[7] This usage has sometimes been related to John's use of *logos*, particularly where *memra* is associated with creation, revelation, and light, or directly identified with God. For example, in Genesis 1.3 the Fragment Targums have the 'Word of the Lord' say, 'Let there be light', and in the Palestinian Targum (Neophyti 1) this light at creation is identified with God's *memra*. In its account of God's appearance to Moses at the burning bush (Ex. 3.12), the same Targum identifies 'word' with God, reading, 'My *memra* will be with you', instead of 'I will be with you' (Boyarin, 2001, p. 256–9). New Testament scholars have generally been wary of making too much of *memra*, arguing that it occurs mostly in genitival phrases like *memra da-yeyah*, 'God's word', rather than absolutely as *logos* in John 1.1, 14. They also point out that it was never regarded as a 'hypostasis' or separate being from God (cf. Barrett, 1978, p. 153, dismissing *memra* as a 'blind alley'). All the surviving Targums are later than John (some much later).[8] Nevertheless, their significance for interpreting his Gospel should not be underestimated. If they were current in the first century CE, then surely at least some Jews must have linked John's divine *logos* – the light that shone in the darkness, through whom all things were created – with the Targumic *memra*.[9]

Further parallels have sometimes been found in the *Hermetica*, where *Logos* comes forth from *Nous*, 'Mind'; it is called 'God's son', and acts as his agent in creation and as a divine intermediary (Dodd, 1953, ch. 2). Alternatively, or in addition, John has been seen as drawing on Mandaean concepts (Bultmann, 1971). Clearly any readers familiar with such texts might have their understanding of John coloured by them. But the images John uses – light, life, word – are found in religious writings of so many periods and backgrounds that strong reasons are needed to postulate direct influence, especially where texts cannot be shown to antedate John. One sometimes feels that the net has been cast too wide in the quest for sources, and that explanations for John's meaning may lie nearer to hand.

One area often neglected is the *Christian* background to John's Prologue. The magnificent opening of the Letter to the Hebrews (1.1–4) proclaims how in the last days God has spoken by [his] Son, through whom he created 'the worlds' (*aiōnes*); it further describes Jesus as reflecting God's glory and upholding all things by his word of power. Some of these ideas come quite close to what John says of the *logos*. In other texts *logos* is used for the preached word: the Sower sows 'the word' (Mk 4.14 par.); Jesus teaches 'the word' (Lk. 5.1, etc.); Paul and Barnabas preach 'God's word' (Acts 13.5), just as Paul preaches 'Christ crucified' (1 Cor. 1.23). The 'word' is not fettered (2 Tim. 2.9), but works within believers (1 Thess. 2.13); it is 'the word of truth, the gospel of your salvation' (Eph. 1.13). In 1 John 1.1–4, the 'word of life' may denote either Jesus Christ, or the message of salvation, or both. It is not such a big step from seeing Jesus as preaching the word, the truth, and the life-giving message of salvation, to describing him *as* 'the Word' (Jn 1.1), or *as* 'the way, the truth and the life' (14.6). While there is no guarantee that John knew any of the above New Testament texts (1 John is probably later than the Gospel), at the very least they provide a context in which an early Christian audience might have understood the Prologue (cf. Barrett, 1978, p. 154).

The Word Incarnate

'And the Word became flesh' (1.14): 'In these five short words the central mystery that John will unfold is stated with absolute simplicity' (Newbigin, 1982, p. 8); 'In these simple words the whole profound mystery and miracle of the Christian faith is expressed' (Richardson, 1959, p. 42). With 1.14 we reach what most people consider to be the climax of the Prologue, the expression of a mystery at which some Christians today still kneel in reverence. Augustine, who had studied the Neoplatonist philosophers, commented that he had found in them many of John's ideas, but 'I did not read in them that the word was made flesh and dwelt among us' (*Confessions*, VII.9). Modern scholars have ransacked ancient Jewish and pagan texts in vain for a text that might have served as John's source. As noted earlier (p. 88), the so-called 'wisdom myth' in which Wisdom seeks a place to dwell among humanity, is too vague to have been John's main inspiration. The

Gnostic 'redeemer myth' is likewise pale in comparison, different in its concepts, and later in attestation.[10] There is nothing precisely like this in Stoicism, the *Hermetica*, the Targums, or even Philo.

So what did inspire John? It has often been noted that the style of the Prologue changes with the use of the 'we' phrases in 1.14, 16: 'The Word became flesh and dwelt among *us*, and *we* beheld his glory ... and from his fulness *we* have received grace instead of grace'. This section's inspiration is not to be sought in recondite allusions to potential Jewish or Gnostic sources, but in the author's own spiritual insights and the experience of the Christian community (cf. Haenchen, 1984, vol. 1, p. 119). It is in the incarnate Jesus Christ that he and they have found a full experience of grace and truth, and have beheld God's glory. Other New Testament writers also speak of this experience of having received God's grace through Jesus Christ (e.g. Rom. 5.15; Eph. 1.3–14; Tit. 2.11–13; cf. Acts 14.3), but John expresses this idea in a unique way.

John says 'the Word became flesh' (*sarx*), not that God became a human being (*anthrōpos*). The Romans and Greeks had legends of gods taking human form, to see for themselves the depths of human wickedness (Ovid, *Met.*, I., 209–43), to give advice (Homer, *Od.*, 1.88–105), or to seduce mortal women (e.g. Hesiod, *Scut.*, 27–36). The incarnation was not like this. It is not like the temporary adoption of human form by angels, such as those entertained by Abraham in Genesis 18, or the archangel Raphael in Tobit, who appears to be a man (5.4), but is really only a vision (12.19). Nor is it the same as when Isaiah, Ezekiel, or Daniel see God in glory, or when Moses talks with God (e.g. Ex. 19.9, 19f.; 33.20–3). In all these examples, the encounter with the Divine is visionary, or for a brief period. By contrast, John speaks of the *logos* actually becoming flesh, and living among human beings. He chooses the word *sarx*, used in secular Greek for animal meat or the human body, and in Paul's writings for physical human nature (cf. Robinson, 1952, pp. 17–26). John may have chosen this term to avoid the misunderstanding that the *logos* only appeared to be human (as the Docetists later claimed), but we cannot be sure of this. Thus his statement is both more robust (to use modern jargon) and in some respects more reticent than Paul's famous 'hymn' which speaks of Christ being in the form of God, but emptying himself to be born 'in the likeness of human beings' (Phil. 2.7f.; cf. Col. 2.9).

John does not explain *how* he pictured the Word becoming incarnate: he makes no mention of the Virgin Birth (more accurately, 'virginal conception'), as in Matthew's and Luke's birth narratives.[11] Nor is it clear whether his language is to be understood as myth, metaphor, or actual fact. In the course of his main narrative he represents Jesus as fully human (Thompson, 1988), yet at the same time as different from other people.

His Jesus displays uncanny or supernatural knowledge (e.g. 2.25; 4.18; 6.6); he refers mysteriously to his origin 'above', and to his not being 'of this world' (8.23; 17.14, 16); he walks on water. Several of his sayings may imply divinity, especially the formula 'I am he' and his statement 'I and the Father are one' (10.30; cf. also 5.17f.; 14.9f.). But he also speaks of the Father as greater than himself (14.28); he prays to God (11.41f.; 17.1–26), and lives his life in complete dependence on God (cf. Davey, 1958, pp. 78f.; Barrett, 1982, p. 22). From the times of the Church Fathers, theologians have sought to understand how Jesus could be both God and human. John does not explain this (see further below, Ch. 12).

Returning to the Prologue, John says that the Word 'dwelt among us, and we beheld his glory' (1.14a–b). The verb for 'dwell' (skēnoō) is the same as used in Revelation's vision of the new Jerusalem, when the seer hears a loud voice saying, 'Behold, the tabernacle of God is with men, and he will dwell [skēnōsei] with them, and they shall be his people ...' (21.3, AV). The Septuagint uses it in its compound form kataskēnoō to translate the Hebrew shakan, 'dwell', in prophecies of God's presence with his people (e.g. Joel 3[4].17; Ezk. 43.7; cf. above, p. 88, on Ecclus). Many scholars see in 1.14 an allusion to Exodus, especially 40.34, where the tabernacle is filled with the Lord's glory. 'Glory' (Hebrew kabod; Greek doxa) is a biblical way of describing the visible manifestation of God's splendour, sometimes under the image of bright light (cf. Acts 22.11).[12] It is a favourite theme of John's. He presents Jesus as disclosing his, or God's, glory during his ministry (2.11; 11.40); Jesus himself says that he was given God's glory before the foundation of the world (17.5, 24), and that Isaiah 'saw' his glory (12.41; cf. above, p. 75) – allusions to his pre-existence. But 'glory' in John is not simply about majesty and splendour: it is also about obedience to the Father and seeking his honour (cf. 7.18; 8.50, 54). As was seen in Chapter 8, John regularly uses doxazomai, 'be glorified' (cognate with doxa), with reference to crucifixion. Jesus' death is not directly mentioned in the Prologue, but discerning readers familiar with the rest of John might detect a pointer to it.

The Prologue also describes Jesus (or less probably his glory) as 'full of grace and truth' (1.14). 'Grace' (charis) occurs four times, twice in the phrase charin anti charitos (1.16), and twice linked with 'truth' (1.14, 17). Its significance has been much discussed. In secular and biblical Greek charis has a wide range of meanings, including a source of delight (cf. chairō, 'rejoice'); outward beauty and gracefulness; favour, kindness, and goodwill extended to others; thankfulness or thanks for favours received. In the New Testament it denotes especially the undeserved kindness and gifts of God (cf. charismata, 'gracious gifts'). Paul is famous for using charis to describe God's gracious action in freely 'justifying' sinners through Jesus' death (Rom. 3.23–5; 5.21; etc.), but one should not assume Pauline doctrine here.

Two slightly different senses for *charis* may be detected in the Prologue. In *charin anti charitos* (1.16) it seems to mean 'gracious gift'. Usually this phrase is translated 'grace upon grace', or 'one blessing after another' (cf. RSV, GNB), and taken to refer to the series of blessings received from Christ. But there are problems with this understanding. Greek linguistic usage seems to demand *anti* to be translated not 'upon', or 'after', but 'instead of' (Edwards, 1988b). If this meaning is adopted, John must be saying that the 'grace and truth' that comes through Jesus Christ now takes the pride of place hitherto occupied by God's gracious gift of the Law through Moses. In 1.14 and 17 'grace and truth' occur as a pair. This probably reflects a Hebrew phrase, *ḥesed we'ĕmet*,[13] where *ḥesed* means 'love' or 'mercy', and *'ĕmet* 'faithfulness' (deriving from *'aman*, 'be firm' or 'binding'), sometimes translated as 'truth'. The Hebrew Bible regularly uses this pair of nouns to refer to God's loving and trustworthy character, and his faithfulness towards Israel (cf. 2 Sam. 2.6; Pss. 25.10; 89.14; etc.). On Sinai God reveals himself to Moses as 'plenteous in mercy and truth' (Ex. 34.6 RV) or 'abounding in steadfast love and faithfulness' (RSV). By describing Jesus as 'full of grace and truth' John suggests not only that he possesses these qualities of God, but that he is also the source of them for others (see further de la Potterie, 1977, 1986).

The Only Son as the Father's 'Exegete'

The Prologue reaches a second climax when John says 'the only Son, who is in the bosom of the Father, he has made him known' (1.18 RSV). The verb translated 'made known' (Greek *exēgoumai*) means literally 'lead out', hence 'explain' or 'interpret' (cf. English 'exegesis'). In secular Greek it is used of priests and prophets giving divine oracles; in Josephus it is a technical term for rabbinic interpretation of Torah (Schnackenburg, 1968, p. 279). John uses it to express his concept of Jesus as the one who reveals God. Jesus is able to do this because he is 'in the Father's bosom'. In English versions of the Bible this old-fashioned word 'bosom' (Hebrew *heq*, Greek *kolpos*) expresses conjugal intimacy, as in the phrase 'wife of your bosom' (e.g. Dt. 13.6; Mic. 7.5; cf. Gen.16.5), and loving care. It is used for a mother, or nurse, holding a child to her breast (1 Kgs 17.19; Ruth 4.16); and for God, as shepherd, carrying his 'lambs' in his bosom (Isa. 40.11). A more modern translation of the phrase in John 1.18 might be 'close to the Father's heart'.

Jesus is able to 'explain' or 'reveal' the Father because he has uniquely seen and known him; hence the apparent polemic in 1.18a, 'Nobody has seen God at any time'. The Hebrew Bible says that Isaiah indeed saw God (Isa. 6.1, 5), and that Moses both talked with him and saw him (e.g. Ex. 3). But later Jewish interpretations softened such anthropomorphisms (picturing God as human) to emphasize his transcendence. Thus in the original Hebrew of Exodus 24.10 Moses and the Elders see 'the God of Israel', but in the reverential Septuagint translation they see only 'the place where the God of Israel stood' (cf. above, p. 90, on *memra*). In 1.18a John aligns himself with those Jews who felt no ordinary human being could see God. He may also be indirectly criticizing Jewish mystics who claimed to have made heavenly journeys to receive divine revelation (Carter, 1990, pp. 43–5; cf. Kanagaraj, 1998, p. 226).

1.18b contains a textual problem. While most English translations refer to Jesus there as 'the only Son' (RSV, NEB, NJB; cf. AV), some important manuscripts, including two papyri, read *(ho) monogenēs theos*, '(the) only-begotten or unique God'. This reading, now adopted in some scholarly Greek texts, has the support of many commentators. But it creates an almost unbearable tension for Jesus to be described as the 'unique' or 'only' God in a sentence that has just referred to 'the Father' as God. Those who adopt this reading are forced to take *monogenēs* and *theos* in apposition to one another, resulting in unnatural translations, e.g. 'the only one, himself God' (NEB, footnote; cf. Fennena, 1985, p. 131) or 'the only Son who is the same as God' (GNB). But there is nothing in the Greek to correspond to 'himself' or 'who is the same as'. This suggests that the traditional reading 'only [or only-begotten] Son' may well be right.[14] It is in keeping with both John's style and theology (cf. 3.16, 18; also 1 Jn 4.9), and has the support of several major uncials. The substitution of *theos* might then be explained as the work of an over-pious Christian scribe.

One should perhaps add that there is no reason to insist, as do several leading commentators,[15] that *monogenēs* here means 'unique' rather than 'only child'. Neither its etymology[16] nor its normal usage requires this. From its earliest attestation *monogenēs* describes 'only children' (so Hesiod, *Op.*, 376, *Theog.*, 426, 448); this use is found in the Septuagint (e.g. Jdgs 11.34; Tob. 3.15),[17] and is the sole meaning in the New Testament (Lk. 7.12; 8.42; 9.38; Heb. 11.17). As a compound meaning 'only-born', *monogenēs* is paralleled by a whole series of words involving the idea of birth, including *agenēs*, 'unborn', *diogenēs*, 'sprung from Zeus', *eugenēs*, 'well-born', *gēgenēs*, 'earth-born', *nothagenēs*, 'base-born', and *prōtogenēs*, 'first-born'. In using this term John describes Jesus' unique relationship to God, rather than his unique deity or absolute uniqueness.

It remains to discuss briefly what John meant by calling Jesus God's 'son'. He clearly did not picture him as physically begotten in the way that gods in Greek mythology fathered children by mortal women. Nor does this image necessarily imply a metaphysical relationship, as in patristic doctrines of Christ. John uses 'the Son' to express Jesus' moral unity with God – his utter obedience to God, his one will with God's, his authority from God, his speaking God's words, his doing God's work, including tasks of life-giving and judgement, and his sharing in God's glory (see Schnackenburg, 1980, pp. 172–86).

Some have suggested that reading *theos* in 1.18 provides a neat chiasmus with 1.1–5 by returning to the same themes (cf. Talbert's analysis above, p. 85). There is indeed a balance between the description of the Word as 'with God' (1.1b) and that of Jesus as 'in the Father's bosom', and between the idea of the *logos* as revelation and that of Jesus as God's 'exegete'. But 1.16–18 does more than echo motifs from the Prologue's opening. It builds on them by identifying the undefined *logos* as a specific individual, Jesus Christ, the source of grace and truth, who as God's only son uniquely knows him, and makes him known. Nor does 1.14 contain 'the whole mystery of the Christian faith' as suggested by Richardson (cf. above, p. 91). For that mystery must also involve both Jesus' sacrificial death on the cross (to be recounted later by John), and his role as God's interpreter.

The Prologue and the Rest of the Gospel

One argument used to support the view that the Prologue incorporates a pre-existing hymn is the occurrence of vocabulary and themes not found again in the Gospel. But, in fact, all its major ideas seem to be picked up later (cf. Robinson, 1962/3, pp. 122f.). Admittedly *logos* never again bears the special sense it has in 1.1 and 1.14; but the concept of Jesus as the one who makes God known, and of his words as God's words, recurs frequently (e.g. 14.8, 24; 17.26). John also regularly refers to Jesus' teaching and authoritative commands as his *logos* (e.g. 4.41, 50; 5.24; 8.31). Jesus is presented as life-giver in his dialogues (e.g. 5.21) and in his miracles (cf. above, Ch. 6). Although the idea of him as God's agent in creation is not precisely repeated, his breathing into the disciples on Easter Day could be an act of new creation (cf. above, pp. 82f.). Several passages represent Jesus as pre-existent (8.58; 17.5, 24; cf. 1.30; 12.41) and pre-existence may also be implied by references to his 'coming' or 'being sent' (e.g. 10.10; 8.29; cf. above, pp. 67–8). The opposition between light and darkness (1.5) is picked up by several later episodes (e.g. 3.19–21; 8.12; 11.9f.) and especially in the healing of the man born blind. The Baptist's 'witness' (1.7, 15) leads nicely into his testimony in 1.19–35 and 3.25–30; the motif of witness also features prominently in subsequent dialogues.

'The world' (*ho kosmos*) is an important theme for John, occurring 78 times in all (contrast Mark, 3 times; Matthew, 9; Luke, 3). In the Prologue it is used with three different nuances, all in 1.10: neutrally, for the world of human affairs (10a), positively, for creation (10b), and, negatively, for those who do not know the *logos* (10c). Later texts speak of God loving 'the world' (3.16f.), of Jesus taking away its sin (1.29), and of Jesus as its Saviour (4.42). It also serves as a generic term for humanity alienated from God (e.g. 7.7; 14.17), and as a sphere to which neither Jesus nor his disciples properly belong (e.g. 8.23; 15.19). 'The world' is judged through Jesus (12.31–3) and conquered by him (16.33) (see further Cassem, 1972/3; Marrow, 2002). Other ideas picked up later are that of 'his own' (10.3f., 12; 13.1), and that of spiritual rebirth (3.3–8). While *charis*, 'grace', is not mentioned again, the themes of God's love and gracious giving recur (e.g. 3.16; 6.32f.). 'Truth' is also a prominent motif, with the noun *alētheia* occurring 25 times and the adjectives *alēthēs* and *alēthinos* 13 and 9 times respectively (contrast their rare appearances in the Synoptics). Some of these words are not always used in precisely the same sense as in the Prologue.[18] 'Glory', as already noted (p. 93), is one of John's favourite motifs. The themes of Moses and the Law (1.17) are picked up quite often (e.g. 1.45; 3.14; 5.45f.; 6.32; 7.19, 22f.; 9.28f.) and there are further allusions where Moses is not mentioned by name (cf. Glasson, 1963; Pancaro, 1975). The idea of the *logos* as divine (1.1) – and the more explicit identification of Jesus as God in 1.18, if *theos* is read – is echoed in Thomas' confession (20.28).

Are there major elements in the Gospel unheralded in the Prologue? The identification of Jesus as the Christ (i.e. messiah) occurs only in the formal reference to 'Jesus Christ' (1.17); but this is enough to alert readers to the theme. The Prologue does not refer to Jesus' being 'sent', but it does allude to his 'coming' (possibly 1.9; 1.11, 15) and to his sonship. The Spirit – important later in the Gospel – is not mentioned (its traditional role in creation being taken by the *logos*), nor are Jesus' miracles. Jesus' kingship does not feature, or his conflicts with 'the Jews', or his passion, death, and resurrection (except perhaps indirectly as his *doxa*). But one cannot expect a writer to include in the introduction every theme that is to occur in a book. In spite of its obscurities the Prologue is an artistic unity; by capturing the reader's imagination, and adumbrating ideas and images that will later be developed, it offers a dramatic and thought-provoking introduction to the Gospel. It is rightly regarded as John's supreme achievement.

10

Characters in John's Story

Literary critics explore how authors use characters in articulating their stories: in recent years some New Testament scholars have examined how the Gospels depict character, applying insights from the study of fiction (e.g. Culpepper, 1983, ch. 5; Conway, 1999; Malbon, 2000). But the Gospels, with their strongly evangelistic and hortatory aims, are bound to represent character differently from modern novels or even ancient epic and drama. The Evangelists show little interest in the 'psychology' of characters, and naturally know nothing of developmental psychology or Freudian analysis. They rarely relate what people thought (though note Jn 2.25; 6.6) and hardly ever describe what they looked like. This chapter considers some of John's characters for their intrinsic interest, for the part they play in his 'plot', and for the light they shed on his theology through possible 'representative' roles. Both groups and individuals will be discussed.

The Disciples

The word 'disciple' (*mathētēs*) means 'learner', or 'pupil'. Jesus' disciples appear in John as a group *c.* 56 times (Mk *c.* 44 times; Mt. *c.* 67; Lk. *c.* 32). They are presented initially like rabbinic students: they seek Jesus out as their master and find fellow-disciples (cf. above, p. 62). They act as his companions (e.g. 2.2; 3.22; 6.3), buy food for him (4.8, 31) – rabbinic pupils often looked after their teachers' physical needs – and are addressed as 'children' (*teknia*, 13.33; *paidia*, 21.5), a term often used by Jewish teachers for their pupils. They continue in this subordinate role throughout John 1—12, and, in contrast to the Synoptics, are not sent out to preach or heal (though note 4.38; 17.18). With the Last Supper, things change: Jesus reverses the roles by washing their feet (13.4–15), and calls them not servants but 'friends' (*philoi*, 15.14f.). He also makes it clear that, although some of them may have taken the initiative in seeking him, he in fact chose them (15.16); they were all entrusted to him by God (17.6, 12).

Do the disciples serve as role models for future believers? At first it might seem as if they do not. Though they put their faith in Jesus at Cana (2.11), they are not represented as particularly perceptive (see, for example, 4.27, 33; 9.2; 12.16). Even during the Last Supper they fail to understand him, asking naive questions (13.6, 36, Simon Peter; 14.5, Thomas; 14.8, Philip; 14.22, Judas, not Iscariot). But such misunderstandings are essentially literary devices, designed to give Jesus the opportunity to clarify his teaching. One is reminded of minor characters in Plato's dialogues who interact with Socrates, enabling him to expound his philosophy; the Gnostic Gospels also use this technique. As the Last Supper proceeds, one becomes increasingly aware of the closeness between Jesus and the disciples as he prepares them for his departure. He tells them that he goes to get ready a place for them (14.1–3) – words that have produced comfort for countless Christians ever since – and promises to come again (cf. above, p. 76). He warns them to expect the world's hatred and persecution (15.18–21; 16.1–4), but promises peace (14.27; 16.33). Their sorrow will turn to joy, like a woman's after childbirth (16.20–2); his desire is that their joy should be 'full' (15.11; 16.24; 17.13; cf. 1 Jn 1.4; 2 Jn 12). He tells them that they will do even greater works than his (14.12), and that whatever they ask in his Name will be granted (14.13f.; 16.23f., 26). He promises them 'another Counsellor', or 'Comforter' (*paraklētos*), the Spirit of Truth, to guide them, bear witness to him, and convict 'the world' (14.16, 26; 15.26; 16.7–15). He bids them love one another, abide in him, and keep his commands (13.34; 14.21, 23f.; 15.4–10, 17); it is by their mutual love that people will know that they are his disciples (13.35). He also assures them of the Father's love (16.27), and prays for them and those who will believe through them (17.9–25).

The intensity and intimacy of Jesus' final words to the disciples come as something of a surprise after their earlier subordinate role. But these are those who have been with him throughout his ministry and stayed faithful when others fell away (6.66). Jesus knows that Peter will deny him, and the others scatter after his arrest (13.38; 16.32; cf. 18.8). Yet he trusts them to be his witnesses, for they have been with him 'from the beginning' (15.27); they know in truth that he came from God and believe that God sent him (17.8).

This changing role of the disciples may explain why scholars assess John's portrayal of them so differently. For Culpepper (1983, p. 115) they are far from exemplars of perfect faith; von Wahlde (1981, p. 404), however, sees them as becoming 'perfect models for the total response to the witness of the Father' (in Jesus). In a sense both are right. Their initial faith, as a group, based on Jesus' first sign was imperfect, but under his loving tutelage and the Spirit's guidance (14.17b) they have grown in understanding. After his 'glorification', when they have been commissioned and further empowered by the Spirit (20.22), they will comprehend and 'remember' more (2.22; 12.16; 13.7).

Sadly, there is one disciple to whom this does not apply: Judas, 'the son of perdition', or 'lost one' (17.12). His character is consistently portrayed negatively: he is made a thief who cares nothing for the poor (12.6); as in the Synoptics, he is repeatedly labelled 'the betrayer' (12.4; 13.11; 18.2, 5; 19.11). Jesus alludes to him as 'a devil' (6.70); at the Last Supper, when he gives Judas the morsel, the devil is said to enter him (13.27); when Judas leaves to betray Jesus, John says dramatically, 'It was night' (13.30). Unlike novelists, playwrights, and some modern scholars, who have speculated why Judas betrayed Jesus, John supplies no psychological, political, or financial motivation. He simply says he was a disciple (12.4), one of the Twelve, who acted on the devil's prompting (13.2), and fulfilled the role allotted him in Scripture (13.18; 17.12). John derived Judas' role as betrayer from tradition; but he heightens his wickedness and his alignment with the powers of evil as a foil to the other disciples and Jesus.[1]

Do the disciples as a group 'represent' future Christian leaders? Before considering this question, it is worth glancing at some other named individuals. Andrew, Nathanael, Philip, Peter, and Thomas all bear witness to Jesus through faith-confessions, but so do others not specifically labelled 'disciple', including John the Baptist, Martha, and the Samaritan woman. Some disciples seem to act as model 'missionaries' and facilitators of others: Andrew fetches his brother Peter (1.42), and brings the lad with the loaves and fishes to Jesus (6.8f.); Philip brings Nathanael and 'the Greeks' to him (1.45; 12.20–2); but neither is depicted in any depth. There is more development in Thomas' portrayal: he moves from being loyal and impulsive in his wish to go to Jerusalem to die with Jesus (11.16), through puzzlement over Jesus' enigmatic sayings (14.5) and doubting (20.25), to robust faith (20.28). He may be intended as a model of a faith that grows but requires strong evidence, in contrast to the 'beloved disciple' and others who believe without even seeing the risen Jesus (20.8, 29).

Of the remaining disciples Peter is most fully portrayed. John names him 39 times,[2] more often than any other individual except Jesus (and more often than in any of the Synoptics). His brother Andrew brings him to Jesus, and Jesus tells him that he will be called Kephas, 'Rock' (1.42); but Peter makes no faith-confession at this point. John's basic characterization is similar to the Synoptists' (from which it may be partly derived). Peter is a fisherman (though this is not apparent until Jn 21). He is keen and impetuous, enthusiastically declaring his willingness to die for Jesus (13.37f.; cf. Mk 14.29–31 par.); but he three times denies him (18.15–27; cf. Mk 14.66–72 par.). Only John describes his 'rehabilitation' (21.15–19), though his special commissioning is partially paralleled in Luke 22.32. John narrates several additional incidents illustrating Peter's impetuousness: in 13.6–10 he protests at Jesus' washing his feet, earning the rebuke, 'If I do not wash you, you have no share with me'; whereupon Peter asks Jesus to wash not just his feet, but his hands and his head. On Jesus' arrest (18.10f.) he draws a sword and cuts off the High Priest's servant's ear, earning another rebuke; in the Synoptics the over-zealous defender is just a bystander (Mk 14.47) or one of those with Jesus (Mt. 26.51; Lk. 22.49f.). In the Appendix Peter leaps into the sea after the 'beloved disciple' has recognized the risen Jesus on the shore (21.7); compare his rash attempt to walk on the water in Matthew (14.28–31). John also describes Peter's running to the tomb with the 'beloved disciple' (20.4), and seeing the linen clothes. He acts as spokesman for the Twelve in 6.68f. (cf. Mk 8.29 par.), when he says, 'We believe and are convinced that you are God's Holy One' (cf. above, p. 66); there is no commendation and no reference to the future Church (contrast Mt. 16.17–19).

Some scholars claim that the 'beloved disciple' outshines Peter whenever they appear together. At the Last Supper Jesus reveals the betrayer's identity to the 'beloved disciple', who reclines on his breast, rather than to Peter (13.23–6). When Jesus is arrested, Peter and 'another disciple' (probably the 'beloved disciple') follow him to the High Priest's house; the other disciple enters, but Peter stands at the door until the other disciple arranges for him to be admitted (18.15f.). The 'beloved disciple' is present at the cross (19.26f.), but not Peter. At the tomb both Peter and the 'beloved disciple' see the grave-clothes, but only the 'beloved disciple' believes (20.8). At Jesus' lakeside resurrection appearance the 'beloved disciple', not Peter, recognizes Jesus first (21.7); later, when Peter enquires about the 'beloved disciple's' fate, he is rebuked (21.22).

These incidents have led to the idea that John depicts a 'rivalry' between these two, reflecting tensions between Jewish Christianity, represented by Peter, and the Gentile Church, represented by the 'beloved disciple' (Bultmann, 1971, pp. 484f., 685), or between 'Apostolic Christians' and 'the Johannine community' (e.g. Brown, 1979, pp. 82–5). Sometimes the whole Gospel is seen as 'anti-Petrine' (Agourides, 1968; Snyder, 1971; cf. Smith, 1985, pp. 143–50). Such hypotheses read too much into the text. Some of the incidents in which Peter is 'outshone' by the 'beloved disciple' are quite trivial or capable of different interpretations. Peter's gesture to the 'beloved disciple' to find out the betrayer's identity (13.24) could indicate his initiative (Quast, 1989, p. 167). The other disciple's success in getting Peter admitted to the High Priest's courtyard may arise from his Jerusalem contacts (contrast Peter's Galilean background). Even the 'beloved disciple's' reaching the tomb first could be a literary device to have the two men arrive at separate points, so that the Evangelist can record different reactions from them (Mahoney, 1974). It is simply not true that

Peter is portrayed in 'a very bad light indeed' (Maynard, 1984, p. 546). He is one of the first disciples to follow Jesus (preceded only by Andrew and one other), whereas the 'beloved disciple' is not even mentioned until John 13. Peter remains loyal to Jesus when other disciples draw back, speaking on behalf of the Twelve (6.68f.). His initial protest at Jesus washing his feet is prompted by a sense of his own humble status compared with his teacher's; his attempt to defend Jesus physically (18.10), though misguided, is surely motivated by devotion. Although he denied Jesus, he is given a special commission, and marked out as a future martyr (21.15–19).

Moreover, nothing in the text connects Peter with 'Jewish Christianity'; nowhere is he linked with 'the Jews', or Jesus' mother (also understood by Bultmann as a symbol of Judaism). The claim to see him or the Twelve as representing 'Apostolic Christians', with which Johannine Christians are in tension, is also dubious. If Peter is linked with the Twelve in 6.67f., it is because he is their spokesman and leader. The idea of the Johannine 'community' at loggerheads with other Christians is a scholarly construct arising from a surfeit of sociological speculation. What then does Peter 'represent'? He represents himself, and in doing so he provides an example for future believers unable to live up to their heartfelt professions, who will be encouraged by the fact that so great a leader failed and was restored.[3]

In contrast to Peter, the 'beloved disciple' is a somewhat colourless personality: his principal trait is his closeness to Jesus, typified by his resting on his breast, and his spiritual perceptivity. He is a model for Christian behaviour, an ideal to which all should aim, and a living example of that love and mutual abiding which Jesus shares with the Father. Although probably based on a real person, his main function is christological, as a human counterpart to Jesus, who abides in the Father's breast and reveals his nature (1.18). He also serves as a witness to the crucifixion and empty tomb, and as 'ideal' author guaranteeing the reliability of John's text (cf. above, pp. 18–26).

We return now to the question of whether the disciples in John serve as models for Christian leadership. It is clear that Peter must do so, at least in John 21. He would be a familiar figure to many of John's readers, having been a leader in the Jerusalem Church, and appearing in many early Christian texts, some of which must antedate John (Synoptics, Acts, Paul's letters, 1 and 2 Peter, and various apocryphal writings). Jesus' command to tend or feed his sheep (or lambs) would readily be understood as referring to pastoral ministry (the same metaphor is applied to other Christian leaders in Acts 20.28; 1 Pet. 5.2; Eph. 4.11; cf. Jesus' role as 'shepherd' in Jn 10). This does not mean that Peter is given 'primacy' over other disciples, as suggested by some

Church Fathers and historically claimed by the Roman Catholic Church.[4] In John 21 Peter is restored because he alone of Jesus' close disciples denied him (18.15–27). The scene of his threefold commissioning carefully balances that of his threefold denials: there is even a charcoal fire (*anthrakia*) on both occasions (a word occurring in the New Testament only here). Jesus' repeated questions establish that Peter has the devoted love essential for discipleship (Brown, 1966, p. 1111), and Jesus' final words to him are 'Follow me' (21.19).

It is difficult to determine how far the other disciples are intended to symbolize the whole believing community, and how far its future leaders. The problem is particularly acute with the commission in 20.23 to forgive or retain sins. This has sometimes been interpreted as appointing the apostles to priesthood, with power to declare and withhold absolution (so the Council of Trent, XIV.3, cited in Hoskyns, 1947, p. 545; Edwards, 1996b, p. 132). More recently it has been seen as addressed to the whole Church, of which the disciples are representatives (von Campenhausen, 1969, p. 128; Hanson, 1979, p. 10). The authority to declare forgiveness cannot be separated from Jesus' 'sending' of this group and the gift of the Holy Spirit, surely intended for the whole Church (Beasley-Murray, 1987, p. 381), nor from Jesus' promises to the disciples in the Farewell Discourses, which are clearly intended for believers in general.[5] Jesus' words in 20.21–3 may be seen as John's equivalent of Matthew's Great Commission (28.18–20; cf. Lk. 24.46–9). There is much more that could be said on this controversial topic: suffice it to say that John does not elsewhere present a hierarchical view of ministry, but rather an ideal of spirit-led service, shared by a faithful community who abide in Jesus' teaching and love.

Other Male Characters

Those addressed at the Last Supper by no means constitute all Jesus' followers. There are others – some lightly sketched and some portrayed in detail. Among the former is the anonymous royal official who 'believed with all his household' (4.53), in a story reminiscent of conversions in Acts (e.g. 16.25–34). He must be a model of faith, even though the practical implications of his believing are nowhere spelt out: how would he practise his new faith in his home? Assuming he is a Jew, would he have been able to continue worshipping in the synagogue? The case is different with the newly sighted man, whose path to faith is so strikingly dramatized, culminating in his acknowledging Jesus as 'Son of Man' and prostrating himself before him (9.38).[6] He comes into conflict with the Jewish authorities because of his loyalty to Jesus: note his sharp retort when they question him a second time about how he received his sight: 'I have told you already and you didn't listen; why do you want to hear it again? Surely you too don't want to become his disciples?' (9.27). Many scholars understand his subsequent 'casting out' (9.34) as expulsion from the synagogue (cf. *aposynagōgos* in 9.22), and interpret him as standing for Johannine Christians who have had the courage to declare their Christian faith openly and so have been excluded from Judaism. Such interpretations remain speculative (cf. above, p. 48). It is safer to read him simply as an example of someone who came to faith after receiving healing from Jesus, and maintained this faith robustly in the face of opposition. As such he would obviously be an encouragement to any Christians suffering persecution.

The newly sighted man is often contrasted with two Jewish leaders who have been seen as lacking courage to come out openly as followers of Jesus – Joseph of Arimathea and Nicodemus. Joseph is explicitly described as 'a disciple of Jesus, but secretly through fear of the Jews' (19.38): Rensberger (1988, p. 40) interprets these words as aligning him with the authorities who were afraid to confess their faith (12.42f.). But Brown (1979, p. 72, n. 128) is probably right to see him as making his faith public by boldly requesting Jesus' body for burial. Thus John's portrait of him as a disciple seems consistent with that of Luke, who describes him as 'a member of the Council [Sanhedrin], a good and upright man, who had not agreed with its decision and action' and who 'was looking for God's kingdom' (Lk. 23.50f.; cf. Mk 15.43; Mt. 27.57).

Nicodemus also has been interpreted negatively as 'a man of inadequate faith and inadequate courage' (Rensberger, 1988, p. 40). He appears in the New Testament only in John (3.1–11; 7.50–2; 19.38–42), and is depicted in more detail than Joseph. The best-known episode is his visit to Jesus by night, when Jesus tells him that only those born *anōthen* – an ambiguous word meaning either 'again' or 'from above' – can 'see' the Kingdom of God (3.1–3). Nicodemus fails to understand and is not helped by Jesus' clarification that only those born of 'water and the Spirit' can enter the Kingdom. Jesus reproaches him for being 'the teacher of Israel' and not grasping his meaning (3.10) – as a Scripture expert he might have been expected to recall passages like Ezekiel 36.25–7 or Psalm 51.2, which link water (or cleansing) with the Spirit. Jesus then speaks enigmatically about 'earthly' and 'heavenly' things, and the Son of Man. Nicodemus fades out of the picture, without the reader knowing exactly when he departed.

As far as Nicodemus' character is concerned, the main interest of this passage is whether John intends him to be understood negatively or sympathetically. He is introduced as 'a man of the Pharisees and a leader of the Jews' (3.1); 'leader' (*archōn*) probably means member of the Sanhedrin. The Pharisees in John have generally a bad press, and 'the

Jews' are often portrayed in a hostile manner. Goulder (1991, p. 153) therefore concludes that John's attitude to Nicodemus is 'solidly negative'. But at this stage no pejorative remarks have been made about Pharisees (in 1.24 they merely investigate the Baptist's claims); 'the Jews' also have been mentioned only neutrally (2.6, 13; in 2.20 they misunderstand Jesus' ambiguous saying, but so do the disciples). Nicodemus' coming 'by night' has sometimes been seen as symbolizing alignment with the world of darkness (cf. Judas in 13.30). But it could have a less sinister significance, since Jewish religious teachers often studied by night; or Nicodemus might be coming out of the darkness into the presence of the true light (Barrett, 1978, p. 205). This section of John concludes with the comment that those who do evil will not come to the light lest their deeds should be exposed, but those who 'do the truth' come to the light (3.20f.). All this suggests that for the Gospel's first readers Nicodemus would not appear obviously as a 'baddy'. A favourable impression is reinforced by his first words to Jesus, 'Rabbi, we know that you have come from God as a teacher'. Far from being greasy flattery (Goulder, 1991, p. 154), this understanding of Jesus is closely comparable to that attributed to the disciples by Jesus at the Last Supper, 'They know in truth that I came from you' (17.8).

Nicodemus appears again in 7.50–2, when the High Priests and Pharisees want to arrest Jesus and have him put to death. Like Joseph in Luke (23.51), he dissents: 'Does our Law condemn a person without first hearing from him and ascertaining what he has done?' This comes in the context of people asking whether any of the authorities (*archontes*) or Pharisees have believed in Jesus; this surely suggests that Nicodemus is a believer rather than the reverse. In 19.38–42 he joins Joseph in bringing a hundredweight of spices for Jesus' burial. Rensberger (1988, p. 40) criticizes him for burying Jesus 'ponderously and with a kind of absurd finality'. But is this how John intends this episode to be understood? The burial is generous – Joseph (Mt. 27.57) and Nicodemus were apparently wealthy men[7] – and nobody at this stage expected Jesus to rise again. Far from being 'a type of unbelief' (Collins, 1976, p. 37) or representing Jews to whom Jesus could not entrust himself (Meeks, 1972, p. 55, citing 2.23f.), Nicodemus is a good man doing Jesus a service.

The example of Nicodemus alerts us to the extraordinary variety of ways in which readers interpret characters. Brown (1966, p. 129) took him as standing for a group of Jewish leaders who came hesitantly to believe in Jesus (citing 12.42). He later decided that Nicodemus did not, after all, represent a group but simply showed that some of those attracted to Jesus did not immediately understand him (1979, p. 72, n. 128). Schnackenburg (1968, p. 363) saw him as 'a well-intentioned representative of the ruling classes'. Bultmann (1971, p. 143) interpreted him more broadly, describing his question in 3.9 as representing 'the inadequacy of the way in which man puts his questions'. Lindars (1972, p. 149) took him as 'an example of official Judaism in a situation of openness'; Bassler (1989) as 'deliberately ambiguous'; Moloney (1998b, p. 97) as on a journey to faith; Conway (1999, p. 103) as a 'pathetic character', lacking courage and conviction. These views may be contrasted with that of the poet Henry Vaughan (1622–1695) in 'The Night':[8]

> Through that pure *Virgin-shrine*,
> That sacred vail drawn o'r thy glorious noon
> That men might look and live as Glo-worms shine,
>   And face the Moon:
> Wise *Nicodemus* saw such light
> As made him know his God by night.

> Most blest believer he!
> Who in that land of darkness and blinde eyes
> Thy long expected healing wings could see,
>   When thou didst rise,
> And, what can never more be done,
> Did at mid-night speak with the Sun!

Women Characters

We turn now to some female characters that have been of special interest to feminist scholars. These often consider John especially sympathetic to women (Scott, 1992; Schneiders, 1999; cf. Brown, 1979, pp. 183–98), sometimes arguing that he depicts an 'alternative' Christian community in which women share fully in leadership (Fiorenza, 1983, pp. 324–33). Some women are indeed sensitively portrayed; others are presented more ambiguously, but none is completely 'bad' like Judas. The fullest portrait is of the Samaritan woman (4.4–42). This episode balances that of Nicodemus, whose encounter with Jesus immediately precedes it. He is a Jew, a teacher and a man of authority; she is a Samaritan (traditionally regarded as heretical and unclean) and a woman, carrying out a woman's regular task of fetching water. He meets Jesus by night, she at mid-day. He is a Pharisee and pillar of respectability; she has been married five times and is living with someone who is not her husband (4.17f.). Both stories involve ambiguity, misunderstanding, and clarification. But they end differently: Nicodemus fails to grasp Jesus' message (though his later conduct suggests a coming to faith); the Samaritan, to whom Jesus reveals himself more openly, recognizes him as a prophet (4.19), and wonders whether he could be 'messiah'. After her encounter, she spreads the word among the townsfolk and many come to faith through her witness (4.39).

The Samaritan's character has been read in different ways. Some earlier commentators tended to treat her as sinful because of her multiple marriages and her living with an unmarried partner. More recently she has been described as level-headed, imaginative, and feisty (Boers, 1988, pp. 163–72). Schneiders is highly critical of her treatment in the major commentaries, describing it as 'a textbook case of the trivialization, marginalization, and even sexual demonization of biblical women' (1999, p. 137), which she sees as reflecting and promoting similar treatment of real women in the Church. O'Day (1992, p. 296) similarly castigates unnamed commentators for 'reflecting their own prejudices against women, not the views of the text'.9 Such comments are unduly harsh. Being married five times would have been unacceptable to Jews and, probably, Samaritans (cf. Schnackenburg, 1968, p. 433); O'Day's comment that she might have been 'trapped in the custom of levirate marriage' (five times?) is just special pleading. Schneiders, following a long-standing exegetical tradition, argues that the woman's marital situation should be interpreted allegorically: the five husbands represent the five pagan gods once worshipped by the Samaritans, while the woman's current partner stands for the Samaritans' imperfect worship of YHWH. The allegory breaks down when one discovers that the pagan deities, supposedly represented by her legal husbands, were seven in number (2 Kgs 17.29–31). It is also most improbable that John would construct an allegory whereby a nation's worship of YHWH is symbolized by an unmarried relationship.10 It is far more likely that the husbands and her partner are to be taken literally for the purposes of the story, and that the interchange in 4.16–18 is designed to reveal Jesus' supernatural knowledge rather than the woman's 'sinfulness', and to facilitate the Evangelist's presentation of her growing faith.

A curious feature of recent interpretation is the attempt to see the conversation at the well as the Samaritan's 'wooing' (e.g. Eslinger, 1993). The Hebrew Bible has scenes where a man approaches a woman at a well and asks for a gift of water; eventually a marriage results (cf. Gen. 24.10–67; 29.1–30; Ex. 2.15–22). Drawing on such materials Fehribach sees the Samaritan as 'entering into a metaphorical betrothal/marital relationship with the messianic bridegroom' (1998, pp. 45–81, esp. p. 69). For Schneiders 'the entire dialogue between Jesus and the woman is the "wooing" of Samaria to full covenant fidelity in the new Israel by Jesus, the new Bridegroom'; she is his 'potential spouse whom he invited to intimacy' (1999, pp. 141, 144). But nowhere in this passage is Jesus pictured as a bridegroom; in John's whole Gospel that image only occurs once, in an analogy on the lips of the Baptist (3.29). This is not scholarly exegesis, but fanciful re-interpretation – without the power to move of Vaughan's beautiful poem.

If we confine ourselves to the woman's character as presented by John, she is practical (4.11); trusting and enthusiastic, if a little naïve (4.15); impetuous and prone to exaggeration (4.28f.), but also theologically aware, perceptive, and persistent (4.19f., 25, 29b). It is, however, a gross exaggeration to speak, as Schneiders does, of her questioning Jesus 'on virtually every significant tenet of Samaritan theology' (1999, p. 139). Perhaps most importantly she provides a model for Christians in her exemplary witness to the Gospel (note *martyreō* in 4.39), a remarkable feature in view of the generally low regard for women's testimony in Jewish law (Maccini, 1996, ch. 3).

Two other women who are sympathetically portrayed are the sisters Martha and Mary, both described, along with their brother Lazarus, as loved by Jesus (11.5). The two episodes in which they appear – Lazarus' raising and the anointing at Bethany – are linked by an unusual reference forward (11.2). In the first episode (11.1–44) Martha is presented as active and outgoing, while Mary appears quieter and more passive (cf. Lk. 10.38–42). Martha goes out to meet Jesus, while Mary stays at home. Martha takes the initiative in speaking to him, expressing her trust in him (11.21) and her faith in future resurrection (11.24); she acknowledges him as 'the Christ, the Son of God, the one coming into the world' (11.27; cf. above, Ch. 7). This confession is made *before* Jesus raises Lazarus. Mary also shows faith: she gets up quickly when her sister tells her that Jesus is calling, goes to him, falls at his feet and weeps (11.28–33). But her only remark is an echo of Martha's first words: 'Lord, if you had been here, my brother would not have died' (11.32).

Many scholars see Martha as an example of full-blooded faith, and her 'confession' as equalling, if not surpassing, Peter's in the Synoptic tradition (Mk 8.29 par.).[11] Moloney, however, argues that she displays only a limited faith compared with Mary, whose unspoken gesture of prostration indicates her 'total trust' in Jesus (1996, p. 165). It is true that Martha's confession may not be wholly adequate (any more than Peter's) because the precise nuance of the 'titles' cannot be determined. But Mary's gesture of falling at Jesus' feet is even more ambiguous: John does not use *proskyneō*, which may denote worship (though it need not do so), but *piptō*, 'fall', the same verb as is used of those arresting Jesus, including apparently Judas (18.6).[12] This gesture could indicate desperate grief, earnest request, or humility, rather than adoration. For Moloney, Mary will always be 'the special sister': has he been unduly influenced by Luke's picture of Mary as the contemplative one (10.39), or by her central role in John's next episode? Or is he reacting against the idealization of Martha by some feminists? The most natural reading is to see Martha in this episode as an example of vibrant faith, while recognizing from John's 'prolepsis' (11.2) that Mary's turn will come.

The description of Mary's anointing of Jesus is much shorter (12.1–8). John's account seems to relate to both Luke's story (7.37–50) of a sinful woman of the town, who washes Jesus' feet with her tears and dries them with her loosed hair, and Mark's story of an anonymous woman anointing Jesus' head just before his passion (14.3–9; cf. Mt. 26.6–13). In Luke, the woman's action comes from penitence, love, and devotion; in Mark it may be intended as a sign of Jesus' kingship (though Jesus' response links it with his burial). John supplies the woman with a name and identity, even though it would have been inappropriate for a respectable woman to loose her hair in public. He keeps Mark's location at Bethany, but transfers the scene to the sisters' house. And he has Mary anoint Jesus' feet (rather than his head), anticipating Jesus' own humility in washing his disciples' feet (Jn 13). Mary's lavish gift of the ointment illustrates her devotion to Jesus (cf. the generosity of Nicodemus and Joseph), though unlike the forgiven 'sinner' in Luke, or the unnamed woman in Mark, she is not directly commended. Her action contrasts with Judas' meanness (12.4f.), and the whole scene points forward to Jesus' death and burial.

John nowhere describes any group of women who travel round with Jesus (contrast Lk. 8.2f.), but he does mention the presence of four women[13] at the cross: Jesus' mother, her sister, Mary [the wife] of Klopas, and Mary Magdalene (19.25; cf. Mk 15.40f.; Mt. 27.55f.; Lk. 23.49). These have presumably followed him from Galilee to Jerusalem for the Passover. Nothing further is said about Mary of Klopas, whom John must have included from tradition. Jesus' mother appeared in the Cana story when she showed confidence in Jesus by telling him of the shortage of wine, and bidding the servants 'Do whatever he tells you' (2.3f.). She has regularly been interpreted as a symbol of the Church by Roman Catholic scholars (see the discussion in Brown, 1966, pp. 107–9), but there is little evidence that John sees her in this way.[14] There is even less to say for the theory that in 19.25–7 Mary represents Israel being absorbed into the Church, despite Bultmann (1971, p. 673) and Brodie (1993a, p. 175). The incident can be interpreted quite simply as illustrating (a) the presence of women at the cross to witness the reality of Jesus' death; (b) Jesus' care for his mother in providing practically for her; (c) Mary's love and faithfulness in being near her son, even at his painful and shaming death.

Mary Magdalene (named after her home-town Magdala in Galilee) appears only at 19.25 and in John's resurrection narrative (20.1f.,

11–18). It seems extraordinary that her initial conduct at the tomb has been interpreted as representing 'unbelief'. Because she fails at first to recognize Jesus, Brodie (1993a, p. 567) sees her as corresponding 'significantly to unbelieving Israel';[15] Moloney (1998a, pp. 158f.) speaks of the darkness when she comes to the tomb as 'a setting of unfaith' and of her 'running away'. But Mary does not run *away*; she runs *to* Peter and the 'beloved disciple' to seek help and share with them her bewilderment that the body has gone. Her devotion to Jesus is illustrated by her early rising, her reference to him as 'the Lord' (20.2; cf. 'my Lord', 20.13), her weeping (20.11, 13, 15), and her willingness to go and fetch the body (20.15; see Bruce, 1983, pp. 388f.). Her initial failure to recognize Jesus is more likely a literary device to heighten the drama (cf. Lk. 24.16, 31) than an indication that she is to be blamed for 'blindness'. Mary's instant recognition of Jesus when he calls her by name, and the fact that he entrusts her with a message for his 'brothers', are sure evidence that she is intended to be understood as a model of faithfulness. Her message to them, 'I have seen the Lord' (20.18), marks her out as an apostle; compare Paul's words: 'Am I not an apostle? Have I not seen the Lord Jesus?' (1 Cor. 9.1). Thus Mary is the first witness of the risen Jesus. One cannot help contrasting her prompt obedience (20.18) with the behaviour of Peter when he sees the empty tomb: although the 'beloved disciple' believes, Peter is not said to do so. Neither of them understands 'the Scripture' that Jesus must rise from the dead, and both rather feebly just 'go away' or 'go home'[16] (20.10).

Mary's part in announcing (*angellō*) the resurrection to the disciples caught the imagination of later interpreters: in the Western Church she became the *apostola apostolorum*, 'apostle of the apostles' (Brown, 1979, p. 190, n. 336; Marjanen, 1996, p. 3, n. 9), and among the Greek Orthodox *isapostolos*, 'equal to the apostles' (Ware, 1983, p. 31). Gnostic writers used her as an interlocutor with Jesus in their dialogues (where she sometimes clashes with Peter) and attributed a Gospel to her (Marjanen, 1996). In later Church art she is represented as proclaiming the resurrection to the male disciples, and even preaching from the pulpit (Moltmann-Wendel, 1982, pp. 73f., with illustrations). She also became identified (by *c.* 6th cent.) with Luke's repentant sinner (7.36–50), understood as a harlot. This identification, without basis in the New Testament, has given rise to countless representations of Mary as a beautiful, long-haired, repentant prostitute. In novels and films she sometimes becomes Jesus' mistress, or at least his 'last temptation' (cf. Scorsese's film, based on Kazantzakis' novel). Despite its long endorsement by the Roman Catholic Church, the identification of Mary Magdalene with Luke's repentant 'sinner' is today repudiated by biblical and feminist scholars alike,[17] though it still continues in popular piety.

Conclusions

John uses a wide variety of characters. Some are 'stereotyped' or 'flat' (to use Forster's terminology, 1962, pp. 73–89), being based on a single readily recognized idea, e.g. the official's faith; Judas' wickedness; the 'beloved disciple's' closeness to Jesus. Others are portrayed in more detail, without necessarily being fully 'round'. Nicodemus, the blind man, the Samaritan woman, Peter, Mary Magdalene, the sisters Martha and Mary, and Thomas are all depicted with liveliness and some subtlety (though they have been read in different ways). Characters quite often serve as foils to Jesus, to set up situations where he may have the opportunity to perform certain actions or deliver particular teaching (cf. Philip's role in the feeding miracle, and in the Supper Discourses; Peter's protests at the foot-washing). Some have 'functional' roles for John's 'plot' – Judas in betraying him; Caiaphas in handing him over to the Romans; Pilate in condemning him;[18] Joseph and Nicodemus in burying him; Mary, Peter, and the 'beloved disciple', in discovering the empty tomb. This does not prevent them also having 'mimetic' qualities, i.e. being portrayed in a realistic, life-like way.[19]

As noted earlier (above, Ch. 7), an important role of many individual characters is to witness to Jesus through christological confessions. As a group, the disciples act as Jesus' companions, pupils, and witnesses of his ministry and resurrection appearances; in the Supper Discourses they may stand for future believers. Theirs is not a perfect faith that comprehends instantly (though the 'beloved disciple' sometimes seems to do this), but one needing correction and nurture. It is doubtful whether John's characters are deliberately designed to reflect specific groups within the Church, e.g. Jewish Christians, Gentiles, 'crypto-Christians', or active female leaders; but in certain situations their behaviour can serve to encourage (or warn) future generations.

Does John portray women and men differently? His basic methods seem to be the same for both: he shows both men and women misunderstanding Jesus (e.g. Nicodemus; the Samaritan woman), and both failing initially to recognize him (Mary Magdalene; Peter). He shows both as loved by Jesus (11.5), both as making faith-confessions and helping bring others to him. No woman denies Jesus, as Peter does, and no woman is depicted as completely 'bad' like Judas. The women are neither stereotyped as 'sex objects', nor presented as weakly subservient to men (though Fiorenza, 1995, pp. 95f., finds Mary of Bethany represented in 'kyriocentric' terms).

Christian interpreters have often attempted to draw inferences about the proper roles for men and women in ministry from their portrayals in the Gospels. Methodologically this is a dangerous exercise, as that is not the purpose of these writings. John depicts women as sharing the faith, as seeing the risen Christ, and as devoted and theologically perceptive. But he should not be taken as offering specific support to the *ordination* of either women or men, since he does not think in these terms (cf. Edwards, 1989, 1996b, pp. 140f.).

11

'Anti-Semitism'/'Anti-Judaism' in John's Gospel?

This chapter tackles a question which has come to the fore in recent Johannine studies. Is John's Gospel 'anti-Jewish' in the sense that it is ideologically opposed to Jewish religion and its adherents, or even 'anti-Semitic', displaying hatred against Jews simply because they are Jews? This must seem a strange question to those who were brought up to respect, and even venerate, John's Gospel. Yet since Ruether's *Faith and Fratricide* (1974) increasing numbers of scholars have condemned it as 'anti-Semitic' or 'anti-Jewish'.[1] She argued that John uses 'the Jews' to symbolize 'a fallen universe of darkness'; they are 'the very incarnation of the false, apostate principle of the fallen world, alienated from its true being in God' (1997, pp. 111–13). Lowry (1977, p. 229) found a direct line of development from John's portrayal of the Jews as 'spawn of the devil' to a Nazi picture-book for children, whose first page is headed '*Der Vater der Juden ist der Teufel*' ('The father of the Jews is the devil'). Beck (1994, esp. p. 295) sees John as 'a message of condemnation' for Jews. Cohn-Sherbok calls it 'a diatribe against the Jews and the Jewish faith' (1992, p. 24). Casey criticizes it not only as 'inaccurate', and 'profoundly untrue', but also as 'anti-Jewish', initiating 'the baleful charge of deicide' [killing God], part of the deplorable history of Christian anti-Semitism, at once 'horrifyingly wicked' and 'centrally deceitful' (1996, pp. 224–9). Are these scholars right?

The criticisms fall under three main heads: (a) John's use of 'the Jews' for Jesus' opponents and to symbolize 'alienated' humanity; (b) his apparent depiction of 'the Jews' as those responsible for crucifying Jesus; (c) their 'hostile' portrayal in John's dialogues and their association with the devil. These topics will form this chapter's main theme. Some scholars see John as also anti-Jewish in his 'replacement theology' and in his 'breach' of Jewish monotheism. These aspects will be discussed in Chapter 12.

John's Use of 'the Jews'

Greek has three words for a Jew: *Israēlitēs* (plural *-ai*), 'Israelite', *Ioudaios* (pl. *-oi*) – conventionally translated 'Jew', but also meaning 'Judaean' – and *Hebraios* (pl. *-oi*), 'Hebrew'. *Israēlitai* was the Jews' preferred term for themselves when speaking with fellow-Jews. *Ioudaioi* was used by Gentiles, and by Jews communicating with Gentiles, to denote both the inhabitants of Judaea and those of Jewish faith more generally. *Hebraios* was an elevated synonym for either term, and also used for language and script. John conforms to this basic pattern: he uses *Hebraïsti*, 'in Hebrew', of language (e.g. 5.2; 19.13); '*Israēlitēs*' and '*Israēl*' in intra-Jewish situations (1.47, 49; 3.10; 12.13), and *Ioudaios* on the lips of outsiders (4.9; 18.33, 35). In this respect his usage parallels the Synoptics. They use 'the Jews' on the lips of the Gentile magi (Mt. 2.2), Pilate (e.g. Mk 15.2 par.), Roman soldiers (e.g. Mk 15.18; Mt. 27.29), and 'king of the Jews' in the Roman superscription on the cross (Mk 15.26 par.; cf. Jn 19.19–22), but 'king of Israel' on the lips of Jewish leaders who deride Jesus (Mk 15.32; Mt. 27.41f.). But even in the Synoptics there are other uses. Mark 7.3 uses the phrase 'of the Jews' to explain Jewish hand-washing customs; Luke 23.51 describes Arimathea as 'a town of the Jews', and the Roman centurion who wants his servant healed sends 'elders of the Jews' to Jesus (Lk. 7.3). In these cases *tōn Ioudaiōn*, 'of the Jews', explains details of the narrative for Gentiles. A slightly different usage is Matthew 28.15, where it is reported that the rumour went round 'among the Jews until this day' that Jesus' disciples had stolen his body from the tomb. Here *hoi Ioudaioi* is used, possibly pejoratively, to distinguish Jews from Christians.[2]

In John *hoi Ioudaioi* occurs *c.* 67 times, much more frequently than in the Synoptics (Mk, 6 times; Mt., 5; Lk., 5).[3] Some examples are on the lips of non-Jews, such as Pilate, but many come from the narrator. A good few occur in explanations of Jewish feasts and customs, rather like Mark's explanation of Jewish hand-washing (e.g. Jn 2.6, 13; 5.1; 11.55). Some (e.g. 7.1; 11.19, 31) appear to be geographical, referring to inhabitants of 'Judaea'.[4] Such uses account for more than half the examples. There remain around 27 instances where *hoi Ioudaioi* appears to be a shorthand way of describing Jesus' opponents. 'The Jews' misunderstand Jesus' actions and sayings (2.18, 20; 6.41, 52; 7.35; 8.22, 57); quibble over his Sabbath healing of the lame man (5.10); disbelieve his restoration of the blind man's sight (9.18). They show themselves ignorant of Jesus' heavenly origin (6.42); they 'persecute' him (5.16), and agree to expel from the Synagogue those who confess him as Christ (9.22); people go in fear of them (7.13; 19.38; 20.19). They accuse Jesus of demon-possession (8.48, 52) and of blasphemy (10.33); they plot to kill him (5.18; 7.1), and attempt to stone him (10.31; cf. 11.8). They choose Barabbas to be released instead of him (18.38b–40); they call for his death (19.7). As well as being associated with the devil (8.44), they are said to be 'from below' and 'of this world', while Jesus is 'from above' and 'not of this world' (8.23). A further contrast may be implied with the disciples, who, like Jesus, are described as 'not of this world' (17.14); hence the suggestion that references to 'the world' as hating the disciples (15.18f.; 17.14) may denote 'the Jews' – though this is never made explicit.

Do such uses constitute sufficient warrant for finding John 'anti-Semitic' or 'anti-Jewish'? Much depends on precisely whom John intended when he spoke of 'the Jews' in this way. Did he mean all ethnic Jews, regardless of whether they practised their religion (which would make him 'anti-Semitic'), or religious Jews as a whole (which would make him 'anti-Jewish')? The problem is that John often uses *hoi Ioudaioi* ambiguously, without distinguishing whether he intends the Jewish religious authorities (or one group among them), a crowd of Jewish people, or even Jews generally. It is rather like a modern writer or speaker referring to 'the British' without defining whether the British government, the British army, or the British public as a whole is intended. In a detailed study von Wahlde (1982) has shown that out of 31 examples, agreed by ten scholars as constituting John's special use of 'the Jews' (mostly 'hostile'), 17 must denote the Jewish religious leadership. These include the places where people, themselves Jews, are described as afraid of 'the Jews' (7.13; 9.22; etc.) and places where 'the Jews' investigate religious matters, when they sometimes seem to be interchangeable with 'the Pharisees' (1.19; 9.18, 22, beside 1.24; 9.13, 15, 40). Compare also 18.14, which states that Caiaphas had counselled 'the Jews' that one man must die for the people, whereas in fact he had given this advice to the Pharisees and chief priests (11.47–52). Von Wahlde therefore proposes that the 14 remaining texts where 'the Jews' are stereotypically hostile to Jesus may also denote the religious authorities. His careful and balanced study demonstrates that John did not intend to denote the whole Jewish people as opponents of Jesus, which must surely clear him of the charge of 'anti-Semitism' (as defined above). It does, however, leave open the question of whether John might still be deemed 'anti-Jewish'.

Other scholars have offered different proposals. Lowe (1976) saw the problem as 'mistranslation', arguing that by *hoi Ioudaioi* John intended the Judaeans rather than 'the Jews' as a whole. But there is no way in which 'the Judaeans' can be substituted wholesale for 'the Jews' in John, and some instances where this translation would be misleading (e.g. 6.41, 52, where 'the Jews' refers to a Galilean crowd). The same applies to Charlesworth's insistence (2001, pp. 489f.) that *hoi Ioudaioi* is properly rendered 'some Judaean leaders/authorities', leading to some bizarre translations (e.g. of 11.54). Others rely on Martyn's 'two-level' reading to suggest that John was targeting not Jews (or Jewish leaders) at the time of Jesus, but specific groups contemporary with the Evangelist. Thus de Jonge (2001) proposes that 'the Jews' refers to Jewish *Christians* of John's own day who could not accept his christology; but his arguments are unconvincing. Others[5] suggest that John intended the 'Torah-fanatic' rabbis of Jamnia, to whom they attribute the expulsion of Christians from synagogues; but we have already seen problems with this view. All these theories depend very much on conjecture, and it may be doubted how many of John's readers could be expected to perceive the allusions.

The theory that causes particular difficulty (and which seems to be accepted by Ruether, Cohn-Sherbok, and others who condemn John as 'anti-Jewish') is that of Bultmann (1971, pp. 86f.), who interpreted 'the Jews' in John as 'representatives of unbelief'.[6] Supporters cite John's association of 'the Jews' with 'the world' (used negatively) and with ignorance, lies, and failure to believe (esp. 8.19, 23, 27, 43f.). It must, however, be stressed that John nowhere simply equates 'the Jews' with 'the world', which has a much broader meaning (cf. above, pp. 96f.). Not all Jews are depicted as ignorant, deceitful, and unbelieving. Nathanael is described as 'truly an Israelite in whom there is no deceit' (1.47). John accepts totally Jews who believe in Jesus (Pryor, 1992, p. 182); all the disciples are Jews, though they are not labelled as such. Additionally many groups of 'Jews', who are so named, come to faith (e.g. 10.42; 11.45; 12.11, 42). John does not associate all Jews with 'the fallen universe (or world) of darkness' (*pace* Ruether, 1974, p. 111; Cohn-Sherbok, 1992, p. 23): he shows no knowledge of 'the Fall' as a doctrine, and Judas alone is associated with 'night' viewed negatively (on Nicodemus, see above, pp. 104–6). Jesus does tell *some* Jews that they are 'from below' and 'of this world' when he warns them that they will die in their sins if they do not believe in him (8.23f.). But he also says to the same group, 'When I am lifted up, then you will know that I am [he]', whereupon 'many believed in him' (8.30).

Sometimes the Prologue's words, 'He came to his own and his own did not accept him' (1.11), are seen as pointing to Jesus' rejection by the Jews. But these words are ambiguous. The first 'his own' (neuter plural) could denote either Israel as Jesus' historic homeland, or the human world as the *logos*' domain, and the second (masculine plural) Jesus' own nation, or humanity in general as belonging to the *logos*; Schnackenburg (1968, pp. 258–61) argues that 'there is no compelling reason' to believe the author had Israel in mind. Even if the second 'his own' in 1.11 is taken as referring obliquely to Israel, it is followed immediately by the words, 'but to as many as received him he gave authority to become children of God'. There can be no one-to-one equation of 'the Jews' with those who reject Jesus; they are among 'his own in the world' whom he loved to the end (13.1).[7]

John's Passion Narrative

Since John's Passion Narrative has often been stereotyped as 'anti-Jewish', the role of 'the Jews' here requires close scrutiny. Their officers are among those who arrest Jesus (18.12); Pilate tells Jesus that his 'own nation and the chief priests' have handed him over (18.35). 'The Jews' choose Barabbas rather than Jesus (18.38b–40), and when Pilate finds Jesus innocent, they respond that he ought to die because he made himself 'Son of God' (19.7). When Pilate asks: 'Shall I crucify your king?' (19.15), the chief priests respond, 'We have no king but Caesar' – a profession of loyalty to the Emperor infringing their loyalty to God as King – while acquiescing in Jesus' condemnation for claiming a kingship 'not of this world'. The chief priests even attempt to change the inscription on the cross (19.21f.). 'The Jews' request Jesus' legs to be broken to hasten his death on the cross, not from pity but so that his body should not remain there on the Sabbath (a 'great day', i.e. solemn feast; 19.31). A similar concern for ritual nicety is reflected in their earlier refusal to enter the Praetorium lest they incur defilement (18.28), a scrupulosity all the more ironical in that they are attempting to have an innocent man condemned.

One should, however, note that some of these negative features are attributed to the 'chief priests'[8] rather than 'the Jews'. Ruether claims that John goes furthest of all the Gospels in depicting Jesus 'as actually being crucified *by the Jews*' (1974, p. 114, her italics); but is this the case? John's account of the procedures leading to Jesus' execution is in some ways less 'anti-Jewish' than Mark's and Matthew's. He has Roman soldiers involved in Jesus' arrest (18.12), while they portray the Jewish leaders as sending the arresting party (Mk 14.43; Mt. 26.47). He describes an informal investigation in the High Priest's house (cf. Lk. 22.54), while they have him condemned by the Sanhedrin, the highest Jewish judicial body (Mk 14.55–64; Mt. 26.59–66; cf. Lk. 22. 66). John makes no mention of jealousy as a motive of Jewish leaders in delivering Jesus to Pilate (contrast Mk 15.10; Mt. 27.18). Whereas Mark (15.13f.) has the (Jewish) crowd shout twice, 'Crucify [him]!', John attributes these words to the 'chief priests and officers', though he later has 'the Jews' cry out 'Away, away [with him]; crucify [him]!' (19.6, 15). John has nothing corresponding to Matthew's dreadful self-curse (27.25), attributed to 'the people' (*laos*), 'His blood be on us and on our children', which opened the way for *descendants* of Jesus' fellow-Jews to be blamed for his death. Unlike some New Testament writers John nowhere accuses Jews not involved in Jesus' crucifixion of being responsible for it (contrast 1 Thess. 2.14f. and Acts 2.22f., where Peter tells those gathered from all over the Jewish world for Pentecost that *they* crucified Jesus; cf. Acts 2.36; 3.14f., 4.10).

The problem of 'anti-Semitism' or 'anti-Judaism' is not unique to John, but affects many New Testament texts (cf. Sanders, 1987, on Luke–Acts; Beck, 1994; Keith, 1997; Farmer, 1999). With the Gospels the situation is complicated by questions about the accuracy of their accounts of Jesus' trial(s). It cannot be 'anti-Jewish' to criticize Jewish leaders for what is genuinely believed to be a miscarriage of justice; but it would be 'anti-Jewish' if such criticisms were invented out of spite, to vilify the Jewish people as a whole. Historical evidence is lacking to confirm (or refute) the details of the Passion Narratives. It is generally recognized that the Jewish priesthood of Jesus' day was corrupt, and that Jesus' appearance before the Sanhedrin transgresses procedures laid down in the Mishnah. But it is also agreed that all four Passion Narratives have been shaped by the desire to find Scripture fulfilment, and that all contain elements of imaginative reconstruction, probably based on hearsay rather than factual information. Jesus' radical teaching, his miracles, and his ability to attract crowds must have disturbed the Jewish religious leadership. There is no hard evidence that he was an insurrectionist. The Jewish leaders were surely involved in engineering his trial by Pilate on a charge of treason (Latin *maiestas*). John's account of their role in Jesus' trial and death is neither an arraignment of the whole Jewish people, nor a covert, malicious depiction of the Jamnia rabbis. Like the Synoptic accounts it is an attempt to explain, in the form of a narrative, how the person Christians believed to be the messiah – who went about doing good – came to be condemned as a criminal.

The Confrontational Dialogues

John's 'hostile' depiction of Jews is not confined to the Passion Narrative. Substantial parts of chapters 5 and 7—10 consist of controversies (confrontational dialogues) between Jesus and 'the Jews', with 8.12–59 being cited more frequently than any other part of the Gospel in arguments about John's 'anti-Jewishness'. In this, first Jesus reproaches the Pharisees for not knowing him or the Father (8.19); next 'the Jews' are said to be from below and of this world (8.23). Then Jesus tells 'the Jews who have believed' (perfect participle) that if they continue in his word, they are truly his disciples; they will know the truth and it will make them free (8.31f.). This precipitates a debate in which they claim to be descended from Abraham and need no freeing, and he accuses them of being slaves to sin because they do what they have heard from their 'father', seeking to kill him (8.33–41). God cannot be their 'father' because they do not love Jesus: they are of their father, the devil, 'a murderer from the beginning' (8.44). They accuse him of demon-possession (8.48; cf. Mk 3.22–7 par.), and the confrontation ends with Jesus claiming, 'Before Abraham was, I am', and his inter-locutors taking up stones to throw at him (8.59).

This passage contains the harshest words that Jesus says anywhere to 'the Jews'. Yet they are, apparently, addressed to Jews who have put their faith in him (8.31). Why should believers be so strongly condemned? Stibbe (1994, p. 124) argues that 'the Jews' here have professed the Christian faith and then fallen away. John, he claims, is satirizing apostasy. But there is nothing in the text to suggest this. These Jews are described as having 'believed' in him, using the verb *pisteuō*, commonly associated with full faith (cf. 2.11; 11.27). There is no qual-ifying comment (as in 2.24), and no reference to any falling away. Stibbe's identification of this passage as 'satire' is also unsatisfactory, since it shows no signs of belonging to such a genre. Nor is there any reason to see the phrase *tous pepisteukotas autō(i)*, 'those who have believed in him', as a gloss (cf. Barrett, 1978, p. 344). John drifts from having Jesus speak to believing Jews into having him confront Jewish opponents more generally, just as John alternates confusingly between 'the Jews' and 'the Pharisees' (cf. above, p. 114), and has Pilate address a question to 'the Jews' and the response come from 'the chief priests' (19.14f.).

So how do we interpret John's confrontational dialogues? Scholars reading his narrative at two levels find in them echoes of bitter debates in the later first century CE between Christians and Jews. Menken (2001) argues that 9.13–17, 24–34 depict the themes of 'false prophet' and 'prophet like Moses' known to be of interest to Jews at this date (and later). This may be so; but the theme of lying or 'false' prophets is embedded in the Hebrew Bible itself (e.g. Dt. 13.1–3; Jer. 14.14; 23.9–40; cf. 1 Kgs 22.19–23), featuring also in the Synoptics (e.g. Mk 13.22; Mt. 7.15; Lk. 6.26). Lively interest in the 'prophet like Moses' is also attested at Qumran well before this date (e.g. 4Q 175; Vermes, 1998, p. 495; cf. also 4Q 339; Vermes, 1998, p. 590, on false prophets). The Synoptic writers regularly depict Jesus in conflict with Jewish religious authorities (e.g. Mk 2.6–12 par.; 3.1–6 par.; 7.1–13 par.). In his confrontational dialogues, especially in those arising out of miracles (Jn 5, 9), John seems to be doing the same sort of thing, but in a more sophisticated and developed manner.

In these John apparently imitates a Jewish literary motif, known as the *rib*, 'case at law' or 'juridical controversy'[9] (Asiedu-Peprah, 2001), in which YHWH accuses his people (cf. Motyer, 1997, esp. pp. 145–8; Lincoln, 2000). The prophets who use this do not mince their words: Hosea says that God has an 'accusation' (*rib*; Septuagint, *krisis*, literally 'judgement') against Israel, denouncing both priests and people for their whoring and idolatry (4.1–19; cf. 2.1–23). In Isaiah 1.2f., God accuses Israel of injustice and unfaithfulness, speaking of its people as 'rebellious sons' (a very serious offence in Jewish law, punishable by death), and claiming that they neither know nor understand him. In Jeremiah, God says that he will contend (*rib*) with the houses of Jacob and Israel and their 'children's children' for forsaking him (2.4–37, esp. 2.9). Micah has God plead with his people to act justly, reminding them of his kindness to them (6.1–8). While the literary forms vary, such passages regularly mention God's accusation of his people, threaten punishment, and, sometimes, promise salvation. The similarities with Jesus' controversies with 'the Jews' are noticeable, including the hyperbole whereby, for example, YHWH says that there is no faithfulness or kindness in the land (Hos. 4.1), and Jesus tells 'the Jews' that they do not have God's love in them (5.42). If Hebrew prophets can accuse their own people in the Scriptures, is it 'anti-Jewish' for John, if he was a Jew (as all the evidence suggests), to use the 'controversy' motif to promote what he believes to be true and right?

This brings us to John 8.44, where Jesus tells some Jews that they are 'of [their] father the devil', a comment which has provoked the most serious criticisms. Tina Pippin felt so strongly about the passage that she wrote, 'to translate John 8 at all is to betray the Jews' (1996, p. 94). Lowry saw it as leading directly to Nazi propaganda against Jews (cf. above, p. 112). This section (8.37–47) reflects a regular pattern of Jewish polemic in which those on the side of truth and right are set against those on the side of evil and deceit, with each group having the source of its actions in supernatural powers. Thus in the Qumran *Community Rule* (? *c.* 100 BCE), humanity is seen as falling into two opposing camps – the 'sons of light' and the 'sons of deceit'. The former are ruled by the 'Prince of Light', but the latter by the 'Angel of Darkness' or 'Spirit of Falsehood', to whom belong lies, pride, lust and other faults, such as 'blindness of eye' and 'dullness of ear' (1QS III.18—IV.26; Vermes, 1998, pp. 101f.). *The Testaments of the Twelve Patriarchs* similarly contrast the 'Spirit of Truth' and the 'Spirit of Error'

(*T.Jud.* 20.1–5). These two 'Spirits' are mentioned again in 1 John 4.6 (and the Spirit of Truth alone in Jn 14.17 etc.). Such texts usually have a strong ethical thrust, urging readers to choose between good and evil, or 'the law of the Lord' and 'the deeds of Beliar' (Satan) (e.g. *T.Levi* 19.1). Von Wahlde (2001) considers that they constitute a definite *topos*, or structured literary form, but he presses his case too far. Nevertheless they vividly illustrate the climate of thought that gives rise to such dualistic oppositions as we see in John 8.42–4, where the murderous desires of Jesus' Jewish interlocutors are attributed to their devilish 'origin', while Jesus' ability to speak the truth results from his 'coming forth' from God. It should be noted that these Jews are not actually called 'offspring' or 'children of the devil' (far less 'spawn', an emotive word, with contemptuous overtones). Jesus says, 'You are *ek* ['of' or 'from'] the devil [your] father'.[10] Motyer (1997, pp. 185–97) cites further examples from Jewish literature where a sharp contrast between God and the Evil One/Beliar/devil is used to urge ethical conduct and religious loyalty, insisting that 'of the devil' in John 8.44 has ethical rather than ontological force, i.e. that Jesus' interlocutors are being criticized for their conduct rather than their inherent nature.

In all this the motivation is vital. Does John depict Jesus as accusing 'the Jews' to vilify them and stir up hatred, or to urge them to repent and make a fresh start, as both Motyer (1997) and Asiedu-Peprah (2001) argue? John 8.12–59 is, in fact, a combination of appeal and warning. Jesus promises those who follow him that they will have 'the light of life' (8.12); he tells 'the Jews' who believed in him that if they continue in his word the truth will liberate them (8.31). But he also expresses frustration at the apparent obstinacy of his audience: 'If I tell the truth, why do you not believe me?' (8.46). The final response of 'the Jews' to his words – the accusation that he is a Samaritan and demon-possessed (8.48; cf. 8.52) and their attempt to stone him – constitute a terrible warning to any who reject or oppose Jesus. The episode is analogous to stories in Acts where those who deceive or oppose the Apostles meet horrible punishment. Compare Ananias and Sapphira (Acts 5.1–11) and Elymas, whom Paul, 'full of the Holy Spirit', physically blinds, calling him 'Son of the devil, full of all deceit and all villainy, enemy of all uprightness' (Acts 13.10).

The depiction of Jesus' Jewish interlocutors in John 8 is likewise unattractive, and unlikely to correspond to historical reality; but ancient standards of what was rhetorically acceptable were very different from today's 'political correctness' (cf. Johnson, 1989). Amos could call Samaritan women 'cows' (4.1) without being accused of sexual harassment; James could address the recipients of his letter as 'adulteresses' (4.4), without fear of dismissal from his pastoral charge. The author of 1 John identified his Christian opponents as 'antichrists' (2.18, 22; 4.3) and still had his epistle accepted into the Christian canon. In Matthew (23.33) Jesus calls the scribes and Pharisees 'Snakes, offspring of vipers!'; in both Mark and Matthew Jesus addresses Peter as 'Satan' when he tries to dissuade him from the path of the cross (Mk 8.33; Mt. 16.23), just as in John he calls Judas 'a devil' (6.70). It is unlikely that John's Jewish contemporaries would have perceived John 8 as constituting uniquely bitter invective.

This episode must also be seen in the light of the Synoptic stories where Jesus comes into conflict with different religious groups – scribes and Pharisees,[11] Sadducees and Herodians, elders and priestly hierarchy. John oversimplifies the Jewish leadership by omitting all reference to the scribes, Sadducees, and Herodians, and using 'the Pharisees', 'the chief priests', or just 'the Jews' as Jesus' opponents. He steps up the polemical tone of Jesus' controversies, possibly influenced by Jewish literary forms like the *rib* and dualistic ethical paraenesis, using them to illustrate the *krisis*, 'judgement' (3.19) caused by Jesus' coming which divides humanity into those who accept his revelation and those who do not. At times 'the Jews' stand for the latter. How far this is 'anti-Jewish' readers must judge for themselves.

Conclusions

There is no simple answer to the question, 'Is John's Gospel anti-Semitic/anti-Jewish?' It is not 'anti-Semitic' in the sense of inciting hatred against Jewish people simply because they are Jews. Nor is it 'anti-Jewish', since where John portrays Jews negatively, this is not because of their religion in itself, but because of attitudes and actions that he deems wrong, especially those of the Jerusalem religious authorities. Such depictions are, to some extent, balanced by references to Jews who believe or become disciples, and his sympathetic treatment of 'the Jews' who come to condole with Martha and Mary on their bereavement (11.19, 31, 33–7, 45). Significantly salvation is said to come from (*ek*) 'the Jews' (4.22);[12] there are also many positive references to things Jewish, including Moses and the Jewish Scriptures. Nevertheless one is left with the general impression that 'the Jews' as a group are treated with hostility, even if less than half the examples of *hoi Ioudaioi* are actually negative.[13]

John follows the Synoptic writers in giving a prominent role to Jewish religious leaders in precipitating Jesus' Roman trial and condemnation; but he nowhere attributes 'deicide' to them or to descendants of those present. In this respect he may be less 'anti-Semitic' (or 'anti-Jewish') than Matthew or some parts of Acts. Nor does he attach blame for Jesus' death to the Jewish people as a whole, except insofar as his use of *hoi Ioudaioi* is ambiguous. By his use of this term, through his stereotyping of 'the Jews' as Jesus' opponents, and through their role in his Passion Narrative, John – like Paul, the Synoptics, and other New Testament writers – unwittingly contributed to 'anti-Judaism' among those who ignored his teaching on love and Christian obedience. But it goes too far to describe his treatment as 'vitriolic' (Casey, 1996, p. 225), or a 'diatribe' against Jews (Cohn-Sherbok, 1992, p. 24). While acknowledging the deep horror rightly felt by sensitive and caring individuals at the appalling history of Christian anti-Judaism, one cannot help observing that some of the literature denouncing John is less scholarly than that defending him. Very few writers on anti-Semitism explore issues of literary form, paraenetic purposes, and the feelings of early Christians living close to the time of Jesus' cruel death and wrestling with the problem (as they saw it) of why so many Jews had failed to recognize Jesus as their 'messiah'.

Modern readers, living in a different age, are mostly unaccustomed to earlier forms of religious polemic – though one still hears violent rhetoric in politics and in time of war – which makes writers like John, Paul, Irenaeus, and Luther seem uncharitable. The literary function of 'the Jews' in John's confrontational dialogues should be frankly recognized, and seen in the context of biblical and other polemic by Hebrews/Jews against fellow-Hebrews/Jews. Even John's linking of 'the Jews' with the devil, so misused by Church Fathers, Luther, Nazis, and neo-Nazis, follows a literary convention widespread in John's time. By today's standards this is unacceptable and repulsive, but is it fair to condemn a first-century writer by these?

12

'Replacement Theology' and Jewish Monotheism

We now consider the two other areas where John's Gospel has been criticized as 'anti-Jewish', namely his 'replacement theology' and his depiction of Jesus as God. Ancient Judaism was not monochrome in its beliefs and practices; some authors prefer to speak of 'Judaisms' in the plural (e.g. Neusner, 1987). Nevertheless Jews were, and are, united, in a common 'ethnicity' and sense of election by God as a covenant community. They share common Scriptures understood as inspired revelation, monotheistic faith, and respect for Torah, embracing both oral tradition and written Law. 'Torah' includes moral injunctions and ritual (ceremonial) prescriptions, as well as liturgical materials and history written from a theological viewpoint. First-century Jews did not drive a wedge between moral and ritual prescriptions, as do many Christians. Among the latter are circumcision, Sabbath, dietary and 'purity' laws, observance of fasts and festivals, and a complex system of sacrifices based on the Temple cult with its priestly hierarchy (ended by the Roman destruction of the Temple). Prayer and Torah-study are taken for granted.[1] How far does John depict Jesus as 'replacing' these beliefs and way of life?

Scripture

We begin with Scripture. For John, there is no idea that this might include Christian texts: 'Scripture' (Greek, *graphē*) for him is the Hebrew Bible (including the Septuagint), for which he displays the utmost respect, regarding it as fully authoritative. In words attributed to Jesus or the disciples, he assumes verbal inspiration (10.35); he presents Moses and the prophets as writing of Jesus and witnessing to him (e.g. 1.45; 5.39b). Jesus always speaks respectfully of Moses, reproaching 'the Jews' for not believing him and not keeping the Law which he gave them (5.46; 7.19). Jesus also refers positively to Isaiah, who 'spoke of him' (12.41), and Abraham, who 'rejoiced to see his day' (8.56), though John clearly presents Jesus as greater than Jacob, Abraham, and Moses (cf. above, p. 3).

John's scriptural interpretation is basically typological (Carson, 1988, pp. 249–51; Hanson, 1991, pp. 238f.). This was a Jewish method of exegesis whereby events or sayings from the past are interpreted as fulfilled in present experience (cf. 'pesher' interpretation at Qumran: Longenecker, 1975, pp. 38–45). Luke uses it when Jesus reads from Isaiah and then says, 'Today this Scripture is fulfilled in your ears' (4.21), and when Peter says in his Pentecost sermon (Acts 2.16–21): 'This is what was spoken by the prophet Joel'. No fewer than twelve of John's Scripture quotations are introduced by phrases like 'as Scripture says' or 'as it is written' (e.g. 2.17; 6.31, 45; 12.14f.) and seven use the word 'fulfil' (Carson, 1988, esp. p. 246). Other passages directly quote biblical texts on the lips of individuals or groups (e.g. 1.23; 12.13) or cite them imprecisely (e.g. 7.38; 19.28). Scripture is 'fulfilled' in the Baptist's ministry (1.23), Judas' betrayal (13.18), the 'triumphal entry' (12.14f.), Jesus' passion (19.24b, 28, 36f.; cf. 2.17), and in his resurrection (2.22; 20.9). Thus John, like Matthew (5.17), shows that Jesus came not to nullify Scripture, but to 'fulfil' it.

Apart from direct quotations, there are numerous scriptural allusions. Jesus' 'lifting up' on the cross is like Moses' raising of the bronze serpent (3.14; cf. Num. 21.9), the point of the comparison being not just the physical lifting up, but also the healing of the Israelites, and Jesus' bringing of life through the cross. Jesus' feeding of the multitude echoes God's provision of manna through Moses, just as his gift of 'living water' may echo the water from the rock (see above, pp. 56f.). 'Moses' was one of the bonds that held Jews together, especially in the Diaspora (Barclay, 1996, pp. 426–8), and John makes many subtle allusions to him. But Jesus' gifts are superior to those of Moses: his water 'wells up for eternal life' (4.14); the food that he provides is 'living bread' that will enable people to live for ever (6.50f.). 'The Jews' search the Scriptures to find eternal life, but it is Jesus who brings it (5.39f.). Jesus alone has seen God (1.18).

Torah

On the moral side Torah includes the Decalogue ('Ten Commandments'), teaching on loving God and neighbour, and many instructions on generosity and kindness. For Casey (1996, esp. p. 133), John's Jesus replaces 'the Old Testament commandments to love God and do the Law' with his new love command. But Jesus in John assumes that God must be honoured (e.g. 5.23). His 'love command' affirms Torah's teaching on human relationships by summing up its essence (cf. Mk 12.28–34 par., quoting Lev. 19.18), just as the rabbis Akiba and Hillel are reported to have done.[2] He gives it a new grounding in his own love (13.34; 15.12, 17), but it is still the 'old' commandment (cf. 1 Jn 2.7). John takes Torah's moral prescriptions for granted, including its teaching on lying, murder, and theft (8.41, 44; 12.6) and, presumably, faithfulness within marriage (4.16–19; see further Carson, 1981, p. 163). He also assumes its doctrines of God as life-giver and judge (5.26f.), holy and righteous (17.11, 25), loving and caring for humanity (3.16; cf. his use of 'father' for God), and as having sovereign authority that he can delegate (e.g. 17.2).

John's statement that 'the Law was given through Moses; grace and truth came through Jesus Christ' (1.17) is sometimes read as depicting an opposition between Torah and Jesus. But 1.17 contains no adversative; rather it explicates 1.16, 'from his fulness we have all received one gracious gift instead of another' (*charin anti charitos*; cf. above, p. 94). John acknowledges Torah as God's gracious gift; but he sees the revelation provided by Jesus as even greater. God's revelation through Moses is still valuable, as Christians recognize in using Jewish Scripture as their 'Old Testament'.[3]

Circumcision and Covenant

For men, circumcision (*peritomē*) was the mark of being Jewish. John never disparages the rite,[4] nor does he 'spiritualize' it (as in Col. 2.11) or depict it as a matter of indifference in Christ (as Col. 3.11; Gal. 5.6; cf. 1 Cor. 7.19). He does not suggest that baptism replaces it as a sign of the covenant community. He makes no allusions to the controversy over whether Gentiles should be circumcised, mentioning the rite only twice, in a single passage (7.22f.), where Jesus describes it as given by Moses, or rather 'the fathers' (a Jewish expression for the patriarchs). Jesus says that it was given 'to you' (i.e. his interlocutors) rather than 'us', not because it is 'an alien custom' (so Casey, 1991, p. 29), but to bring home to 'the Jews' the inconsistency between their seeking to kill him (7.19) and membership of the covenant people. Like John the Baptist in Matthew (3.7–10), Jesus argues that being Abraham's descendants does not in itself bring salvation. That depends on 'knowing' God, through spiritual birth (3.3–5) and his emissary Jesus (17.3). The fact that Jewish law permitted circumcision on the Sabbath is also part of Jesus' defence against criticisms for his healing on that day. Although John nowhere uses the word 'covenant' (*diathēkē*), the concept is not far beneath the surface (cf. Pryor, 1992).

Sabbath

Some scholars claim that John's Jesus abrogates Sabbath: for example, Casey (1991, p. 29) claims that it is 'explicitly removed' in 5.18. But the words in question, *eluen to sabbaton*, are not given as John's own views, but those of Jesus' opponents; and *eluen* clearly means 'was breaking' (the Sabbath) rather than 'destroying' it (cf. RSV, NEB, GNB, etc.). The passage resembles a Synoptic 'controversy story', though Jesus' defence is different (cf. above, p. 54). It is not about 'abrogating' the Sabbath, but rather an intra-Jewish dispute about how its laws are to be observed. The same applies to Jesus' healing of the man born blind, when the Pharisees accuse him of not 'keeping' the Sabbath (*tēreō*; 9.16). By treating restoration to full health as an appropriate Sabbath activity Jesus offers a humane alternative to more rigid scribal and pharisaic interpretations of Torah. He is concerned with its heart, not its letter (7.21–4). There is no hint in John of the replacement of Sabbath by the Christian Sunday.

Dietary Laws

John's Gospel says nothing about dietary observances. This contrasts with Mark (7.19b), where Jesus is said 'to make all foods clean', and with the disputes in Acts (e.g. 10.9–16; 15.28f.) over whether Gentiles should keep Jewish food laws (cf. also 1 Cor. 10.25–8; Rom. 14.14f.). John presumably takes them for granted, or else sees them as irrelevant to his message. It is improbable that he writes so late that Jewish–Christian controversies over dietary laws are past and forgotten.

Purity Laws

In his story of the Cana miracle John says that the water-jars were there for 'the Jewish purificatory rites' (2.6). Some commentators have interpreted this water as representing 'ritualistic' Judaism being replaced by the splendid 'new wine' of Christianity; but there is no need to read the narrative this way (cf. above, p. 52). This incident cannot be taken as a rejection of the entire holiness code, any more than Jesus' foot-washing (13.10) and cleansing through the 'word' (15.3) can be seen as replacing Jewish purity prescriptions with Christian ones (*pace* Casey, 1996, p. 114). John's Jesus never teaches that purity laws are superseded, and, in contrast to the Synoptics (where he touches a leper and a funeral bier, and is touched by the haemorrhaging woman), he never incurs ritual 'uncleanness'.

Festivals

John's Jesus regularly observes the Jewish festivals (which feature far more often than in the Synoptics). He is present at Jerusalem for Passover (2.13; cf. 12.12), an unnamed feast (5.1), Tabernacles (7.10), and Dedication (10.22); but in 6.4 he is in Galilee near Passover time, when commentators think he should have left already for Jerusalem.[5] John mentions Passover to facilitate his typological interpretation of the feeding miracle; Jesus could have gone up later (but that is outside the story). In 7.10 he goes up 'privately', after his brothers, for Tabernacles, appearing publicly at the feast (7.14, 28, 37). John nowhere mentions fasting (a controversial issue between Jews and Christians).

The festivals are occasions for significant actions, miracles, or special teaching by Jesus. Casey and others (e.g. Brown, 1966, p. 104; Dunn, 1991, pp. 93–5; Kerr, 2002, ch. 7) interpret this as John's way of showing Jesus as superseding these feasts. Yee (1989, p. 26) speaks of him 'nullifying' Jewish liturgical institutions; Motyer (1997, p. 124) of him 'hijacking' each festival in turn for the Christian faith. Is this really John's intention? In 5.1 the feast is not even named: it is simply a means of getting Jesus to Jerusalem, enabling John to describe the controversies with the Jewish authorities generated by the Sabbath healing. Nor can it seriously be argued that Jesus 'replaces' Passover simply because

Passover motifs appear in the crucifixion narrative (cf. above, p. 79) and Jesus is called 'Lamb of God' (see above, p. 69). This is typology, not supersession (Hanson, 1991, p. 239).

Some scholars understand Jesus' promise of rivers of living water at Tabernacles (7.37), and his saying about 'the light of the world' (8.12), as 'taking over' this festival. Motyer describes Jesus as proclaiming himself 'the centre of an *alternative* Tabernacles' (1997, p. 127, his italics). But this reads too much into the text. It is true that according to the Mishnah (*c.* 200 CE) the rituals included fetching water from the pool of Siloam, pouring it out before the Temple, and filling the Women's Court with lights (*mSukkah* 4.9—5.2). But John nowhere refers to these rites. He simply develops the theme of 'living water' featuring already in 4.10–14. Nor can the image of 'light', used by John about 20 times, be tied to Tabernacles symbolism. In describing Jesus as 'the light of the world' (8.12; 9.5) John probably draws on Isaiah's metaphorical use of light for 'salvation' (42.6; 49.6; etc.; Williams, 2000, p. 266). It is not even clear that John intends these 'light' sayings to be understood as uttered at Tabernacles. He makes no mention of other prominent motifs, including the temporary shelters (*sukkoth*), from which it derives its Hebrew name, or palm-waving (which John uses on another occasion: 12.13). Nor does he take advantage of Tabernacles' Greek name, *skēnopēgia*, 'tent-pitching' (7.2), to develop his theme of Jesus' tabernacling among humankind.

There is even less to commend the idea that Jesus 'replaces' Dedication (*Hanukkah*; Greek, *ta enkainia* or 'Renewal').[6] John makes nothing of its processions with palms and other leafy branches, or its use of lights; rather Jesus repeats his earlier 'shepherd' theme (10.1–18), and contends with 'the Jews' by speaking of his unity with the Father. There is only one possible, oblique allusion to a Hanukkah motif, in the reference to the Father's 'consecrating' Jesus (*hagiazō*; 10.36); but this theme features much more prominently in John 17 (set in a different context). To sum up: the idea that John's Jesus 'replaces' every major Jewish festival is unfounded.[7]

Temple and Worship

Loyalty to the 'Temple' was another identity factor for pre-70 CE Jews (Dunn, 1994, pp. 441f.).[8] Many scholars, including Moloney (1993, p. 101), Coloe (2001), and Kerr (2002, esp. p. 374), see John as portraying the abolition of its sacrifices in Jesus, and its replacement with his person and/or the Church. Both Dunn (1991, p. 95) and Casey (1996, p. 10) speak of the Temple being made 'redundant' in John. In the Synoptics Jesus had foretold its destruction (Mk 13.2 par.; cf. 14.57f. par.), but in

John the 'Temple saying' takes a different form: 'Destroy this temple, and in three days I will raise it' (2.17). 'Destroy' here has conditional force, 'If you destroy'. John makes it clear that Jesus speaks of 'the temple of his body', i.e. foretells his own death and resurrection (cf. above, Ch. 7). Sometimes Jesus' driving out of the traders (2.15f.) is taken as symbolizing God's rejection of Jewish worship (so Nereparampil, 1978, p. 18), or as portending the Temple destruction as an act of divine judgement (so Sanders, 1985, pp. 61–71, with critique of other views). But is this John's interpretation?

Traditionally this incident is known as 'the cleansing of the Temple', and this is how John presents it. Money-changers and animal vendors were defiling the Temple precincts; Jesus, moved by zeal for his Father's house, drives them out (2.17, citing Ps. 69.9). By so doing, he does not 'abolish' the sacrificial system (the coins could have been exchanged and the animals sold elsewhere); he acts out of concern for the cult's *purity* (cf. Mk 11.16). John probably saw this cleansing as 'messianic' (cf. above, p. 67): 'house of trade' (2.16) recalls Zechariah's prophecy that 'on that day' (i.e. in the end-time), 'there shall no longer be a trader in the Lord's house' (14.20f.). It may also fulfil Malachi 3.1–3: 'The Lord whom you seek will suddenly come to his Temple'; 'but who can stand when he appears? For he is like a refiner's fire ... and will purify the sons of Levi'. Ezekiel (40—47) also hoped for a new, purified cult, as did the Qumran covenanters (cf. the 'New Jerusalem Scroll': Chyutin, 1997; Crawford, 2000).

Unlike some Church Fathers, John never attacks Jewish worship as idolatrous. Rather Jesus contrasts it favourably with Samaritan worship saying to the Samaritan woman: 'You worship what you do not know; we worship what we know, for salvation comes from the Jews' (4.22) – notice how Jesus associates himself here with 'the Jews'. But he also foretells a new eschatological worship, taking place neither in Jerusalem nor 'this mountain' (the site of the Samaritan temple), but in spirit and in truth (4.21–4).[9] By at least the later stages of John's writing, the Jerusalem Temple had been destroyed (see above, Ch. 5); like his Jewish contemporaries he had to cope with a situation when sacrifices could no longer be performed there. Something new was required. Some Jews took refuge in apocalypticism; some, like Johannan ben Zakkai, emphasized the need for repentance and deeds of kindness; some sought to apply the Temple purity rules to the home. John saw the possibility of new 'spiritual' worship through Jesus, the symbol of God's abiding presence. His understanding coheres remarkably with Revelation's picture of the heavenly city where there is no temple, for 'God's dwelling [*skēnē*] is with humankind' and 'its Temple is the Lord God Almighty and the Lamb' (21.3, 22). What the seer saw in a vision of the future, the Evangelist finds already happening.

Ethnicity

There is little to add here. John depicts Jesus as a Jew; he appears to write from a group including many Jews, and for a broad audience of Jews and Gentiles (see above, Ch. 5). A hope of Judaism was that one day the Gentiles would come to acknowledge Israel's God (cf. Isa. 11.9f.; 49.60f.; Tob. 14.6).

Monotheism

Monotheism has been left until last, because it is the most complex issue. Several scholars (including Casey, 1996, p. 31) find John 'anti-Jewish' in breaching this by representing Jesus as 'God'. It will be necessary to explore both the character of first-century Jewish monotheism and the ways in which John represents Jesus as divine. By 'monotheism' is understood belief in, and worship of, only one deity, being distinguished from 'monolatry' (worship of one deity, while recognizing the existence of other deities) and polytheism (belief in, and worship of, a plurality of deities). First-century Jews were clearly monotheists in this sense: the first clause of the *Shema*, recited daily by the devout, is 'Hear, O Israel, the Lord your God is one' (Dt. 6.4; cf. Mk 12.29). But this monotheism did not preclude belief in the existence of other spiritual beings, both good and evil – angels, cherubim, and other ministering spirits, Satan and evil angels/demons. In the Hebrew Bible God is sometimes pictured as having a heavenly court, with both good and evil spirits present (1 Kgs 22.19–22; cf. Job 1.6). Angels are pictured as carrying out God's commands in relation to mortals, and it can be hard to tell when an appearance is of God himself or of his angelic messenger. Sometimes the angel of the Lord appears to be YHWH himself (e.g. Gen. 16.7–13; 32.24–30; Ex. 23.20–2).

After the Exile, speculation about such spiritual beings grew, with angels being given individual names and functions. Michael was 'the great prince' and protector of Israel (Dan. 12.1); Raphael reportedly appeared as a man and travelled with Tobias to Ecbatana and back, only revealing his angelic identity after Tobias had safely returned to his aged father (Tob. 5.4—12.22). Other angels were identified with exalted patriarchs, like the angel Israel, who was identified with Jacob (*Prayer of Joseph*, frag. A: Charlesworth, 1985, p. 713) and 'the heavenly prince' Melchizedek at Qumran, who may be intended to be the same person as the mysterious priest-king of Genesis 14 (11Q 13; Vermes, 1998, pp. 500f.) – described in 'quasi-messianic' terms as the one who will act as judge at the Jubilee, when atonement will be made. The text identifies him with *'ĕlohim* and *'el* (usually translated 'God'), citing

Psalms 82.1 and 7.7f., and saying that he will comfort the mourners and proclaim peace and salvation, exacting vengeance on the wicked. Some of the texts quoted concerning him are the same as are used of Jesus, notably Isaiah 61.1–3 (cf. Lk. 4.18f.) and Isaiah 52.7 (cf. Rom. 10.15). Sometimes the 'messiah' or 'Elect One'/'Son of Man' is seen as part of this heavenly company, having been chosen by 'the Lord of the Spirits' and given a name before the creation of the sun, moon, and stars. *1 Enoch* (46, 48, 51, etc.) describes him as 'a light to the Gentiles', and predicts that he will sit on God's throne and reveal 'all the secrets of wisdom' (cf. above, pp. 66f., with n. 9).

Jews occasionally spoke of biblical patriarchs in quasi-divine terms, notably Adam, Abraham, and Moses. The Bible itself calls Moses 'god' when YHWH says (Ex. 7.1), 'See, I will make you god to Pharaoh (Hebrew *'ĕlohim*; Greek *theos*). Commentators point out that Moses is not being given divine power, merely appointed to act towards Pharaoh as God or a god (many translators supply 'as' or 'like'). But Philo took this text to mean that God had deemed Moses 'worthy to be named god and king' (*Mos.*, 1.158). Alluding to Ex. 20.21, he describes him as entering into the darkness where God is, and beholding what is hidden from mortal nature, and then displaying in his life a model for human beings to imitate. For other texts treating Moses as divine see Jeremias (1967, pp. 848–73); Meeks (1967, p. 195), citing a midrash (on Dt. 33.1) describing him as 'a man' when he ascended on high, and 'god' when he descended below.

Jews who speculated about 'the host of heaven' and exalted patriarchs did not perceive themselves as 'breaching' monotheism. Their aim was to protect God's transcendence and majesty by ascribing to him the service of numerous angels and spirits, who could act as intermediaries with mortals. Another way of expressing reverence for God's transcendence was by avoiding the pronunciation of his Name (YHWH) by substituting periphrases like *maqom* (place), *yeqara* (glory), *memra*, and *shekinah* (cf. above, pp. 88, 90). Creation was described as occurring through Wisdom or *logos* rather than directly by God. Angels were believed to have delivered the Law; Moses was said to have seen the *logos*, or an angel, at the burning bush. It is against this background that we have to understand John's attribution of 'deity' to Jesus.

So how does John present Jesus as divine? He does so with delicacy and reticence, more by hints and suggestions than by brash or dogmatic statements. Jesus walks on water, recalling YHWH's making his path in the deep (cf. above, p. 56), but also echoing the Israelites' crossing the Red Sea and the Jordan dryshod. He heals on the Sabbath, claiming to work as his Father does (5.17). He speaks like YHWH in some of his confrontational dialogues (cf. above, p. 119, on the *rib* motif); but in none of these incidents does he actually claim divinity. He also uses the phrase 'I am' (*egō eimi*), often supposed to depict him as God. But the 'I am' sayings are not all of the same type. The phrase itself is normal Greek, appearing on the lips of other individuals where identity is in doubt (9.9; and, in the negative, 1.20f.; 18.17, 25). In some of his 'I am' sayings Jesus reveals something about himself, e.g. 'I am the bread of heaven'. Such 'revelatory' sayings are paralleled in Revelation (1.8; 22.13, 16, etc.) and in Hellenistic religious literature, where, for example, the goddess Isis claims, 'I am Isis, ruler of every land' (Horsley, 1981, pp. 18f.). John may be employing the formula as a memorable way of presenting Jesus' functions and enhancing his role as the dominant personality of his narrative (Ball, 1996, p. 255). More significant parallels are those from the Hebrew Bible, especially YHWH's self-disclosure to Moses at the burning bush: 'I am the God of your father, the God of Abraham ...' (Ex. 3.6) and 'I am who I am'[10] (Ex. 3.14; Septuagint: *egō eimi ho ōn*). God's 'I am' is often linked to affirmations of his deeds: 'I am the Lord your God, who brought you out of the land of Egypt, out of the house of bondage' (Ex. 20.2; cf. Dt. 5.6).

But John is not 'setting up' Jesus as a separate 'deity', in rivalry with God, by attributing to him these sayings. Their basic message is that Jesus feeds his people, as God did through Moses (6.35, 48, 51; cf. 6.32). He cares for them like an ideal shepherd (10.11), as Moses and David did (Isa. 63.11 Septuagint; Ezk. 37.24) and as God does (Ps. 23.1f.). He shows them the way to God, as the prophets did before him, revealing truth and enabling salvation (10.7, 9; 14.6; cf. 8.12; 11.25). None of these revelatory 'I am' sayings equates him directly with God. They show him as acting *like* God.

Other 'I am' sayings lack a complement, consisting only of pronoun and verb. Some of these are 'recognition' or 'identification' formulae, such as 'It is I; don't be afraid' (6.20; cf. Mk 6.50) and 'I am [he]', i.e. 'the one you are looking for' (18.5). The latter has been taken as indicating divinity, since those arresting Jesus fall to the ground; but similar reactions are recorded at appearances of angels (cf. Tob. 12.16; Bauckham, 1993a, pp. 121f.) and at other uncanny happenings (e.g. Lk. 5.8). In 4.26 when Jesus says to the Samaritan woman, 'I who speak to you am [he]' (*egō eimi ho lalōn soi*), 'he' is readily understood as the 'messiah' about whom the woman has just been speaking (4.25). Possibly 8.24, 8.28, and 13.19 should be taken similarly (cf. Mk 13.6 with Mt. 24.5). But in 8.58, 'Truly, truly, I say to you, before Abraham was, I am', 'messiah' cannot readily be supplied. The present tense is also remarkable, implying that Jesus existed before Abraham, presumably as *logos* (cf. 17.5), and exists permanently.

This raises the question whether some or all of these sayings deliberately recall the Septuagint's use of *egō eimi* to translate the Hebrew *'ani hu'*, literally 'I [am] he'. The formula, though occasionally used by human beings, is associated with God's self-disclosure, sovereignty, and saving presence in Deutero-Isaiah (e.g. 41.4; 48.12; cf. Dt. 32.39; Williams, 2000). The parallel between Isaiah 43.10, 'so that you may know and believe me and understand that I am [he]', and John 13.19 is striking. It has even been suggested that in 8.58f. John depicts Jesus as using the divine Name (cf. Ex. 3.13–16), and that this is why 'the Jews' are ready to stone him for blasphemy. But he has made no *direct* claim to be God, nor has he pronounced the ineffable Name YHWH. He says simply *'egō eimi'*, 'I am', not *'egō eimi ho ōn'*.[11] We conclude that, while John has Jesus speak in ways that recall divine pronouncements, Jesus does not identify himself with YHWH explicitly.

What about Jesus' descriptions of himself as 'the Son' and his references to God as his 'Father'? Traditionally several of these have been treated as indicating Jesus' 'deity', regularly appearing in patristic discussions. Most significant is Jesus' claim: 'I and the Father are one' (10.30). But this must be read in context: Jesus has said that nobody can snatch his 'sheep' because God has given them to him, and he and God are one. It is by no means clear that a metaphysical unity is intended (Barrett, 1978, p. 382; 1982, pp. 24f.). The statement 'the one who has seen me has seen the Father' (14.9) may well mean that people can best perceive God's character in Jesus. He may be 'in' the Father and the Father 'in' him (14.10 etc.) because to know God is to share his nature; mutual indwelling is promised also to believers who trust in Jesus (14.20; 17.21); compare Paul's phrase 'in Christ' (see further Malatesta, 1978; Jerumanis, 1996). Jesus' reference to 'the Son' being honoured like the Father (5.23) may arise from his role as the Father's emissary, since in Jewish thought one sent with full authority was honoured equally with the sender (Borgen, 1986). One of the most striking features of Jesus' references to God as his 'Father' is how often he stresses his subordination to God, and his executing the tasks entrusted to him by God (cf. above, p. 54). This is part of his work as God's 'messiah'.

We turn now to the Prologue. Even here there is no one-to-one equation of Jesus with God. In 1.1 the *logos* is said to be god (*theos*), but is also described as 'with God' (*pros ton theon*), the repetition in 1.2 adding emphasis. The Word cannot therefore be identical with God. Moreover, god (*theos*) in 1.1c is anarthrous,[12] reminding us of Philo's distinction between *ho theos* – God in the absolute sense – and *theos* for others so called (*Somn.*, I.229f.), a distinction also observed by Origen (*Comm. Jo.*, II.2), citing John 17.3, where Jesus himself calls his Father 'the only true God'. For English-speaking Christians this distinction is hard to grasp, because we are so accustomed to using 'God' (with a capital letter) for the Supreme Being/Israel's God that we do not realize that Greek *theos* and Hebrew *'ĕlohim* can be used in other senses. In the Graeco-Roman world Greek *theos* (also Latin *deus/divus*) was used in literary texts for philosophers and rulers, and in the East for Hellenistic monarchs and the Roman Emperor. While Jews would reject such uses, *'ĕlohim* (grammatically plural) appears in the Hebrew Bible (and the Dead Sea Scrolls) for beings other than YHWH. These include the ghost of Samuel (1 Sam. 28.13), pagan gods (e.g. Ex. 20.3), the king (Ps. 45.6), judges (e.g. Ex. 21.6), and angels/heavenly court (e.g. Pss. 82.1; 97.7; cf. 4Q 400; Vermes, 1998, p. 322). This usage is often obscured in English translations (compare Ps. 8.5 AV, RSV). In John 10.34 Jesus defends himself against a charge of blasphemy by quoting Psalm 82.6 (81.6 Septuagint), where *theoi* is used for pagan gods (later interpreted as angels). All this suggests that John's use of *theos* for Jesus would not seem so harsh or radical as it might at first appear.

To return to the Prologue, John does not say that *God* became a *man*, but that the *logos* became *flesh* (1.14). Some manuscripts do refer to Jesus as 'God' in 1.18, but it has been already argued that the reading 'the only Son' is to be preferred (see above, p. 95). Even if *theos* is read there, the more reliable sources lack the definite article, so that our earlier arguments apply. This means that the only place where Jesus is directly and definitely called '*ho theos*' is in Thomas' words to the risen (and possibly ascended) Jesus, 'My Lord and my God' (20.28). These may be a direct address to Jesus, with a Hebraistic use of the nominative with article for the vocative, or an exclamation (see Harris, 1992, pp. 106–9). But in either case Thomas gives Jesus a title belonging to YHWH (cf. Rev. 4.11, where 'our Lord and God' is used in heavenly worship). Yet even this is no dogmatic formulation of 'deity' for Jesus, but shows that Thomas has recognized in the risen Christ the one in whom he found God truly present (cf. Grayston, 1990, p. 170). It should be noted that John does not presuppose worship of Jesus (sometimes seen as evidence for acknowledgement of his divinity) except, doubtfully, in 9.38 (see below, p. 160, n. 6).

Is this presentation of Jesus anti-Jewish? We have seen that Jewish ideas of monotheism were more flexible than often supposed (though certain texts cited may stem from esoteric groups). Some of the figures discussed above provide parallels to John's usage (cf. Hurtado, 1998), but none is exact. John does not have an 'angel christology' (except in the broadest sense that Jesus is sent by God and declares God's message). The patriarchs who are identified as angels are human beings believed to have ascended into heaven, not pre-existing beings who came down from heaven to be incarnate.[13] Angels who visit human beings in the appearance of men do so temporarily, not for a life-time of thirty years or more.

One angel ('the angel of the Lord'/Yaoel) is said to have 'God's Name' in him, but (*pace* Fossum, 1995, pp. 109–23) it is a far cry from this to John's Jesus. Despite all attempts to find external parallels, John's under-standing of Jesus remains closer to that of other early Christians than it does to near-contemporary Jewish texts. This does not make it *anti*-Jewish; rather it shows John using Jewish categories of thought to explain what was, and still is, a mystery – how Jesus of Nazareth, a first-century Jew, could reveal God so fully that he came to be acknowledged as *theos*.

Conclusions

This chapter has focused on two related questions: is John anti-Jewish in his 'replacement theology'? Is he anti-Jewish in 'breaching' Jewish monotheism? In response to the first we have argued that John does not have a programmatic 'replacement theology'. The emphasis is on 'fulfil-ment'. John presents Jesus as the realization of Judaism's deepest hopes and beliefs, fulfilling Scripture in his role as 'messiah', 'saviour', 'son', 'shepherd', 'king', sent with authority to carry out God's work and make God's nature known to humanity (cf. above, Ch. 8). These roles of Jesus are not set out in ways antagonistic to Judaism, but build on traditional Jewish beliefs, using Jewish symbolism and categories of thought. While John sometimes explains terms for Gentiles among his intended audi-ence, his main orientation is towards Jews. 'Fulfilment' may involve 'supersession': for example, if Jesus is the expected deliverer, then one does not need to look for another; but that is not its prime purpose.

As for 'monotheism', John does not set out to 'breach' this in his chris-tology, but to present Jesus in ways that are consistent with it. John's Jesus never asserts his 'equality' with God, though he is accused of this. He prays to God, acts in unity with God, performing his Father's will as an obedient 'son'. As *logos* he is God's heavenly agent and emissary, who became human to reveal God's nature; as 'messiah' he acts for God on earth; by his life, teaching, death, and resurrection, he draws humanity to God. Jews who became Christians must have seen this presentation as falling within the constraints of Jewish monotheism; others evidently did not.[14]

John is not alone in the New Testament in calling Jesus 'God'. Hebrews does so twice (1.8f., in a citation from Ps. 45.6f.); Philippians describes him as being 'in the form of God' (2.6); Colossians as 'the image of the invisible God' (1.15). Several texts *may* call him God, but are ambiguous (e.g. Rom. 9.5; Tit. 2.13; 2 Pet. 1.1); Matthew describes Jesus as being worshipped (2.11; 28.9, 17) and may imply divinity in 1.23 and 28.19. If John is considered 'anti-Jewish' in treating Jesus as part of God's identity, then these texts also must come under scrutiny. What cannot be denied is the *effect* of John's christology. Along with other texts it contributed to the much more explicit, closely defined recognition of deity for Jesus in later Trinitarian theology, just as his 'fulfilment' motif readily lent itself to Christian 'supersessionism'. But it should not be seen as the root cause of the split between Judaism and Christianity. That separation had complex causes, including the controversial admission of the Gentiles (in which Paul played a large part), the development of *worship* of Jesus, and the emergence of Christianity's own religious leadership, festivals, sacraments, and sacred texts.

13

Conclusions: The Value of John's Gospel Today

Our Introduction highlighted problems felt by some contemporary readers of John's Gospel. It has been condemned as 'inaccurate', with a portrait of Jesus that does not correspond to historical reality. It has been read as 'sectarian' in outlook, with a negative world-view and limited ethical teaching, as 'androcentric' and over-individualistic. It has been found 'anti-Jewish' and 'exclusive' in its claims. By contrast it has also been received as the climax of New Testament theology, and a foundation document for Trinitarian faith. It has been perceived as inspiring Church unity, women's ministry, humble service, and communion with God. This final chapter seeks to evaluate John in the light of these contrasting views, and to come to a balanced assessment.

Historical Accuracy

It is not easy to recover verifiable historical data from John other than in very broad outline. His Gospel embodies the results of long reflection on the Jesus traditions, his own life-experiences, including his presumably Jewish upbringing, his Christian faith, and Jewish–Christian tensions. Probably influenced by a broader background of Jewish, Christian, and 'Hellenistic' thought than the Synoptists, John came to particular convictions about Jesus as messiah, prophet, teacher, saviour, and revealer, seeing Jesus as sharing God's very identity. He sought to put over these ideas in a narrative where history and theology are inextricably intertwined. Faith-confessions, dramatic dialogues, and controversies with 'the Jews' mingle with sayings and discourses on the lips of Jesus – a mixture of historically authentic and imaginatively created materials. To these are added Passion and Resurrection Narratives, Prologue and Appendix, and personal reflections.

Each of the Evangelists adapted traditions he received of Jesus' words and actions, and provided his own narrative framework. They grouped together miracles, parables, sayings, and other teaching materials (cf. Matthew's 'Sermon on the Mount'), and shaped Jesus' story to suit their particular aims (cf. Luke's motif of Jesus' great journey to Jerusalem). John's framework, centred on Jesus' signs, the Jewish festivals, and the passion perceived as 'glorification', differs from both those of the Synoptists and, almost certainly, from historical reality. He seems to have felt at liberty to remodel earlier traditions, attributing to Jesus fresh theological ideas and a distinctive speech-style: sometimes (but only sometimes) this style seems closer to 'Gnostic' revelatory discourses than to Jesus' parables, wisdom sayings, and other utterances in the Synoptics. In so doing John followed literary conventions of the Graeco-Roman world, where historians, biographers, and philosophical writers regularly attributed conversations or speeches to figures like Socrates or Pericles, when they had no written record of what had been said.[1] They also related anecdotes which they saw as in keeping with the characters they portrayed, even if they could not prove authenticity.

John also wrote in the context of Jewish religious historiography, where authors created quasi-historical narratives to express their theology, and freely reported events and dialogues about which they had very limited information. They rewrote earlier 'histories' from fresh viewpoints (cf. 1 and 2 Chronicles, *Jubilees*, and Josephus' *Jewish Antiquities*). They attributed proverbs, wisdom literature, songs, and psalms to Solomon; edifying 'testaments' to the patriarchs; apocalyptic revelations to Enoch and Ezra. Christians followed suit with apocryphal 'Gospels' and 'Acts', and other 'apostolic' writings (e.g. the *Didache*), and 'Gnostic' texts where Jesus utters sentiments far removed from his Synoptic sayings, e.g. 'Blessed is the lion which becomes man ...' (*Gos. Thom.*, 7) and 'Pray in the place where there is no woman' (*Dial. Sav.*, 144). John must be interpreted in this context: it is unfair to castigate him for telling 'untruths', when a wholly factual description of Jesus' life and teaching was not his aim. The question is whether his account of Jesus is close enough to what can be deduced from other sources to be a fair presentation of Jesus' abiding significance.

Portrait of Jesus

While once deemed 'the perfect portrait' (cf. above, p. 1), John's Jesus is now often found less attractive than the Jesus of the Synoptists. This is because modern people prefer their heroes to be 'human', readily accessible, and self-deprecating rather than conscious of their dignity (cf. Edwards, 1997, esp. pp. 104f.). They like them to have a sense of humour, to be kind and considerate, open in their attitudes, accepting of outcasts and the unloved. John's omniscient, majestic, authoritative Jesus seems closer to the cosmic *Christos Pantokratōr* ('Christ all-powerful') of Byzantine fresco and mosaic than the 'Galilean peasant' or 'marginal Jew' of recent scholarship (e.g. Crossan, 1991; Meier, 1991, 1994, 2001). Why does John's Jesus not express care for the poor, heal the lepers, dine with tax-collectors and sinners? Why does he not tell homely parables? Why is he so sharp with 'the Pharisees' and 'the Jews'? Why is he never said to feel compassion?

John's stylized portrayal is designed to convey his distinctive understanding of Jesus as heavenly revealer and Israel's true king, who brings salvation but also judges by his coming. Many think it impossible that the historical Jesus thought and spoke as presented by John, with a self-conscious awareness of his divine origin and unity with 'the Father'. Yet several of the characteristics deemed unhistorical in John's portrayal have counterparts in the Synoptics. The latter also show Jesus aware of a special relationship with God (e.g. Mk 1.11 par.; Mt. 4.3; Lk. 2.49): Jesus calls him 'Abba' or 'Father' (e.g. Mk 14.36 par.), and himself 'the Son' (Mk 13.32 par.; Mt. 11.27; Lk. 10.21f.). They portray Jesus' sense of mission and authority (e.g. Mk 2.17b; Mt. 15.24; 28.18) and show him being harsh to 'hypocrites', including scribes and Pharisees (e.g. Mt. 7.5; 23.13; Lk. 11.42–52) and those who reject his message (e.g. Lk. 10.10–15). They also depict him as the glorious 'Son of Man', who will come as judge (e.g. Mk 8.38 par.; 13.26 par.).

John's method seems to have been to take traditional sayings and features of Jesus' character and develop them in the light of broader thought. The resulting figure shares characteristics with Hellenistic gods and 'divine men', exalted Jewish patriarchs, personified wisdom, Philo's *logos*, and 1 Enoch's pre-existent, glorified 'Son of Man'/'messiah'. His portrait is also probably influenced by contact with sophisticated Christian interpretation of Jesus, exemplified in Hebrews and some Pauline letters, and by his own experience of Jesus as 'Lord' and his membership of a worshipping Christian community.

It has been alleged that John's Gospel is 'untrue' factually and theologically. But one has to ask what is meant by 'true'. 'True' does not mean merely 'historically accurate'. It can also mean 'corresponding to reality'. The 'truths' claimed by John are not verifiable by historical investigation or the application of ruthless logic. Nobody can *prove* that this first-century Galilean peasant was 'Son of God', pre-existent *logos*, or 'light of the world'. These are perceptions that have to be experienced in faith. For some people these images of Jesus are helpful and inspiring; for others they are not.

'Sectarianism' and World-View

John's Gospel and the Johannine Epistles have often been categorized as 'sectarian'. Part of the problem lies in reconstructions of the 'Johannine community' that exaggerate its isolation from other Christian groups and its alienation from surrounding culture, concentrating excessively on texts about the disciples 'being hated' or not belonging to 'this world'. The Synoptic Gospels also refer to the persecution and hatred of disciples,[2] and other New Testament writings mention the trials and tribulations they will have to face (e.g. Jas 1.2; 1 Pet. 4.12; Rev. 2.9; 7.14). Historically this is what happened to Christians at least in some places; at times their social environment must indeed have seemed hostile and threatening. John's warnings are no more extreme than the others cited – if anything his language is less colourful. Nevertheless it must be acknowledged that John's basic world-view is 'dualistic' in its polarization of opposites – good and evil, truth and falsehood, faith and unbelief, etc. Sometimes one wants to protest: 'Life is not like that! People are a mixture of good and bad; the same actions may have both positive and negative results; truth is hard to discover and multi-faceted; there are *degrees* of faith and unbelief.'

Dualism of this sort is characteristic of many religions, occurring in the Hebrew Bible, the Dead Sea Scrolls, Jewish Pseudepigrapha, the *Hermetica*, the Nag Hammadi and Mandaean texts, and elsewhere. Like many religious teachers, John urges people to choose between two courses presented as stark alternatives (cf. Dt. 30.15, 19: 'I have set before you this day life and good, death and evil'; 'I have set before you life and death, blessing and curse; therefore choose life').[3] His dualism is not absolute, as in Zoroastrianism (where good and evil wage war with uncertain outcome), but moral and ethical with eschatological overtones. Jesus and Satan, the 'ruler of this world', are diametric opposites; but in the death of Jesus good prevails over evil. John's emphasis on the distinction between believers and unbelievers, and between Jesus (and the disciples) and 'the world', is part of an evangelistic strategy designed to encourage people to come to faith. He does not present everything in black-and-white terms, as is evident from his more nuanced character portrayals; but his depiction of Judas as 'a devil', and the 'beloved disciple' as a model of faith, warns how easy it is to demonize opponents and idealize one's own group, with potentially disastrous consequences.

Nor is John's attitude to the physical world and 'the flesh' entirely negative, as in Manichaean thought. If he describes 'the world' as made through the *logos* and loved by God, he cannot see it as wholly evil; but his Gospel expresses no appreciation of the natural world's beauty as God's creation. Sometimes John betrays a certain 'pessimism' in his rhetorical use of 'the world' as a catch-phrase or teaching tool, to refer to humanity alienated from God.[4] For modern readers this usage is unfortunate, because it makes the Gospel sound negative towards culture and society. It is also true that John shows little interest in social concerns ('the poor' are mentioned only in connection with Judas' complaint about 'wasted' ointment: 12.4–6).

John's contrast between *sarx*, 'flesh', and spirit (e.g. 6.63) is sometimes seen as expressing this 'world-denying' outlook. In today's culture, where a fine and healthy body is highly esteemed (in athletics, health care, the beauty trade), such language may suggest an 'ascetic' or negative attitude to physical things. This is unlikely to be intended – though in common with many religious writers John evidently saw the things of the Spirit as of greater importance. The strongest argument against the idea that he had a negative attitude to the body is his description of the incarnation: 'the Word became flesh'. On the other hand some interpreters have exaggerated the idea that John held material things as 'sacred' because of the incarnation.

Ethics and the Love Command

John gives less 'moral teaching' than Matthew, Luke, or most New Testament epistles. His ethics centre on Jesus' repeated command that 'you love one another as I have loved you' (15.12, etc.). This has been interpreted as narrowing the scope of the Synoptic injunction, 'You shall love your neighbour as yourself'; but it is doubtful if John saw his formulation as restricting love to the Johannine 'community' or 'the saved'. The love command, though addressed to the disciples at the Last Supper, applies to the whole Church; and it is rooted in Jesus' self-giving love. As for the broader issue of why John gives so little other moral teaching, one can only reply that people think ethically in different ways. Some like to give (and receive) detailed instructions for behaviour (cf. the Pauline 'Household Codes', Eph. 5.22—6.9; Col. 3.18—4.1); others prefer general principles. The ethical content of New Testament narratives is not limited to explicit 'moral teaching' (cf. Hays, 1996, p. 140). Some modern ethicists also preach 'love' as the supreme guide to life (though one may question whether this is adequate).

'Androcentrism' and 'Patriarchy'

It is widely recognized that most biblical writings are 'androcentric' in that they often focus on men's lives, rather than women's, and 'patriarchal' in depicting men as leaders and encouraging (or enjoining) women to be subordinate. This male-centredness stems in large measure from the cultural environment in which the Bible was written (cf. Edwards, 1989, esp. chs. 2–4). John is often perceived as an exception to this rule in that he depicts female characters sympathetically and gives them important roles in faith-confessions and in spreading the good news. Fehribach (1998, esp. pp. 180–4) disagrees, seeing John's Gospel as 'androcentric' in its focus on Jesus – a male – as its central figure and in its presentation of women, e.g. by portraying Mary as the 'mother of an important son'. Although Fehribach exaggerates women's subordination to Jesus, and distorts the text to depict them as his 'brides', she makes valid points about the absence of women among 'the disciples' and the possible disregard in 21.14 of the risen Jesus' appearance to Mary Magdalene. She proposes strategies for applying a 'hermeneutic of suspicion', and 'resisting' the text by reading it as affirmative of women. Reinhartz (1994, esp. pp. 594–7) similarly suggests reading John subversively to avoid 'compliant' readings that marginalize people, and concentrating on 'liberating' texts like 8.32, 'the truth will make you free', An alternative is to recognize 'androcentrism' as part of John's cultural dress, and not essential to its message. Some express hurt at John's constant references to God as 'Father' and Jesus as 'Son', which they see as excluding or devaluing women, regretting a lost opportunity in the Prologue to present Jesus under the 'feminine' image of *sophia* rather than as masculine *logos*. Here the late Barnabas Lindars (a Franciscan) offers helpful thoughts: all Father–Son language is analogical; Jesus reveals God's character and glory through the image of 'family likeness'; in the realm of understanding 'sexual differentiation is transcended' (1990, p. 17).

Individualism and the Church

John vividly describes encounters of people with Jesus, employing 'faith-confessions' to highlight the importance of personal faith. Like Mark and Luke, he does not use *ekklēsia*, 'congregation', 'church' (contrast Mt. 16.18; 18.17) or *koinōnia*, 'fellowship' (contrast 1 Jn 1.3, 6f.). He makes few allusions to Christian baptism or Eucharist, and those that have been detected are disputed. This has led to the suggestion that John overstresses individual faith at the expense of Church life. Marshall (1982, p. 1090) argues that this emphasis on individual faith is not something for which the expositor need apologize: 'The modern stress on the corporate nature of Christianity can easily be carried too far'. Brown (1966, pp. cv–cxi) says that John cannot be expected to use anachronistic ecclesial vocabulary when he is writing about Jesus' historical ministry; but he sees John as offering deep understanding of Christian sacraments despite the disputed nature of the relevant passages.

We would argue that it is a mistake to read into the text everything one might hope to find there. John does not provide a blueprint for Christian worship and ecclesiastical organization; he works within the essential framework of Judaism (cf. above, Ch. 12). But he does depict Jesus as 'training' the disciples, and preparing them for mission and service through the example of his sacrificial death and his gift of the Spirit. John is aware of the danger of disunity (cf. Jesus' prayer 'that they should be one': 17.21). He promotes an ideal of harmony and mutuality in his image of the 'one flock' (10.16), the vine with its branches (15.1–8), and his language of 'indwelling'. Jesus' words, 'I go to my Father and your Father, and my God and your God' (20.17), evoke covenantal imagery (cf. Ex. 6.7, 'I will be your God'). Believers are described in 'inclusive' language as *tekna theou*, 'children of God' (1.12f.; cf. 11.52).

'Anti-Semitism' and 'Anti-Judaism'

This subject has already been discussed in detail (Chs 11–12). It was concluded that John is not 'anti-Semitic', in that he does not deliberately incite hatred against Jewish people simply because they are Jews. But he can be seen, in a limited sense, as 'anti-Jewish' inasmuch as his 'plot' stereotypes 'the Jews' as Jesus' opponents, and at times he uses them to symbolize unbelief. By deploying the same phrase, 'the Jews', for Judaeans, Jewish religious leaders, and Jewish people more generally he lays himself open to misinterpretation. We did not see John as advocating a wholesale 'replacement' theology, but rather presenting Jesus as 'fulfilling' Scripture, using essentially Jewish interpretative methods. It was also argued that John does not 'breach' Jewish monotheism, in that he does not present Jesus as 'a second God', but rather portrays him as sharing God's identity. Nevertheless we recognize that his portrayal of Jesus contributed to the separation of Christianity from Judaism (in which the admission of Gentiles, so passionately advocated by Paul, was a major factor).

Those wishing to avert 'anti-Jewish' misuse of John need to adopt strategies to avoid misunderstanding, like putting 'the Jews' in inverted commas ('scare quotes'), as done in this book, to signal that this is a special usage. Some scholars recommend more drastic steps, such as changing 'the Jews' to 'the Judaeans' or 'the religious leaders'. The problem is that this can distort John's meaning in the interests of 'political correctness', just as some 'inclusive language' versions of the Bible give the impression that women in ancient Jewish society were treated equally with men. Others suggest omitting offending passages from lectionaries; but this is difficult since 'the Jews' feature so often in John, and even passages which do not mention them by name have been judged polemical, including the Prologue (which cannot lightly be dispensed with). A better way forward is through education: by drawing attention to potential misunderstanding; by adding brief introductions to passages read in Church; through scholarly and popular writing, and sensitivity in preaching or speaking generally about Jewish people. More strenuous efforts could also be made to deepen Christian knowledge of Judaism by building friendship with Jews, reading Jewish writings, and joining groups concerned with promoting good interfaith relations.

Johannine 'Exclusivism'

A further problem concerns Christianity's relation to other world faiths. John is often seen as 'exclusive' in offering a stark choice between faith in Jesus and unbelief, whereas other religious thinkers were more tolerant of differing beliefs. Ancient religions often absorbed features from surrounding cultures by the process known as 'syncretism': thus Greeks and Romans adopted oriental cults; the Romans identified their own gods with Greek ones; and so on. Few faiths made such exclusive truth claims as did Jews and Christians. The world today is different: most of us live in pluralist, multicultural societies, composed of men and women from a variety of ethnic origins and with a mix of religious beliefs. We are all too aware of the dangers of intolerance leading to such horrors as racism, sectarian violence, 'ethnic cleansing', and imperialist aggression. The tensions and violence between Israelis and Palestinians, Catholic and Protestant in Northern Ireland, the affluent, materialist West and the Muslim world, and the internecine strife between tribal or religious groups in parts of Africa and India, all alert us to the perils of religious self-confidence and bigotry.

A few years ago texts like 'I am the way, the truth, and the life; no one comes to the Father except by me' (Jn 14.6) would not have been regarded as problematic. Today some see this verse as a 'stumbling block' and as wrongfully denying salvation to adherents of world faiths such as Islam, Buddhism, Hinduism, Sikhism, and Judaism. But it does not have to be so understood. 'The way' (Greek *hodos*; Hebrew *derek*) means 'road' or 'journey' (cf. Isa. 40.3); hence 'behaviour', or 'teaching' (Pss. 1.6; 86.11): the Qumran community interpreted it as the study and practice of Torah; Luke used it for the Christian way of life (Acts 9.2). John 14.6 does not express 'an insensitive imperialism', but indicates that Jesus shows the way to God, reveals truth, and demonstrates life

(Grayston, 1990, pp. 116f.). As Jesus says in another context, 'I came that they might have life, and have it to the full' (10.10). Other sayings, too, can be interpreted inclusively: 'I have other sheep not of this fold, and I must lead them' (10.16); 'When I am lifted up, I will draw all people to me' (12.32; cf. 6.37); 'In my Father's house are many rooms' (14.2). The 'true light' that enlightens everyone (1.9) has often been seen as indicating that all human beings share in the divine light (though some choose darkness: 3.19).

Using these texts to see Jesus as the 'constitutive mediator' of salvation for all humankind, with people of other faiths as latent or 'anonymous' Christians, is reading them 'subversively'. Some are unhappy with such interpretations, either because they see them as unfaithful to John's original meaning or because they feel this approach does not go far enough in recognizing the spiritual value of other religions (Haight, 1999, ch. 14; Fergusson, 2001; Whaling, 2002). It must be frankly recognized that John, writing in the first century CE, was not concerned about 'world religions' in the modern sense. He shared the attitudes of other New Testament writers (e.g. 1 Pet. 2.9f.; cf. Eph. 5.8–14) who understood conversion from paganism to Christianity as moving from darkness to light, from ignorance to knowledge, and from being outside God's mercy to being within it; some Pauline texts (e.g. 2 Cor. 6.14–18; Rom. 1.18–25) condemn Gentile religion much more explicitly than does John's Gospel (though note 1 Jn 5.21). Christianity's relation to other faiths involves far more than Johannine interpretation, and is an urgent question for today's Church.

Storytelling Skill

We turn now to some positive assessments of John. Many people admire his narrative skill. His story captures the imagination, as evidenced by the numerous works of creative art inspired by it. Those who hear or read it can identify themselves with its characters – Nicodemus, the Samaritan woman, the official, Martha and Mary – and consider how they would react in comparable situations. John has the gift of making scenes live before our eyes – Andrew's bringing forward the lad with his picnic; the charcoal fire by which Peter warms himself; Jesus' confrontation with Pilate; the barbecue by the lake. Mary Magdalene's meeting with the risen Jesus and his calling her by name never fails to move, making the resurrection more credible than many a philosophical discussion. His Passion Narrative, with its understanding of Jesus' crucifixion as his exaltation, has inspired courage, gratitude, self-dedication, compassion, and hope that evil may be conquered through love.

Love and Service

John presents inspiring ideals for the Christian life. Jesus' teaching on love, though sometimes criticized, is usually seen as a very positive feature, especially for its theological grounding in the prior love of Jesus (13.34; 15.12) and ultimately in God's love (17.26) – a theme made explicit in 1 John (4.7–11). The supreme example of God's love is his giving of his Son: 'God so loved the world ...' (3.16), a text rightly cherished by Christians through the ages. John does not spell out how Christians should apply the love command in their lives (though note 1 Jn 3.17f.); but Jesus' washing of the disciples' feet constitutes a practical example of humble, loving service. This 'acted parable' brings home the same message as the Synoptic sayings – 'I am among you as one who serves' (Lk. 22.27; cf. Mk 10.45; Mt. 20.28), and 'Whoever wants to be first shall be last of all and servant of all' (Mk 9.35) – but with greater vividness. Jesus' own example shows that the love required by God involves total self-giving: 'Greater love hath no man than this, that a man lay down his life for his friends' (15.13, AV). These words (unique to John) have inspired countless men and women to acts of heroism and self-sacrifice, foreshadowing as they do Jesus' voluntary giving of his own life. The same teaching is reflected in the saying about the grain of wheat that has to 'die' so that it may 'bear fruit' (12.23–6).

Discipleship and Friendship

John pictures discipleship as a learning process: after all the time Peter has spent with Jesus, after his denials and his forgiveness, he is still bidden, 'Follow me' (21.19). But the disciples are not just pupils; they are also Jesus' 'friends' (15.14f.; cf. Lazarus in 11.11). John is unique among the Evangelists in using this term, with its echoes of God's calling Abraham 'his friend' (Isa. 41.8) and speaking with Moses 'as a man talks with his friend' (Ex. 33.11). This focus on friendship offers potential for fresh, 'inclusive' understandings of what it means to be a Christian.[5] In John's portrayal of the disciples many have detected a pattern of ministry in which people serve as equals under Christ rather than being ranked hierarchically. In particular his depictions of women's faith and service have been seen as affirming of the call of women to witness and ministry alongside men. In fairness one must add that Christians have used John to support almost every type of ecclesial organization from the papacy to the ideals of the Religious Society of Friends (Quakers).

Holy Spirit

John lays special emphasis on the Holy Spirit. New birth 'from above' occurs through water and the Spirit (3.5); the Spirit is *to zōopoioun*, literally 'the life-giving one' (6.63). As Paraclete, or 'Spirit of Truth', the Spirit proves 'the world' wrong about sin, justice, and judgement, encourages the disciples, and leads them into truth (14.16, 26; 16.7–15). It is the risen Jesus' gift (20.20). John is often valued for the personal way he speaks about the Spirit, and for his contribution to the development of the doctrine of the Trinity.[6]

Evocative Symbols and 'Sublime Truths'

John's use of symbols has been much praised, especially in Jesus' 'I am' sayings and 'titles'. Images like light, life, bread, vine, shepherd, word, and 'saviour of the world' strike chords with people of varied backgrounds, evoking different thoughts and emotions. This is their strength; the 'downside' is that because his images are multivalent, John's intentions are sometimes obscure. Most of all John has been admired for his grand concepts, seen as 'sublime truths'. In the medieval period this admiration reached such an extreme that Eriugena, the Irish scholar, described John as being 'transmuted into God' as he revealed the mystery of the Trinity (*Hom. Prol. Jo.*, 5: Bamford, 1990, p. 26).

Today scholars make a more sober assessment. Some still perceive John as uniquely inspired, taking his words about the incarnation of the *logos* quite literally and elucidating them from patristic exegesis and the Church's traditional faith. Others understand John's ideas in the light of their historical, literary, and religious context, and suggest that they (and their patristic exegesis) need reinterpretation for today. Some talk quite freely of the 'myth' or 'metaphor' of God incarnate (Hick, 1977, 1993), or of Jesus as the 'symbol' of God (Haight, 1999). Others work with concepts of 'presence' or *kenōsis*, understanding the incarnation as a divine self-abasement reflecting the self-giving of the immanent Trinity (see Fergusson, 2001, p. 78). Others again are more attracted to the 'historical Jesus' (as reconstructed in critical scholarship), seen as prophet and radical social critic rather than a divine figure. Yet others propose models of a 'Christa' ('female Christ'), embodying elements of equality and mutuality. Many find in Jesus the perfect expression of God's love.

These developments remind us that no single understanding of Jesus can convey all truth. John's portrait must be set beside the Synoptic portraits and the insights of other Christian writers. One of the strengths of the New Testament is precisely its varied pictures of Jesus, its diverse christologies, and its different ways of understanding redemption.[7] John's distinctiveness is 'sheer gain' for Christian theology, spirituality, and ecclesiology (so Barton, 1993, p. 301).

John's Achievement

So what is John's special achievement? He has written a work which presents Jesus as God's revelation to humanity. Jesus reveals what God is like – not so much by what he says about God, though he does say important things, as by all that he is and does. In his Jesus John offers readers an ideal of love, service, and obedience toward which they can strive, and an ideal of a community of friends bound together in mutual love. He affirms that there is such a thing as truth, that there are spiritual realities beyond the material world – important perceptions today in a culture of 'postmodernism', where abiding values are no longer cherished and everything seems to be understood relatively. It is John's belief that in Jesus God acted in history – that he became part of human history – and that by his teaching and sacrificial death Jesus opened up a new way to salvific knowledge of God. To those who can trust without the kind of proof required by contemporary science, philosophy, and historiography, he offers hope of life in communion with God, not just now but for eternity. Of course, there are shadows, e.g. John's treatment of 'the Jews' and the question of those who fail to accept Jesus or who adhere to other faiths; and John's world of thought which presupposes a 'dualism' unacceptable to many today. There are tensions with the sophisticated thinking of modern sociologists and historians of religion, and with recent trends in systematic theology. But John deals with 'narrative', not propositional, theology, and with 'narrative' ethics. His is a Gospel of 'encounter', in which readers are invited to meet Jesus as John has discovered him. It is hoped that this exposition may have helped readers not only to 'discover' John, but also to discover something of the God who inspired him.

Appendixes
Notes
Bibliography
Indexes

Appendix 1

The Structure of John's Gospel

I. Proem

1.1–18   *Prologue*: Jesus in his cosmic setting, as divine *logos*, life, true light, revealer of God, and giver of salvation to believers

1.19–51   *Testimony*: witness of John the Baptist, Andrew, and Nathanael; Jesus as Lamb of God, Son of God, Messiah, and King of Israel

II. Jesus' self-revelation and ministry
sometimes called 'The Book of Signs'

(i)   *Jesus Inaugurates the New Order and Gives New Life*

2.1–12   First 'sign': water into wine at Cana

2.13–25   Temple 'Cleansing' at *Passover* time

3.1–36   New birth and the Spirit (Nicodemus); further witness of the Baptist

4.1–42   Living water and 'Saviour of the World' (Samaritan woman)

4.43–54   Second 'sign': life for the official's son

(ii)   *Further Miracles and Conflict with 'the Jews'*

5.1–47   Lame man healed on Sabbath; Jesus' authority questioned; Jesus and the Father; Jesus as life-giver and judge

6.1–71   Feeding at *Passover* time; walking on the water; Jesus as 'the bread of heaven'

7.1—8.59   *Feast of Tabernacles*; increasing opposition; Jesus' identity, pre-existence, and mission; Jesus as 'light of the world' [7.53—8.11 Independent pericope: the woman taken in adultery]

9.1–41   Healing of the man born blind: spiritual sight and blindness

10.1–42   Jesus as the 'Good Shepherd'; *Feast of Dedication*; further controversy with 'the Jews'; accusation of blasphemy

11.1–57   Raising of Lazarus; Jesus as 'the Resurrection and the Life'; Chief Priests and Pharisees plot his death

(iii)   *Scenes Preparatory to the Passion*

12.1–50   Anointing at Bethany; 'triumphal entry'; teaching on death and sacrifice; conflict of light and darkness; summary of Jesus' teaching

III. The Passion Narrative
sometimes called 'The Book of Glory'

(i)   *Last Supper and Discourses, Preparing the Disciples for Jesus' Departure*

13.1–38   Foot-washing and love command; Judas leaves to betray Jesus; Peter's denials predicted

14.1–31   First Farewell Discourse: Jesus and the Father; Jesus as 'the way, the truth, and life'; promise of Paraclete

15.1—16.33 Second Farewell Discourse: Jesus as 'the True Vine'; teaching on love, Spirit of Truth, and prayer; warning of persecution; promise of joy

17.1–26   'High-Priestly' Prayer for disciples and future believers: may they be kept safe, sanctified, and united. Jesus has declared God's glory and love

(ii)   *Jesus' Arrest, Trial, Scourging, Death and Burial*

18.11—19.42 Appearances before Annas and Caiaphas; Peter's denials; trial before Pilate; Jesus' obedience to God, witness to truth, and kingship; Jesus is scourged and crucified; he commends his mother and the 'beloved disciple' to one another; Jesus dies on eve of *Passover*, his work accomplished; Nicodemus and Joseph bury him sumptuously

(iii)   *Resurrection and Main Conclusion*

20.1–29   Mary Magdalene, Peter and the 'beloved disciple' at the tomb; appearance to disciples; gift of Spirit and commissioning; appearance to disciples with Thomas

20.30–1   Conclusion on purpose of Gospel, 'that you may believe that Jesus is the Christ, the Son of God, and that believing you may have life in his Name'

IV. Epilogue or Appendix

21.1–25   Appearance by the lake; miraculous catch of fish; Peter restored; the fate of the 'beloved disciple' (identified as the author); final conclusion

Appendix 2: Jesus' Burial and Resurrection in the Gospels

Material in square brackets is found only in some manuscripts

	John	Mark	Matthew	Luke
Jn 19.38–42 Mk 15.42–6 Mt. 27.57–60 Lk. 23.50–4	Joseph of Arimathea, a secret disciple, requests body from Pilate; Nicodemus and Joseph bind it in cloths (*othonia*) with 100 lbs of myrrh and aloes, and bury it, on Day of Preparation, in new tomb (*mnēmeion*) in garden.	Joseph of Arimathea, a respected councillor, requests body from Pilate; Pilate checks Jesus is already dead; Joseph buys shroud (*sindōn*), wraps body, and places it in rock-cut tomb (*mnēmeion*); rolls stone against door.	Joseph of Arimathea, a rich man who was a disciple, requests body from Pilate; wraps it in clean linen shroud (*sindōn*), places it in his own new tomb (*mnēmeion*), rolls great stone against door.	Joseph of Arimathea, a councillor and a good and righteous man who had not consented to the deed, requests body from Pilate; takes it down, wraps it in linen shroud (*sindōn*), and buries it, on Day of Preparation, in new rock-hewn tomb (*mnēma*).
Mk 15.47 Mt. 27.61 Lk. 23.55f.		Mary Magdalene and Mary mother of Joses see where he is laid.	Mary Magdalene and the other Mary are there, sitting opposite the sepulchre (*taphos*).	The women from Galilee see where he was laid; prepare spices and myrrh; then rest on Sabbath.
Mt. 27.62–6			At request of Chief Priests and Pharisees Pilate grants guard at sepulchre; stone is sealed.	
Jn 20.1f., 11–13 Mk 16.1–8 Mt. 28.1–8 Lk. 24.1–11	On first day of week Mary Magdalene comes to tomb, while still dark, and finds it empty. She runs and tells Peter and 'beloved disciple'. She stands by tomb weeping; she sees two angels in white, who ask her why she is weeping; she says it is because they have taken away her Lord.	Mary Magdalene, Mary mother of James, and Salome buy spices; very early on first day of week go to tomb after sunrise; find stone rolled back; enter and are amazed to see young man in white on right side. He tells them Jesus is risen, and bids them tell the disciples and Peter that Jesus is going before them to Galilee, where they will see him. They flee and tell nobody out of fear.	Towards dawn on first day of week Mary Magdalene and the other Mary go to see sepulchre; earthquake; angel in dazzling raiment descends and rolls back stone; guards tremble. Angel tells women Jesus is risen, bidding them tell the disciples Jesus is going before them to Galilee, where they will see him. They depart quickly in fear and great joy to tell his disciples.	On first day of week at early dawn the women go to tomb, taking spices, find stone rolled back, enter. Two men in dazzling white ask why they seek the living among the dead, reminding them of Jesus' predictions in Galilee. Mary Magdalene, Joanna, and Mary mother of James tell the Eleven and the rest, but the apostles take their words as an idle tale.
Jn 20.3–10 [Lk. 24.12]	Peter and other disciple run to tomb; the other sees linen cloths (*othonia*) lying. Peter enters tomb, sees cloths and napkin rolled up separately; other disciple enters, sees and believes; the disciples go home.			[*Peter runs to tomb, stoops and looks in, and sees linen cloths (othonia) lying by themselves; goes home wondering what has happened.*]
Jn 20.14–18 [Mk 16.9–11] Mt. 28.9f.	Mary turns and sees Jesus, but takes him for gardener; he calls her by name; she recognizes him. He forbids her to cling to him, saying she must tell the brethren that he is ascending to the	*Longer ending: Jesus appears to Mary Magdalene; she tells those who had been with him; they do not believe her.*	Jesus meets and greets them; they grasp his feet and worship him; he bids them tell his brethren that he is going to Galilee where they will see him.	

and elders, who bribe them to say the disciples stole the body.

Reference	Matthew	Mark	Luke	John
[Mk 16.12f.] Lk. 24.13–35		*Jesus appears in another form to two of them walking in the country.*	The same day Jesus appears to two walking to Emmaus and interprets Moses and the prophets to them. They recognize him as he blesses the bread at supper. They return to Jerusalem and tell the Eleven and those with them.	
Jn 20.19–23 Mk 16.14–18 Lk. 24.36–49		*Jesus appears to the Eleven as they sit at table; upbraids them, commissions them to preach the Gospel to all creation, promising that believers will cast out demons, heal the sick, speak in new tongues, pick up serpents, and drink deadly poison without harm.*	Jesus appears [*and says, 'Peace be to you'*]. They are frightened. He shows them his hands and feet. They disbelieve for joy, but he requests food, and eats some fish. He explains the Scriptures, commissions them, and bids them stay in the city until they are clothed with power from on high.	The same evening, the doors being shut for fear of 'the Jews', Jesus appears to the disciples, says 'Peace be with you' and shows his hands and side. They are glad. He says, 'As the Father has sent me, even so I send you'; then breathes on them, saying, 'Receive Holy Spirit', giving them authority to forgive or retain sins.
Jn 20.24–9				The disciples tell Thomas, who disbelieves. A week later, Jesus appears, and asks Thomas to put his fingers in his hands and side. Thomas acclaims him as Lord and God. Jesus blesses those who believe without seeing.
Jn 21.1–24 Lk. 5.1–11			(Parallel story early in Jesus' ministry) The disciples catch a miraculous draught of fish; Jesus calls Peter, James and John; special words to Peter.	Jesus appears to seven disciples by the Sea of Tiberias. They catch a miraculous draught of fish; Jesus feeds them. Note that this is Jesus' third resurrection appearance. Jesus forgives and commissions Peter. Predictions of Peter's martyrdom; saying about the 'beloved disciple' remaining, and note on his witness. Final conclusion to Gospel.
Mk 16.19f. Mt. 28.16–20 Lk. 24.50–52	Jesus appears to the Eleven in Galilee; Great Commission to make disciples, baptize, and teach in Name of Father, Son, and Holy Spirit. He promises to be with them until close of age.	*Jesus ascends to heaven and sits at God's right hand. They preach the Gospel and work miracles.*	Jesus leads them to Bethany, blesses them, is carried up to heaven. They [*worship him,*] return to Jerusalem with joy, and continually bless God in the Temple.	

Notes

1 Introduction: A Distinctive Gospel

1 For convenience, the traditional name 'John' is used for the main author and for his book, without prejudice as to who actually composed it.
2 *Hom. Prol. Jo.*, 4, tr. Bamford (1990). The image of the eagle is found in many earlier Church writers, including Augustine.
3 For a definition of these terms, see Ch. 11.
4 This name has been traced to David Chytraeus (1530–1600), but already Cyril of Alexandria (d. 444) saw Jesus here as serving as High Priest (Beasley-Murray, 1987, p. 294). It is also known as the 'Prayer of Consecration' (Westcott, 1919, p. 236; cf. Hoskyns, 1947, p. 494).
5 Apart from excursions into the Decapolis and to the Syro-Phoenician coast; Luke alone has the boy Jesus visit Jerusalem (2.41–50).
6 *Apostolos* occurs only in a general saying about 'envoys' (13.16).

2 The Reception of John's Gospel

1 Probably by *c.* 200 CE, if this is the right date for the Muratorian fragment (an early list of documents accepted by the Church in Rome): see Bruce 1988, p. 159.
2 Casey (1996, p. 226); cf. Ruether (1974); Cohn-Sherbok (1992, pp. 25–8). Chrysostom's sermons contain some virulent anti-Jewish polemic.
3 Reproduced in Schwartz (1991, pl. 73). Rembrandt's contemporary Jan Lievens also painted this theme.
4 Hermes, the messenger god of the Greeks, was identified with the Egyptian god Thoth.
5 These rather beautiful poems, dating to the late first or early second century CE (Charlesworth, 1985, pp. 725–71), are written in Syriac (with some Greek fragments). Charlesworth ascribes them to a Jewish-Christian group, from the same area as John's 'community'; others postulate dependency on John.
6 See Cullmann, in Stendahl (1958, pp. 18–32, esp. p. 27); Charlesworth (1972, pp. 76–106, esp. p. 105, with his n. 128). On the Dead Sea Scrolls and the New Testament, see further VanderKam (1994, pp. 159–185); Vermes (1999, pp. 182–91).
7 A Greek text purporting to be the final words of the twelve sons of Jacob, dating possibly to the second century BCE, but with later additions (Kee, in Charlesworth, 1983, pp. 775–828). A few Aramaic fragments of the *Testament of Levi* have been found at Qumran.
8 The contrast between Jewish and Hellenistic is to some extent artificial, since many Jews in the Palestinian cities and the Diaspora were quite Hellenized (cf. Hengel, 1974; Barclay, 1996).
9 The theory of 'community' differs slightly from Culpepper's (1975) concept of a Johannine 'school', and Cullmann's (1976) of a Johannine 'circle'.
10 See, for example, Martyn (1979; 1st edn 1968); Meeks (1972); Brown (1979); Woll (1981); Neyrey (1988); Malina and Rohrbaugh (1998).

3 The Question of Authorship

1 'These things' in 21.24 (Greek *toutōn*, *tauta*) could refer to either the resurrection appearance of Jn 21 and subsequent conversations, or, more probably, the whole Gospel.
2 When Judas appears in lists of apostles he is called the 'son of Jacob' (Lk. 6.16; Acts 1.13).

3 However, most scholars today postulate separate authors for John and 1–3 John.
4 Cf. Lieu (1986, pp. 55–7). Hengel (1989) maintains, improbably, that John combines material from both the apostle and 'John the Elder'.
5 The 'Alogoi' denied the divinity of the *logos*; hence Epiphanius' ambiguous nickname for them, meaning either 'without *logos*' or 'unreasonable'.
6 Schnackenburg (1968, p. 201) speculates that they may have denied apostolic authorship through concern over John's differences from the Synoptics.
7 Point (c) should not be pressed, as the idea may have arisen out of a false interpretation of Mk 10.39.
8 See Cullmann (1976, ch. 8), further arguing that one should distinguish the identity of the main author from that of any editor or redactor.
9 See Gunther (1980), referring to Irenaeus, Proclus, the Muratorian Canon, Tertullian, and the *Acts of John*.
10 E.g. 'the Teacher of Righteousness' and 'the Wicked Priest' in the Dead Sea Scrolls; 'the man alien to our race' or 'Lawless One' (Pompey) in *Ps. Sol.* 17.7–14.
11 'The disciple whom Jesus loved' always appears with the masculine form of the noun for 'disciple' (*mathētēs*), and the masculine forms of the definite article (*ho*) and relative pronoun (*hon*). Other masculine forms used to describe this figure are *ekeinos*, 'that', and *allos*, 'other', and the participle *parestōta*, 'standing'. Schneiders tries to get round this by claiming that *mathētēs* is 'a happily ambiguous term, which in Greek is female [*sic*] in form' (1999, p. 220); but this is untrue. *Mathētēs* is a masculine noun of the a-stem (first) declension, analogous to other words of similar type (e.g. *stratiōtēs*, 'soldier', *prophētēs*, 'prophet'). When used in the plural, it can stand collectively for both men and women disciples; but in the singular it would have been understood as denoting a male.
12 Greek *sophia*, 'wisdom', is a feminine noun, and was sometimes personified in Jewish literature as a woman. But there is no evidence that John perceived it as a specially 'feminine' term (it never appears in his Gospel). See further Ch. 9.
13 Berkowitz and Squitier (1990) give only a tiny handful of women among over 3,000 male authors. Most female authors were lyric poets (notably Sappho, Corinna, and Erinna). The Neo-Pythagorean treatise *Perictione* and the *Gospel of Mary* (3rd–5th cent. CE) have sometimes been ascribed to women, but were probably composed by men in the *persona* of a woman.

4 Traditions, Sources, and the Nature of John's Writing

1 See VanderKam (2001); Wintermute, in Charlesworth (1985 pp. 35–142), with English translation of *Jubilees*; Carson and Williamson (1988, esp. ch. 7), with further examples of Jewish rewriting of scriptural texts.
2 On the Gospel genre, see Burridge (1992). Although the Gospels share qualities with ancient *Bioi*, 'Lives', it must be stressed that they are not biographies in the modern sense. They are documents designed to promote faith (and this applies to non-canonical as well as canonical Gospels).
3 The parallel in Mk 16.14–18 is an addition to the original text.
4 For this conclusion compare Barrett (1955, 1978); Kümmel (1975, pp. 202f.); Neirynck (1977), with further references; for arguments that John knew Matthew, see Brodie (1993a, esp. ch. 7). John's independence of the Synoptics is maintained by Dodd (1963), Morris (1972), and Smalley (1978, 1998). Brown (1966) mostly supports independence, but postulates cross-influence from Lucan traditions; Lindars (1972) acknowledges familiarity with 'the Synoptic tradition', and the possibility of common sources with the Synoptics.
5 Talbert (1992, pp. 267–74), though not all of his parallels are equally convincing.
6 The identification of these sayings is a complex task. Indicators are vocabulary and other characteristics of Jesus' Synoptic speech style. Thus 3.3, 5 may be a

radicalization of the saying in Mt. 18.3 (par. Mk 10.15; Lk. 18.17): 'Unless you turn and become like children, you will never enter the Kingdom of Heaven'. This is one of the rare cases where Matthew has the closest Synoptic parallel; it is the only occurrence in John of 'the kingdom of God/heaven' (so frequent in the Synoptics). The use of *amēn* to preface a saying (doubled in John) may be a characteristic of Jesus' own speech (Jeremias, 1971, pp. 35f.). But John's version is unlikely to be authentic as it stands, since it involves a pun dependent on Greek, rather than Aramaic, usage. See further Lindars (1981, pp. 84–7).

7 Though especially associated with Bultmann (1941; 1959; 1971), this hypothesis originated earlier (Ashton, 1991, p. 33; van Belle, 1994, ch.1); for some recent theories see Fortna (1970); Becker (1970); Nicol (1972).

8 The same applies to Jesus' Bread of Life discourse following the feeding miracle in Jn 6, and the conflicts with the Jewish authorities arising from the healings of the lame man and the man born blind (5.2–9; 9.1–12).

9 Ruckstuhl (1977, pp. 132–41); van Belle (1994, p. 374 with n. 37).

10 Literally 'divine man', a controversial term much overused in New Testament scholarship; see Blackburn (1991).

11 Thus, at Cana Jesus' disciples 'believe' in him after he has revealed his glory (2.11), whereas Nicodemus is rebuffed when he speaks positively of Jesus' 'signs' (3.1–3).

12 Jn 4.54 is not actually inconsistent with 2.23 and 3.2. It says that this is the second sign that Jesus did after he had come from Judaea to Galilee, not that it was the second sign he did altogether.

13 The phrase 'for the third time' (21.14) refers to Jesus' resurrection appearances and not the number of the miracle, which is not even called a 'sign'.

14 Some have defended a historical basis for both these episodes.

5 Purpose, Audience, Place and Date of Composition

1 Or the 'messiah' as Jesus: see Carson (1987, 1991, pp. 662f.).

2 The word translated 'believe', *pisteu[s]ēte*, occurs in two different forms in the manuscripts, and could mean either 'come to believe' or 'continue to believe'; but John's intention cannot be determined by tense alone.

3 LSJ, p. 2007. Pagans sometimes understood *christos* as a proper name, interpreting it as *chrēstos*, 'useful', pronounced almost identically (Bauer, 1979, p. 887).

4 Freed (1970) proposed that John was aimed partly at Samaritan converts, to whom the episode of the Samaritan woman (4.1–42) would obviously appeal. Brown (1979) thought that Samaritans formed a significant element in John's 'community' and influenced his christology. However, John's knowledge of Samaritan theology has been over-estimated (see Ch. 7).

5 The idea that the *Hellēnes* were Gentiles is refuted by the fact that they were in Jerusalem to worship at Passover; but they could have included proselytes and God-fearers.

6 Only Jn 1.1, 14 uses *logos* absolutely of Jesus; 1 Jn 1.1–4 speaks of 'the word of life' (which could mean 'the preached Gospel'); Rev. 19.13 depicts 'the Word of God' as an apocalyptic horseman, called 'Faithful and True', leading the heavenly armies.

7 These traits include redundant pronouns, a limited range of connecting particles with overuse of 'and' (features of Aramaic and Hebrew); sentences of fixed patterns; and a narrow vocabulary with repetition of favoured words (Turner, 1976, pp. 64–79, 132–8).

8 John does, however, refer to future judgement and future resurrection (e.g. 5.28f.; 6.39f.); 1 Jn 2.18, etc. and 2 Jn 7 both refer to the 'Antichrist' (expected in the last days), and 1 Jn 3.2 mentions Jesus' future 'appearance'.

9 Turner (1976, pp. 150–4); Thompson (1985); see also Aune (1997–8, vol. 1, pp. clx–ccvii).

10 They are formally letters from the presbyter (not further identified) to 'an Elect Lady', either a personified congregation or a female Church leader, and Gaius, presumably a house-church leader.

11 So Ashton (1991, 195f.), arguing that evidence is lacking for a single founder and leading teacher (he does not consider that the 'beloved disciple' fits this role).

12 Cf. above, Ch. 2, n. 10. See further Culpepper (1975); Smith (1976); Segovia (1981); Rensberger (1988; 1998). In British popular usage 'sect' denotes a religious group viewed as separate from the mainstream Church. In North America, 'sect' is often used in a technical sense for an exclusive group that sees itself as separated from society and holds negative views of the world.

13 Cf. Carson (1991, p. 88). The relationship of Johannine and Pauline theology has been neglected, though note Barrett (1978, pp. 54–9) and Brodie (1993a, ch. 12). McGrath (2001) cites much Pauline material, but does not tackle the complex questions of authenticity, dating, and evidence for and against literary dependency.

14 Possible 'Semitizing' features include redundant pronouns (e.g. 13.26); frequent use of the *casus pendens*, where a hanging phrase is picked up by a pronoun later in the sentence (e.g. 3.26; 10.1); third-person impersonal verbs (e.g. 15.6); and expressions like 'to come for a witness' (1.7); 'to do the truth' (3.21); 'to believe on' (*pisteuō eis*, occurring *c.* 33 times); 'answered and said' (over 30 times), 'walk' in the sense of 'behave' (e.g. 8.12); and *thalassa*, 'sea', for lake (21.1). There are also double meanings dependent on Aramaic (e.g. *hypsoō*, meaning both 'lift up' and 'crucify'). See further Brown (1964); Turner (1976, pp. 64–79); Barrett (1978, pp. 8–11); Martin (1989); also Colwell (1931), with criticisms of earlier work on Aramaisms.

15 Ephesus is only one of seven Asiatic cities featuring in Revelation (on which see Hemer, 1986); apart from tradition there is no more reason to link it with John than, say, Pergamon many miles to the north. There were numerous Pauline churches in the Ephesus area.

16 First Cairo Geniza form (Horbury, 1998b, p. 68).

17 A general 'curse' is quite different from a prayer which some Jewish-Christians would find hard to say (this Synagogue prayer was recited only by free, male Jews).

18 Martyn (1979, pp. 54f., with n. 69) himself conceded that he had dated the *birkat* too early, but not before his arguments had profoundly influenced Johannine scholarship. On the *birkat* see further Kimelman (1981); Horbury (1982, 1998b, pp. 1 14); Katz (1984); Smith (1995, p. 55); Reinhartz (1998).

6 Jesus' Miracles as Narrative Theology

1 *Erga* includes other actions beside miracles; in the singular it generally denotes Jesus' whole mission, culminating in the cross (Moloney, 1996, p. 22, n. 97). See further Ensor (1996).

2 An early second-century Syriac text, based on earlier Greek and Hebrew versions (Charlesworth, 1983, pp. 616f.).

3 Mt. 22.1–14; 25.1–13; Lk. 14.15–24; cf. Mk 14.25 par.; also the image of Jesus as bridegroom: Jn 3.29; Rev. 19.7–9; etc.

4 Jewish readers might see a link with God's revelation of his glory on Mount Sinai 'on the third day' (Ex. 19.16): cf. Moloney (1993, pp. 83f., 91).

5 So Eve (2002, p. 289, n. 39), who sees Hanina as praying for a miracle rather than actually performing one. The Babylonian Talmud is generally dated to *c.* 600 CE.

6 Taylor (1966, pp. 219f.) cites rabbinic parallels, including Simeon ben Menasya's

saying, 'The Sabbath is delivered to you; you are not delivered to the Sabbath'.

7   Cullmann (1953, pp. 84–8), following various Church Fathers, takes it as alluding to baptism; but the man never enters the water, nor does he show the characteristics of a newly committed Christian.

8   The Galilaean setting causes problems, because John nowhere mentions when Jesus returned from Jerusalem (the scene of the last miracle). Some critics transpose Jn 5 and 6, so that Jn 6 follows immediately after 4.54, when Jesus returns from Judaea to Galilee. This may, however, be 'improving' on John.

9   Jewish texts attest the expectation of a second outpouring of manna in the last days, e.g. 2 Bar. 29.8 (almost contemporary with John); also the later Midr. Rabbah Eccles 1.9, Mekhilta on Ex. 16.25, and other texts cited in Odeberg (1929, pp. 242–7); Brown (1966, pp. 265f.); Barrett (1978, 288f.).

10 'Typological' interpretation means seeing scriptural sayings and events as foreshadowing future realities.

11 Bultmann (1971, pp. 234f.), who thought John uninterested in sacraments, or even anti-sacramentarian, attributed 6.51c–8 to an editor; others find these verses essential to Jn 6's structure, which may reflect a synagogue sermon (Borgen, 1965; see further Culpepper, 1997). The style is Johannine, and the multivalent imagery consistent with John's writing elsewhere.

12 Cf. Odeberg (1929, pp. 238–42), citing texts including Mekhilta on Ex. 13.18, '"And God led the people about (through the way of the wilderness of the Red Sea)" in order to do signs and mighty deeds through the manna, the quails, and the well.'

13 Spittle was believed to have curative powers; the emperor Vespasian reputedly used it to restore a blind man's sight (Suetonius, Vesp. 7).

14 Some manuscripts read 'Son of God'; but 'Son of Man' is better attested (Metzger, 1971, pp. 228f.).

15 Cf. Stephen's martyrdom and ensuing persecution (Acts 6.9—8.3); Peter's imprisonment following the killing of James, son of Zebedee (12.1–3); and attempts on Paul's life (e.g. 14.19).

16 Brown (1966, p. 1098) sees it as the 'dramatic equivalent' of Matthew's Great Commission (28.19f.).

7 Christological Confessions and Titles for Jesus

1   'Title' is used here in a general sense to include designations, modes of address, and ways of describing Jesus.

2   Rabbi, literally 'my great one' (cf. Hebrew rab, 'great', 'chief'), appears, along with rab and rabban, as a title for teachers in Jewish inscriptions (late 1st–2nd cent. CE) and in the Mishnah (Lohse, 1968, pp. 961–3). It is sometimes seen as anachronistic in Jesus' ministry, but note Albright (1956, pp. 157f.). In Mt. 23.7f. Jesus forbids his disciples to be addressed as 'Rabbi'.

3   Ribboni occurs for God in Jewish literature (Dalman, 1902, p. 325), including the Targum Onkelos (possibly authorized in Babylon, 3rd–5th cent. CE); anyone familiar with this usage could therefore understand rabboni as a divine name. In the Palestinian Targum (Neophyti 1) rabbuni is applied to human beings (Brown, 1966, p. 991). The dating of these Targums, their dependence on earlier oral materials, and the extent to which they were known in Palestine, are uncertain. The spelling variations are unimportant, since the original texts were unvocalized.

4   The Greek could mean either 'a' prophet or 'the' prophet, but the context supports an indefinite understanding; so too in 9.17.

5   Theoretically 'the Prophet' could refer to Elijah, whose return was expected in the end-time (Mal. 3.1–4; 4.5f.; Ecclus 48, esp. 48.10), but John has already distinguished these two (1.21).

6   John himself distinguishes 'the Prophet' from 'the Christ' in 1.19–25; 7.40f.
7   Horsley (1984), however, makes a sharp sociological distinction between popular movements led by 'kings' and those led by 'prophets'.
8   4Q 161, frs 8–10; 4Q 285, fr. 5 (both citing Isa. 11.1); 4Q 174 (4QFlor.), I.10–14 (citing 2 Sam. 7.11); Vermes (1998, pp. 467, 189, 493f.). The Hebrew text can be found in Lohse (1981); Martínez (1996) gives an alternative English translation.
9   These chapters come from the 'Similitudes' (or 'Parables'), whose dating is disputed: they are widely believed to stem from a Jewish work from around the late first century CE (Isaac, in Charlesworth, 1983, pp. 5–7; cf. Nickelsburg, 1981, pp. 221–3). 1 Enoch (Ethiopic Enoch) is a composite work whose manuscripts date to the fifteenth century, but with much earlier Greek and Aramaic fragments; parts of 11 different copies were found at Qumran (though none include the 'Similitudes').
10 In the Synoptics, 'God's Holy One' occurs on the lips of the demon-possessed, who display an uncanny awareness of Jesus' identity (Mk 1.24; Lk. 4.34); it is quite gratuitous, however, to suppose that John wished to align Peter with Satan here.
11 Some manuscripts of Jn 1.34 (including some early witnesses) have 'God's Elect One' (ho eklektos tou theou) instead of 'God's Son' (cf. NEB, NJB). This too could be messianic (cf. e.g. 1 En. 39.6), though 'Elect' is also applied to Moses, Jacob, David, and the Isaianic 'Servant' (cf. Isa. 42.1). On this reading, the Proem never uses the same title for Jesus more than once ('God's Son' occurs in 1.49). However, 'God's Son' is found in early witnesses and may well be right (cf. Aland et al., 1993; RSV; GNB).
12 The woman's reference to 'messiah (who is called Christ)' who 'will disclose all things' (4.25) has been seen as alluding to the Samaritan Taheb, 'he who returns', expected to reveal truth (cf. Schnackenburg, 1968, p. 441). But the source for this belief, the Tibat Marqe or Memar Marqar (IV.12), is no earlier than the fourth century CE, and may be later; the term 'messiah' does not occur in ancient Samaritan theology (Williams, 2000, pp. 258f. with n. 14). On the Taheb's supposed identification with the 'prophet like Moses' see also Moloney (1998b, pp. 133f.).
13 The function of the Passover lamb was originally apotropaic (to ward off evil), but by Jesus' time it had become associated with sacrifice. In Palestine it was slain by the Temple priests; cf. Brown (1966, p. 62).
14 Others have seen allusions to the ram substituted for Isaac (Gen. 22); the scapegoat, driven into the wilderness to bear people's sins (Lev. 16.21f.; in Hebrew the same word means both 'lamb' and 'kid'); or Jeremiah's description of himself being led to the slaughter like a gentle lamb (11.19). See further Barrett (1978, pp. 176f.); Carson (1991, p. 176).
15 The phrase also appears in 6.27, 53, where Jesus speaks of the Son of Man giving people lasting food and of the need to eat his 'flesh', and in the dialogue with the newly sighted man. Here Jesus asks him if he believes in the Son of Man, but the man does not know who this is; Jesus clarifies that he means himself, and the man expresses his faith in him (9.35–8).
16 See Borsch (1970, pp. 78–83) on the Gospel of Philip; Dodd (1953, pp. 69–73, 109–12, 241–4) on the Hermetica, Philo's concept of a 'heavenly man' representing ideal humanity, and various Gnostic ideas; also Schnackenburg (1968, pp. 538–62).
17 Malina and Rohrbaugh (1998, pp. 57, 62–4), are so taken with the 'heavenly' character of John's Son of Man that they suggest it should be translated 'Sky Man', seeing the phrase as part of what they call John's 'antilanguage', intelligible only to insiders. But this exaggerates the phrase's obscurity and over-emphasizes one aspect of the Son of Man's functions in John.

18 Some think *ho anthrōpos* here may be intended messianically, e.g. Brown (1966, p. 876), citing Zech. 6.12 LXX, 'Behold the man [*idou anēr*] whose name is Branch', and Num. 24.17 LXX, 'a star shall rise from Jacob and a man [*anthrōpos*] shall arise from Israel' (both 'messianic' texts).

19 See further Hurtado (1998), and the standard works on New Testament christology. Bultmann (1955, p. 36) mistakenly says that 'the Kyrios-title is completely missing' in John.

8 Jesus' Passion and Resurrection

1 So Bernard (1928, p. 641) and many other commentators. It is most improbable that these words denote a release of the Spirit to the disciples.

2 On the shame of crucifixion, see Hengel (1986, pp. 93–102).

3 John may be working from both the Hebrew and the Septuagint.

4 In 12.38 John's quotation corresponds exactly to the Septuagint; in 12.40 it is nearer the Hebrew, which it abbreviates. In the Targum on Isa. 6.5, the prophet sees 'the glory of the *shekinah* [presence] of the King of the Ages', rather than God himself – an interpretation which may have influenced John. See further Barrett (1978, p. 432); Hanson (1991, pp. 170, 217f.); Bauckham (1998a, pp. 49f.); Williams (2000, pp. 300f.).

5 This is the only place, apart from 21.14, where John uses the passive to describe Jesus' resurrection (contrast Mk 14.28 par.; 16.6 par.; Rom. 6.4, 9; 1 Cor. 15.4).

6 John most often uses *hypagō* in this sense; less frequently *anabainō, erchomai* and *poreuomai*; occasionally *aperchomai* and *metabainō*; details in Nicholson (1983, p. 58).

7 Bultmann (1955, p. 39) sees all these references to future eschatology as ecclesiastical editing; but this is a 'desperate expedient' (Ladd, 1982, p. 137).

8 Lk. 24.50f., however, mentions no time-interval, nor does Mt. 28.16–20 (Mk 16.19 is part of an addition to the text).

9 So Aland (1993), but many manuscripts add 'who is in heaven' (cf. AV), which may well be original (Barrett, 1978, p. 213; Beasley-Murray, 1987, p. 45). Presumably the scribes who omitted it did so because they found the idea of Jesus being both in heaven and on earth too difficult; but in 1.18 the Word, just described as incarnate, is also said to be 'in the Father's bosom'.

10 The clearest example of a sacrificial understanding is probably Mark's use of *lutron* (cognate with *lutroō, lutrōsis*) in his 'ransom' saying (10.45; cf. Mt. 20.28). Luke lacks this, but note 1.68; 2.38; 24.21.

11 In Lk. 24.12 (only in some manuscripts) Peter goes to the tomb and sees the linen bandages (*othonia*) lying: this use of *othonia*, rather than *sindōn*, strongly suggests contact with the Johannine tradition.

12 Bultmann (1971, p. 691 with n. 2) cites classical parallels, including *h.Hom.*, IV.145–9, where the god Hermes passes through a keyhole. In Luke (24.31, 36) Jesus mysteriously disappears and reappears, but there is no mention of closed doors.

13 The authentic text ends with the words, 'For they were afraid' (Mk 16.8). Recent scholars argue that this abrupt conclusion (*ephobounto gar*, ending with a weak conjunction) is deliberate; but there is much to be said for the older view that Mark intended to describe some resurrection appearances (cf. 14.28; 16.7, 'he is going before you to Galilee and you will see him there').

14 Many scholars consider that 1 Cor. 15.5–8 contains older and more reliable traditions than the Gospel stories of an empty tomb; others argue that the women's witness is not likely to be invented. On the resurrection, see further Fuller (1972); Ladd (1975); Lindars (1986); Carnley (1987); D'Costa (1996). On Jesus' trials see Légasse (1997); and, in more detail, Brown (1994, pp. 311–877).

15 It is odd that John, if he felt so free to modify the Jesus tradition as many scholars

maintain, did not incorporate any post-resurrection revelatory discourses of the sort favoured by Gnostics, e.g. the *Gospel of Mary* (see Robinson, 1977, pp. 470–8).

9 Jesus: Word Incarnate and Father's Son

1 The phrase 'turned toward' over-interprets *pros*, which John uses in its Hellenistic sense of 'with' (Schnackenburg, 1968, p. 234); cf. Mk 6.3; Mt. 26.18; etc.

2 Burney (1922, pp. 40–2) reconstructed the whole Prologue in Aramaic, with verse and prose sections. Though impressive, his work has not met with widespread acceptance.

3 E.g. the Qumran *Hymns* (Vermes, 1998, pp. 243–300) and the *Odes of Solomon* (Charlesworth, 1985, pp. 725–71, ascribing them to a late 1st or early 2nd cent. Jewish-Christian group, from the same area as John's 'community'). The *Odes* could, however, be partially dependent on John.

4 For further arguments against a pre-Johannine 'hymn', see Barrett (1971); Brodie (1993b, pp. 133f.); Boyarin (2001, esp. pp. 262–7).

5 Accepting the traditional punctuation of 1.3f. (cf. AV, RSV, NIV); for a different view, see NEB, NJB, GNB (all with peculiar translations). The commentators are similarly divided.

6 This passage probably influenced Rev. 19.11–16, where the 'Word of God', riding on a white horse, 'judges and makes war'. But in John's Prologue the image is creative rather than military or destructive.

7 Etheridge (1862, p. 19) noted over 150 examples of *memra* in periphrases for God in the Targum Onkelos alone.

8 See above, Ch. 7, n. 3. Apart from a few fragments from Qumran, the surviving manuscripts are all substantially later than John; but influence on him cannot be excluded, since the Targums may embody older traditions.

9 See further Burney (1922); McNamara (1968, pp. 102–6); Morris (1972, pp. 119f.); Young (1988, p. 733); Boyarin (2001) – all linking John's *logos* in some way with *memra*.

10 In Gnosticism the Redeemer clothes himself in human form to disguise himself from the evil powers (Bultmann, 1971, p. 61, n. 1); see further Schnackenburg (1968, pp. 543–57). There are some parallels in the *Odes of Solomon*, notably 12.12: 'For the dwelling-place of the Word is man, and his truth is love' (Charlesworth, 1985, p. 747); but 'man' is here generic rather than denoting a specific individual. In any case the *Odes* are probably a Christian composition, potentially influenced by John.

11 Attempts to find the Virgin Birth in 1.13, by reading 'who *was* born ...' (with a singular for the plural), are mistaken. This reading (adopted by JB) is not found in the Greek manuscripts, and appears to be an early interpretation of the Latin Church.

12 *Doxa* is also used of God's glory manifested at Jesus' birth (Lk. 2.9), and of Jesus' glory at his transfiguration (Lk. 9.32) and resurrection (e.g. Rom. 6.4; cf. Heb. 2.9), and at his coming as judge (e.g. Mk 8.38; Mt. 24.30).

13 So, for example, Brodie (1993b, p. 143). The link between *charis* and *ḥesed* has been disputed because *charis* in the Septuagint usually renders Hebrew *ḥen*, 'favour'. But in later Hebrew *ḥen* and *ḥesed* converged in meaning (Conzelmann and Zimmerli, 1974, p. 381), with *charis* replacing *eleos*, 'mercy', as a translation of *ḥesed* (Dodd, 1963, p. 175). The Septuagint shows awareness of *'ĕmet*'s range of meanings by translating it as *dikaiosynē*, 'righteousness', and *pistis*, 'faith', as well as by *alētheia*, 'truth'.

14 An alternative is to read, with some ancient versions, *monogenēs* alone, without either *theos* or *huios*, but the external attestation for this is weak.

15 E.g. Brown (1966, p. 13); Beasley-Murray (1987, p. 14); cf. Moody (1953).

16 From *monos*, 'only', 'alone', and either *genesthai*, 'become', 'be born', or *genos*, 'race', 'stock', 'offspring', 'kin', 'kind'.

17 The Septuagint also uses *monogenēs* to render Hebrew *yaḥid*, 'precious', and of wisdom (Wisd. 7.22), probably in the sense of 'unique'.

18 *Alēthinos*, used in 'the true light' (1.9), later often stands for what is real, e.g. 6.32, 'the true bread from heaven', 15.1, 'the true vine'; but it may also describe what is reliable (e.g. 8.16; 19.35; cf. Hebrew *'ĕmet*, discussed above, p. 94). It is often hard to determine the precise denotation: when God is described as 'true' (7.28; 17.3), does this mean he is the 'real' God, as opposed to false gods, or the God who can be relied upon? *Alētheia* is later sometimes used in an abstract way (e.g. 18.38); but it often relates to God's saving revelation in Jesus and the gospel (8.32, 44; 14.6; 17.17, 19).

10 Characters in John's Story

1 See further Collins (1976, pp. 118–20); Klassem (1996, esp. ch. 8). For Culpepper (1983, p. 125), Judas is 'the representative defector'; but John nowhere indicates that he represents other defectors.

2 'Simon Peter', 17 times; 'Peter', 17; 'Simon, son of John', 4; 'Simon', 1.

3 See further Brown (1973, pp. 129–47); Barrett (1982, pp. 159–67), both suggesting that Peter and the 'beloved disciple' represent different types of discipleship; Perkins (2000, pp. 95–103), stressing Peter's weaknesses.

4 See Edwards (1996b, p. 135), citing the First Vatican Council of 1870; also ARCIC (1982, pp. 64–7).

5 Cf. the promises to prepare a place for them; the warnings of persecution; promises of answered prayer and future joy.

6 Some major manuscripts omit 9.38–9a (referring to the prostration), but its authenticity is defended by many scholars (e.g. Metzger, 1971, p. 229; Schnackenburg, 1980, p. 499 n. 51). The verb *proskyneō* can mean either 'do obeisance' or 'worship' (Bauckham, 1993a, pp. 122–49). On the reading 'Son of Man', see above, Ch. 6, n. 14.

7 John's Nicodemus, though often assumed to be a literary fiction, may be based on a real person: Bauckham (1996) argues that he was a member of a rich and prominent Jerusalem family, and related to Naqdimon ben Gurion (known from independent Jewish sources).

8 Full text in Fogle (1965, pp. 323–5). Kermode (1986, pp. 33f.) cites this poem as an example of acceptable misinterpretation.

9 In fact, most of the major commentators are quite cautious. Barrett (1978) makes no judgment; Brown (1966, p. 175) quotes Lagrange's odd characterization of the Samaritan as 'mincing and coy, with a certain light grace', but he also recognizes her role as a missionary and her 'quasi-apostolic function' (1979, pp. 188f.). Schnackenburg (1968, pp. 432f.) refers to her 'sinful way of life' and 'guilt' (in connection with her sexual history), but he also sees her as having 'religious questings and yearnings'.

10 As noted by Bernard (1928, vol. 1, p. 144); the allegorical interpretation is likewise rejected by Bultmann, Brown, Schnackenburg, Beasley-Murray, and Haenchen.

11 So Schnackenburg (1980, pp. 332f.); Fiorenza (1983, p. 329); Edwards (1989, p. 45); Scott (1992, pp. 202–6).

12 The difference is that Mary falls 'at his feet', whereas those arresting Jesus fall 'to the ground'.

13 Or three if Mary of Klopas is the same person as Jesus' mother's sister: the Greek is ambiguous.

14 The only grounds for understanding Mary symbolically as the Church are Jesus'

address to her as 'woman' (2.4; 19.26; cf. Rev. 12.1–6), John's failure to name her, and a long tradition of Catholic exegesis. But none of these arguments is compelling: see Beasley-Murray (1987, pp. 349f.); Aune (1997–98, vol. 2, 680). On Mary in the New Testament, see further McHugh (1975, pp. 361–432); Brown (1978); Culpepper (1983, pp. 133f.); Carson (1991, pp. 616–18).

15 Citing Rom. 11.25, 28–31 and 2 Cor. 3.12–18 for the image of Israel as 'temporarily blind' and 'veiled in mind', but eventually receiving mercy. Rom. 11.25, however, refers to Israel's *pōrōsis*, 'hardening', not blindness (which appears in the Vulgate).

16 *pros hautous/autous*; see Lindars (1972, p. 603); Fitzmyer (1985, p. 1548) on Lk. 24.13.

17 E.g. Fitzmyer (1981, p. 688); Thompson (1995, esp. pp. 4f.). See also de Boer (1997, pp. 2–9) on changes in the Roman Missal effectively acknowledging the scholarly consensus. The identification was accepted by Bernard (1928, p. 412), and still influences some interpretations of Mary (e.g. Fehribach, 1998, pp. 144–67).

18 Space precludes discussion of Pilate's character in John. Many interpret him as representing the State or the power of Rome (cf. Rensberger, 1988, p. 98, 'a cruel advocate' of Caesar's kingship). Brown (1966, p. 864) sees him as typical of 'the many honest, well-disposed men that would try to adopt a middle position in a struggle that is total'. On the historical Pilate, see Bond (1998, esp. pp. 174–93).

19 Modern literary critics debate whether characters have 'functional' or 'mimetic' roles: see Conway (1999, pp. 50–8), with some conclusions on John's characters.

11 'Anti-Semitism'/'Anti-Judaism' in John's Gospel?

1 On these terms, see Keith (1997, pp. 2–4); Rensberger (1999, p. 120); Schoon (2001, p. 145).

2 The term *Ioudaioi* is very common in Acts, over 70 times: see Gutbrod in von Rad (1965, pp. 379f.); Gasque (1982); in more detail, Sanders (1987, esp. ch. 7).

3 These figures exclude the masculine singular *Ioudaios*, and the feminine singular *Ioudaia*, 'Judaea', as a geographical term (with or without *gē/chōra*, 'land').

4 The Gospel writers generally distinguish Judaea in the south (the territory round Jerusalem, comprising what was once 'Judah') from Samaria and Galilee in the north; but the term is sometimes used in a wider sense to include Samaria and even Galilee (e.g. Lk. 4.44).

5 E.g. Thyen (1980, pp. 179f.); Ashton (1991, p. 158), tracing the term 'Torah-fanatic' to Bornhäuser (1928, p. 141).

6 Cf. Lindars (1990, p. 16); Smith (1995, p. 56); Kelber (1996, p. 132).

7 Sometimes 'his own' in 13.1 is interpreted exclusively of the disciples; but Lindars (1972, p. 448) is surely right to identify them as Jesus' 'own sheep' (10.3f.), i.e. all believers, whom the disciples represent at the Last Supper.

8 There was only one *archiereus*, 'Chief' or 'High Priest'. But the term was used also for former High Priests, like the deposed Annas, and, in the plural, for senior members of the Jewish establishment, who were prominent members of the Sanhedrin, over which the High Priest presided (Jeremias, 1969, pp. 147–81).

9 Also translated 'lawsuit', 'charge', 'accusation'; the root means 'strive' or 'contend'.

10 The text is obscure: there is no word for 'your'; grammatically the phrase could mean 'the devil's father', as some Gnostics took it (assuming a reference to the Demiurge). See further Bultmann (1971, pp. 318–20); Beasley-Murray (1987, p. 135); Motyer (1997, pp. 184f.).

11 Many scholars consider the Synoptic depiction of these groups to be distorted: see Beare (1981, pp. 447–61) on Mt. 23; on Pharisees, see further Jeremias (1969, pp. 246–67); Sanders (1992, pp. 380–451); Westerholm (1992).

12 The Nazis sought to suppress 4.22b as pro-Jewish: see van Belle (in Bieringer *et al.* (2001)), esp. pp. 394–8).

13 It is sometimes hard to determine when uses are 'positive', 'neutral', or 'negative', as study of scholarly discussions shows.

12 'Replacement Theology' and Jewish Monotheism

1 On the definition of 'Jewishness', see Casey (1991), who draws up eight 'identity-markers' (mostly ritual-based, but including monotheism), with Dunn's critique (1994, pp. 439–52); Wright (1992, pp. 244–79), based mostly on beliefs; Sanders (1992), covering both practice and belief.

2 Akiba: 'You shall love your neighbour as yourself; this is the greatest principle in Torah'; Hillel: 'What is hateful to yourself, do not do to your neighbour: this is the whole Torah; the rest is commentary' (see Taylor, 1966, p. 487; Hooker, 1991, p. 288).

3 It is sometimes argued that Jesus has a 'Gentile' perspective when he refers to 'your Law' rather than 'our Law' (8.17; 10.34; cf. 15.25, 'their Law'). But the usage may be dictated by literary context: Jesus distances himself from religious leaders who made much of the Law's prescriptions but failed to keep its more radical demands.

4 Contrast the word-play in Phil. 3.2f., paralleling it with *katatomē*, 'mutilation'.

5 Attendance was officially obligatory for Jewish males, but it was impossible for all to attend every year. John does not say that Jesus failed to attend, but only that he was in Galilee when the Passover feast was 'near' (*engus*).

6 Commemorating Judas Maccabaeus' re-dedication of the Temple in 164 BCE after its desecration by Antiochus Epiphanes (1 Macc. 4.52–9).

7 Moreover, John says nothing about Pentecost, a 'feast of obligation' for men, or the Day of Atonement (with its possibilities for Christian reinterpretation).

8 Some were unhappy about the contemporary hierarchy (e.g. the Qumran covenanters). Casey does not include 'Temple' among his eight criteria for Jewishness (1991, ch. 2; 1996, ch. 7).

9 Compare Tobias' hopes for a rebuilt Temple to which the nations will come, truly 'fearing' God, and all who love God will rejoice 'in truth and righteousness' (Tob. 14.5–7).

10 Or, 'I am what [or that] I am' or 'I shall be who [or what or that] I shall be'.

11 When Ex. 3.14b refers back to the Name revealed to Moses, it uses the formula *ho ōn*, not *egō eimi*. The Mishnah confines 'blasphemy' to uttering the Divine Name (*mSanh.* 7.5); but before this it seems to have been understood more widely (Williams, 2000, pp. 247f.).

12 This is probably not for purely grammatical reasons (following 'Colwell's law', 1933, that, in the New Testament, complements preceding verbs usually drop the article); see Harris (1992, pp. 59–70).

13 In the *Prayer of Joseph*, frag. A (known from Origen), the angel Israel is said by Uriel to have descended to earth and tabernacled (*kataskēnoō*) among human beings; but the text is obscure, almost certainly later than John, and may be anti-Christian polemic.

14 On Jewish monotheism, see further Hayman (1991); Barker (1992) with Adler (1993) and Hurtado (1993); Gnuse (1997); Horbury (1998a).

13 Conclusions: The Value of John's Gospel Today

1 E.g. the historians Herodotus, Thucydides, Polybius, and Livy; Plato and Xenophon in their presentations of Socrates; the biographers Diogenes Laertius, Plutarch, and Suetonius.

2 E.g. Mk 13.12f.; Mt. 10.16–23; 24.9; Lk. 21.12–17; cf. Mt. 5.10f.; Lk. 6.22f.

3 Cf. the Synoptic ('Q') images of the 'narrow gate' and 'broad path to destruction'

(Mt. 7.13f. par.), and the two house-builders (Mt. 7.24–7 par.), and similar stark choices in James, the *Didache*, Paul's teaching, and Stoic ethics.

4 Cf. the negative uses of 'the/this world' in 1 Cor. 1.21; Jas 1.27; 2 Pet. 2.20; 1 Jn 2.15–17; 4.4f.; 5.19; etc.; also 'this generation' (Mk 8.12 par., 38; Mt. 12.42; etc.) and 'this age' (Rom. 12.2; 1 Cor. 1.20; etc.).

5 E.g. Ringe (1999); Ford (1997, esp. p. 111), seeing the incarnation as 'God's supreme act of friendship'.

6 E.g. Gruenler (1986). In Greek *pneuma* is neuter, and the Synoptic Gospels tend to speak of the Spirit impersonally, as does John for the most part. But in the Supper Discourses (14.26b; 15. 26b; 16.13f.) he uses masculine pronouns with reference to *paraklētos* (a masculine noun), encouraging readers to think about the Spirit more personally. In Hebrew 'Spirit' (*ruaḥ*) is usually feminine, and some modern critics regret the loss of Spirit as a potentially female image.

7 Cf. Dunn (1977); Haight (1999, ch. 6). On the Gospel portraits of Jesus, see Burridge (1994); Hedrick (1999); Marsh and Moyise (1999); Weren (1999).

Bibliography

Selected Primary Sources
For authors not cited below, see Easterling and Knox (1985) and Kenney and Clausen (1982) for classical writers; Charlesworth (1983, 1985) for Jewish Pseudepigrapha; Williams (2000, pp. 311–18) for other Jewish sources; Cross and Livingstone (1997) for Christian writers.

Apostolic Fathers, see Lightfoot (1891); Lake (1912–13).
Augustine, see *NPNF*; Pine-Coffin (1961).
2 Baruch, see Charlesworth (1983).
Calvin, see Parker (1959, 1961).
Chrysostom, see *NPNF*.
Cyprian, see Bévenot (1971).
Dead Sea Scrolls, see Lohse (1981); Martínez (1996); Vermes (1998).
1 Enoch, see Charlesworth (1983).
Epiphanius, see Dummer (1980).
Eusebius, see Lake and Oulton (1926–32).
4 Ezra (2 Esdras), see Charlesworth (1983).
Hermetica, see Nock and Festugière (1945–54).
Irenaeus, see *ANF*.
Josephus, see Thackeray (1926–65).
Jubilees, see Charlesworth (1985).
Justin, see *ANF*.
Luther, see Pelikan (1957, 1959); Sherman (1971).
Midrash, see Hammer (1995).
Mishnah, see Danby (1933); Neusner (1988).
Nag Hammadi texts, see Robinson (1977).
Odes of Solomon, see Charlesworth (1985).
Origen, see Brooke (1896); Blanc (1966–75).
Philo, see Colson (1929–62); Marcus (1953).
Pirke Aboth, see Danby (1933); Neusner (1988).
Psalms of Solomon, see Ryle and James (1891); Charlesworth (1985).
Septuagint (LXX), see Rahlfs (1935).
Talmud (Babylonian), see Epstein (1948).
Testaments XII Patriarchs, see Charlesworth (1985).
Theophilus of Antioch, see Grant (1970).
Vulgate, see Weber (1983).

Modern Scholarship
Adler, W. (1993), review of Barker (1992), *CBQ* 55, 795–7.
Agourides, S. (1968), 'Peter and John in the Fourth Gospel', *SE* 4, 3–7 = *TU* 102.
Aland, B., *et al.*, eds (1993), *The Greek New Testament*, 4th edn. Stuttgart, Deutsche Bibelgesellschaft, UBS.
Albright, W. F. (1956), 'Recent Discoveries in Palestine and the Gospel of St John', in *The Background of the New Testament and its Eschatology:* Studies in Honour of C. H. Dodd, ed. W. D. Davies and D. Daube, 153–71. Cambridge, Cambridge University Press.
Alter, R., and Kermode, F., eds (1987), *The Literary Guide to the Bible.* Glasgow, Collins/Fontana.
ARCIC [Anglican–Roman Catholic International Commission] (1982), *The Final Report: Windsor, September 1982.* London, SPCK and Catholic Truth Society.

Ashton, J. (1985), 'The Identity and Function of the *Ioudaioi* in the Fourth Gospel', *NovT* 27, 40–75.
——, ed. (1986), *The Interpretation of John*. Philadelphia, Fortress, and London, SPCK.
—— (1991), *Understanding the Fourth Gospel*. Oxford, Clarendon Press.
—— (1998), 'John and the Johannine Literature: The Woman at the Well', in Barton (1998), 259–75.
Asiedu-Peprah, M. (2001), *Johannine Sabbath Conflicts as Juridical Controversy* (*WUNT*, 132). Tübingen, Mohr-Siebeck.
Aune, D. (1988), 'Son of Man', *ISBE* 4, 574–81.
—— (1997–8), *Revelation* (*WBC*), 3 vols. Dallas, Word, and Nashville, Nelson.
Aus, R. (1988), *Water into Wine and the Beheading of John the Baptist* (*Brown Judaic Studies* 150). Atlanta, Scholars Press.
Ball, D. M. (1996), *'I am' in John's Gospel: Literary Function, Background and Theological Implications* (*JSNTSup* 124). Sheffield, Sheffield Academic Press.
Bamford, C. (1990), *The Voice of the Eagle: Homily on the Prologue to the Gospel of St. John – John Scotus Eriugena*. Hudson, NY, Lindisfarne Press, and Edinburgh, Floris Books.
Barclay, J. M. G. (1987), 'Mirror-Reading a Polemical Letter: Galatians as a Test-Case', *JSNT* 31, 73–93.
—— (1996), *Jews in the Mediterranean Diaspora from Alexander to Trajan (323 BCE–117 CE)*. Edinburgh, T. & T. Clark.
Barclay, W. (1956), *The Gospel of John*, 2nd edn (*Daily Study Bible*), 2 vols. Edinburgh, St. Andrew Press.
Barker, M. (1992), *The Great Angel: A Study of Israel's Second God*. London, SPCK.
Barrett, C. K. (1955, 1978), *The Gospel according to St John*, 1st edn. London, SPCK; 2nd edn. Philadelphia, Westminster Press.
—— (1971), *The Prologue of St John's Gospel*. London, Athlone Press.
—— (1975), *The Gospel of John and Judaism*. ET London, SPCK.
—— (1982), *Essays on John*. London, SPCK.
—— (1987), *The New Testament Background: Selected Documents*, 2nd edn. London, SPCK.
Barton, J., ed. (1998), *The Cambridge Companion to Biblical Interpretation*. Cambridge, Cambridge University Press.
Barton, S. (1993), 'The Believer, the Historian and the Fourth Gospel', *Theology* 96, 289–301.
Bassler, J. M. (1989), 'Mixed Signals: Nicodemus in the Fourth Gospel', *JBL* 108, 635–46.
Bauckham, R. (1993a), *The Climax of Prophecy: Studies on the Book of Revelation*. Edinburgh, T&T Clark.
—— (1993b), 'The Beloved Disciple as Ideal Author', *JSNT* 49, 21–44.
—— (1996), 'Nicodemus and the Gurion Family', *JTS* 47, 1–37.
—— (1998a), *God Crucified: Monotheism and Christology in the New Testament*. Grand Rapids and Cambridge, UK, Eerdmans.
——, ed. (1998b), *The Gospels for All Christians: Rethinking the Gospel Audiences*. Grand Rapids, Eerdmans, and Edinburgh, T&T Clark.
Bauer, W. (1957, 1979), *A Greek-English Lexicon of the New Testament*, 4th edn, ed. and tr. W. F. Arndt and F. W. Gingrich; 5th edn rev. F. W. Gingrich and F. W. Danker. Chicago, University of Chicago Press, and Cambridge, Cambridge University Press.
Beare, F. W. (1981), *The Gospel according to Matthew*. San Francisco, *et al.*, Harper & Row.
Beasley-Murray, G. R. (1987), *John* (*WBC*). Waco, Word.
Beck, N. A. (1994), *Mature Christianity in the 21st Century: the Recognition and Repudiation of the Anti-Jewish Polemic of the New Testament*, rev. edn. New York, American Interfaith Institute/World Alliance, Crossroad (orig. edn 1985).

Becker, J. (1970), 'Wunder und Christologie: zum literarkritischen und christologis-chen Problem der Wunder im Johannesevangelium', *NTS* 16, 130–8.

Berger, P. L. and Luckmann, T. (1967), *The Social Construction of Reality*. Harmondsworth, Penguin Books.

Berkowitz, L., and Squitier, K. A. (1990), *Canon of Greek Authors and Works*, 3rd edn (*TLG*). Oxford and New York, Oxford University Press.

Bernard, J. H. (1928), *The Gospel according to St John (ICC)*, 2 vols. Edinburgh, T. & T. Clark.

Bévenot, M., ed. and tr. (1971), *Cyprian*, De Lapsis *and* De Ecclesiae Catholicae Unitate (*Oxford Early Christian Texts*). Oxford, Clarendon Press.

Bieringer, R., *et al.*, eds (2001), *Anti-Judaism and the Fourth Gospel: Papers of the Leuven Colloquium, 2000*. Assen, Royal Van Gorgum.

Black, M. (1967), *An Aramaic Approach to the Gospels and Acts*, 3rd edn. Oxford, Clarendon Press.

Blackburn, B. (1991), *Theios Aner in the Markan Miracle Traditions (WUNT 40)*. Tübingen, Mohr-Siebeck.

Blanc, C., ed. (1966–75), *Commentaire sur Saint Jean*, vols 1–3 (*Sources Chrétiennes* 120, 157, 222). Paris, Éditions du Cerf.

Boer, E. (1997), *Mary Magdalene – Beyond the Myth*. London, SCM Press.

Boers, H. (1988), *Neither on This Mountain nor in Jerusalem: A Study of John 4 (SBLMS 35)*. Atlanta, Scholars Press.

Boismard, M. -É. (1993), *Moses or Jesus: An Essay in Johannine Christology (BETL 84a)*. ET Leuven, Peeters, and Leuven University Press.

—— *et al.* (1977), *L'évangile de Jean (Synopse des quatre évangiles*, vol. 3). Paris, Éditions du Cerf.

Bond, H. K. (1998), *Pontius Pilate in History and Interpretation (SNTSMS 100)*. Cambridge, Cambridge University Press.

—— (2002), 'Caiaphas: Reflections on a High Priest', *ExpT* 113, 183–7.

Borgen, P. (1965), *Bread from Heaven: An Exegetical Study of the Concept of Manna in the Gospel of John and the Writings of Philo (NovTSup 10)*. Leiden, Brill.

—— (1986), 'God's Agent in the Fourth Gospel', repr. in Aston (1986), 67–78 (orig. edn, 1968).

Bornhäuser, K. (1928), *Das Johannesevangelium: Eine Missionsschrift für Israel*. Gütersloh, C. Bertelsmann.

Borsch, F. H. (1970), *The Christian and Gnostic Son of Man (SBT* 2nd ser. 14). London, SCM Press.

Bothe, J. E. (1993), 'John 4. 16a: A Difficult Text Speech Act Theoretically Revisited', in Stibbe (1993a), 183–92.

Bousset, W. (1970), *Kyrios Christos: A History of the Belief in Christ from the Beginnings of Christianity to Irenaeus*, 6th edn. ET Nashville, Abingdon (orig. German edn 1913).

Boyarin, D. (2001), 'The Gospel of the *Memra*: Jewish Binitarianism and the Prologue to John', *HTR* 94, 243–84.

Bradley, I. (1995), *The Power of Sacrifice*. London, Darton, Longman & Todd.

Brodie, T. L. (1993a), *The Quest for the Origin of John's Gospel*. Oxford and New York, Oxford University Press.

—— (1993b), *The Gospel according to John: A Literary and Theological Commentary*. Oxford and New York, Oxford University Press.

Brooke, A. E. (1896), *The Commentary of Origen on S. John's Gospel*, 2 vols. Cambridge, Cambridge University Press.

Brown, R. E. (1965), 'The Johannine Sacramentary' and 'The Eucharist and Baptism in John', in R. E. Brown, *New Testament Essays*, 51–77, 78–95. London, Chapman.

—— (1966), *The Gospel according to John (AB)*, 2 vols. Garden City, NY, Doubleday, and London, Chapman [1971].

—— (1979), *The Community of the Beloved Disciple: The Life, Loves, and Hates of*

an Individual Church in New Testament Times. New York, *et al.*, Paulist Press.
—— (1982), *The Epistles of John (AB)*. Garden City, NY, Doubleday.
—— (1994), *The Death of the Messiah*, 2 vols. Garden City, NY, Doubleday.
—— (1997), *An Introduction to the New Testament*. New York, London, *et al.*, Doubleday.
—— *et al.*, eds (1973), *Peter in the New Testament*. New York, Paulist Press.
—— *et al.*, eds (1978), *Mary in the New Testament*. Minneapolis, *et al.*, Paulist Press.
Brown, S. (1964), 'From Burney to Black: The Fourth Gospel and the Aramaic Question', *CBQ* 26, 323–39.
Bruce, F. F. (1983), *The Gospel of John*. Basingstoke, Pickering Books.
—— (1988), *The Canon of Scripture*. Glasgow, Chapter House.
Bultmann, R. (1925), 'Die Bedeutung der neuerschlossenen mandäischen und manichäischen Quellen für das Verständnis des Johannesevangeliums', *ZNW* 24, 100–46.
—— (1941), *Das Evangelium des Johannes*. Göttingen, Vandenhoeck & Ruprecht.
—— (1955), *Theology of the New Testament*, vol. 2. ET London, SCM Press.
—— (1959), 'Johannesevangelium', in *RGG* 3rd edn, vol. 3, cols. 840–50.
—— (1964), see Quell *et al.* (1964).
—— (1971), *The Gospel of John*. ET Oxford, Blackwell (ET of Bultmann, 1941).
—— (1986), 'The History of Religions Background to the Gospel of John'. ET in Ashton (1986), 18–35 (orig. German edn 1923).
Burney, C. F. (1922), *The Aramaic Origin of the Fourth Gospel*. Oxford, Clarendon Press.
Burridge, R. A. (1992), *What are the Gospels? A Comparison with Graeco-Roman Biography (SNTSMS 70)*. Cambridge, Cambridge University Press.
—— (1994), *Four Gospels, One Jesus? A Symbolic Reading*. London, SPCK.
Butler, S. (1897), *The Authoress of the Odyssey*. London, Jonathan Cape.
Caird, G. (1980), review of Brown (1979), *Theology* 83, 146–7.
Calvin, J. (1553), *Commentary on the Gospel of John*, tr. T. H. L. Parker, 2 vols. Edinburgh, Oliver & Boyd and St Andrew Press, 1959–61.
Campbell, D. A., ed. (1996), *The Call to Serve: Biblical and Theological Perspectives on Ministry in Honour of Bishop Penny Jamieson*. Sheffield, Sheffield Academic Press.
Carnley, P. (1987), *The Structure of Resurrection Belief*. Oxford, Clarendon Press.
Carson, D. A. (1981), *Divine Sovereignty and Human Responsibility: Biblical Perspectives in Tension*. Atlanta, John Knox Press.
—— (1987), 'The Purpose of the Fourth Gospel: John 20. 31 Reconsidered', *JBL* 106, 639–51.
—— (1988), 'John and the Johannine Epistles', in Carson and Williamson (1988), 245–64.
—— (1991), *The Gospel according to John*. Leicester, Inter-Varsity Press, and Grand Rapids, Eerdmans.
—— and Williamson, H. G. M., eds (1988), *It is Written: Scripture Citing Scripture (Essays in Honour of Barnabas Lindars, SSF)*. Cambridge, *et al.*, Cambridge University Press.
Carter, W. (1990), 'The Prologue and John's Gospel: Function, Symbol, Definitive Word', *JSNT* 39, 35–58.
Casey, M. (1991), *From Jewish Prophet to Gentile God: The Origins and Development of New Testament Christology*. Cambridge, James Clarke, and Louisville, Westminster John Knox Press.
—— (1996), *Is John's Gospel True?* London and New York, Routledge.
—— (1998), *Aramaic Sources for Mark's Gospel (SNTSMS 102)*. Cambridge, Cambridge University Press.
Cassem, N. H. (1972/3), 'A Grammatical and Contextual Inventory of the Use of *kosmos* in the Johannine Corpus', *NTS* 19, 81–91.

Charlesworth, J. H., ed. (1972), *John and Qumran*. London, Chapman.
——, ed. (1983, 1985), *The Old Testament Pseudepigrapha*, 2 vols. London, Darton, Longman & Todd.
——, ed. (1992), *The Messiah: Developments in Judaism and Christianity*. Minneapolis, Fortress.
—— (1995), *The Beloved Disciple: Whose Witness Validates the Gospel of John?* Valley Forge, Pa., Trinity Press International.
—— (2001), 'The Gospel of John: Exclusivism Caused by Social Setting', in Bieringer *et al.* (2001), 479–513.
Chyutin, M. (1997), *The New Jerusalem Scroll from Qumran* (*JSPSS* 25). Sheffield, Sheffield Academic Press.
Cohn-Sherbok, D. (1992), *The Crucified Jew: Twenty Centuries of Christian Anti-Semitisim*. San Francisco, HarperCollins.
—— (1997), *The Jewish Messiah*. Edinburgh, T&T Clark.
Collins, R. F. (1976), 'The Representative Figures in the Fourth Gospel', *Downside Review* 94, 26–46, 118–32.
Coloe, M. L. (2001), *God Dwells with Us: Temple Symbolism in the Fourth Gospel* Collegeville, Minn., Liturgical Press.
Colson, F. H. *et al.* (1929–62), *Philo* (*LCL*), 10 vols. Cambridge, Mass., Harvard University Press, and London, Heinemann.
Colwell, E. C. (1931), *The Greek of the Fourth Gospel: A Study of its Aramaisms in the Light of Hellenistic Greek*. Chicago, University of Chicago Press.
—— (1933), 'A Definite Rule for the Use of the Article in the Greek New Testament', *JBL* 52, 12–21.
Conway, C. M. (1999), *Men and Women in the Fourth Gospel: Gender and Johannine Characterization* (*SBLDS* 167). Atlanta, Scholars Press.
Conzelmann, H., and Zimmerli, W. (1974), '*Charis, etc.*', *TDNT* 9, 372–6.
Crawford, S. W. (2000), *The Temple Scroll and Related Texts* (*Companion to the Qumran Scrolls* 2). Sheffield, Sheffield Academic Press.
Cross, F. L., and Livingstone, E. A., eds. (1997), *The Oxford Dictionary of the Christian Church*, 3rd edn. Oxford, *et al.*, Oxford University Press.
Crossan, J. D. (1991), *The Historical Jesus: The Life of a Mediterranean Jewish Peasant*. Edinburgh, T&T Clark.
Cullmann, O. (1953), *Early Christian Worship*. ET London, SCM Press.
—— (1963), *The Christology of the New Testament*, 2nd edn. ET London, SCM Press.
—— (1976), *The Johannine Circle*. ET London, SCM Press.
Culpepper, R. A. (1975), *The Johannine School* (*SBLDS* 26). Missoula, Mont. Scholars Press.
—— (1980), 'The Pivot of John's Prologue', *NTS* 27, 1–31.
—— (1983), *Anatomy of the Fourth Gospel: A Study of Literary Design*. Philadelphia, Fortress.
—— (1994), *John, the Son of Zebedee: The Life of a Legend*. Columbia, SC, University of South Carolina Press (repr. Edinburgh, T&T Clark, 2000).
——, ed. (1997), *Critical Readings of John 6*. Leiden *et al.*, Brill.
Dalman, G. (1902), *The Words of Jesus*. ET Edinburgh, T. & T. Clark.
Danby, H., tr. and ed. (1933), *The Mishnah*. Oxford, Oxford University Press.
Davey, J. E. (1958), *The Jesus of St John*. London, Lutterworth.
Davies, M. (1992), *Rhetoric and Reference in the Fourth Gospel* (*JSNTSup* 69). Sheffield, Sheffield Academic Press.
Davies, W. D. and Allison, D. C. (1988, 1991, 1997), *The Gospel according to Saint Matthew* (*ICC*), 3 vols. Edinburgh, T. & T. Clark.
D'Costa, G., ed. (1996), *Resurrection Reconsidered*. Oxford, Oneworld.
de Boer, M. C. (2001), 'The Depiction of "the Jews" in John's Gospel: Matters of Behavior and Identity', in Bieringer *et al.* (2001), 260–80.

de Jonge, H. J. (2001), 'The "Jews" in the Gospel of John', in Bieringer *et al.* (2001), 239–59.

de Jonge, M., ed. (1977), *L'Évangile de Jean* (*BETL* 44). Gembloux, Duculot, and Leuven, Leuven University Press.

—— (1997), *Jesus: Stranger from Heaven and Son of God*. Missoula, Mont. Scholars Press.

de la Potterie, I. (1977), *La vérité dans Saint Jean* (*AnBib*. 73). Rome, Bib. Inst.

—— (1986), 'The Truth in Saint John'. ET in Ashton (1986), 53–66 (orig. pub. 1963).

de Vaux (1965), *Ancient Israel: Its Life and Institutions*, 2nd edn. ET London, Darton, Longman & Todd.

Dodd, C. H. (1953), *The Interpretation of the Fourth Gospel*. Cambridge, Cambridge University Press.

—— (1963), *Historical Tradition in the Fourth Gospel*. Cambridge, Cambridge University Press.

—— (1967), 'The Portrait of Jesus in John and in the Synoptics', in *Christian History and Interpretation: Studies Presented to John Knox*, ed. W. R. Farmer *et al.*, 183–98. Cambridge, Cambridge University Press.

Dokka, T. S. (1999), 'Irony and Sectarianism in the Gospel of John', in Nissen and Petersen (1999), 83–107.

Dummer, J., ed. (1980), *Epiphanius*, vol. 2, *Panarion, Haer. 34–64* (*GCS* 25. 2), 2nd edn. Berlin, Akademie-Verlag (orig. edn by K. Holl, 1922).

Dunn, J. D. G. (1977), *Unity and Diversity in the New Testament*. London, SCM Press.

—— (1989), *Christology in the Making*, 2nd edn. London, SCM Press.

—— (1991), *The Partings of the Ways between Christianity and Judaism*. London, SCM, and Philadelphia, Trinity Press International.

——, ed. (1992), *Jews and Christians: The Parting of the Ways A. D. 70–135*. Tübingen, Mohr-Siebeck.

—— (1994), 'The Making of Christology – Evolution or Unfolding?', in Green and Turner (1994), 437–52.

—— (2001), 'The Embarrassment of History: Reflections on the Problem of "Anti-Judaism" in the Fourth Gospel', in Bieringer *et al.* (2001), 47–67.

Easterling, P. E. and Knox, B. M W., eds (1985), *The Cambridge History of Classical Literature I: Greek Literature*. Cambridge, *et al.* Cambridge University Press.

Edwards, R. B. (1988a), 'Word', *ISBE* 4, 1101–7.

—— (1988b), '*Charin anti Charitos*: Grace and the Law in the Johannine Prologue', *JSNT* 32, 3–15; corr. repr. in Evans and Porter (1997), 190–202.

—— (1989), *The Case for Women's Ministry*. London, SPCK.

—— (1992), 'John and the Johannines: A Survey of Some Recent Commentaries', *BT* 43, 140–51.

—— (1994), 'The Christological Basis of the Johannine Footwashing', in Green and Turner (1994), 367–83.

—— (1996a), *The Johannine Epistles* (*New Testament Guides*). Sheffield, Sheffield Academic Press (updated edn in Lindars *et al.* (2000), 109–203).

—— (1996b), 'Ministry and Church Leadership in the Gospel of John', in Campbell (1996), 117–41.

—— (2000), 'Feeding on Jesus', *ExpT* 111, 344–5.

Elliger, K., Rudolph, W., *et al.*, eds (1983), *Biblia Hebraica Stuttgartensia*, 2nd edn. Stuttgart, Deutsche Bibelgesellschaft.

Ensor, P. W. (1996), *Jesus and His 'Works'* (*WUNT*, 85). Tübingen, Mohr-Siebeck.

Epstein, I., ed. (1948), *The Babylonian Talmud: Zer'aim I, Berakoth*, tr. M. Simon. London, Sonchino Press.

Esler, P. F. (1994), *The First Christians in their Social Worlds: Social-Scientific Approaches to New Testament Interpretation*. London and New York, Routledge.

Eslinger, L. (1993), 'The Wooing of the Woman at the Well', in Stibbe (1993), 165–82.

Etheridge, J. W. (1862, 1865), *The Targums of Onkelos and Jonathan ben Uzziel on the Pentateuch*, 2 vols. London, Longman, Green, Longman & Roberts.

Evans, C. A., and Porter, S. E., eds (1997), *New Testament Backgrounds*. Sheffield, Sheffield Academic Press.

Eve, E. (2002), *The Jewish Context of Jesus' Miracles* (JSNTSup 231). Sheffield, Sheffield Academic Press.

Farmer, W. R., ed. (1999), *'Anti-Judaism' in the Gospels*. Harrisburg, Pa., Trinity Press International.

Faure, A. (1922), 'Die alttestamentliche Zitate im vierten Evangelium und die Quellenscheidungshypothese', *ZNW* 21, 99–121.

Fehribach, A. (1998), *The Women in the Life of the Bridegroom: A Feminist Historical-Literary Analysis of the Female Characters in the Fourth Gospel*. Collegeville, Minn., Glazier/Liturgical Press.

Fennena, D. A. (1985), 'John 1. 18: "God the Only Son"', *NTS* 31, 124–35.

Fergusson, D. (1992), *Bultmann*. London, Chapman.

—— (2001), 'The Doctrine of the Incarnation Today', *ExpT* 113, 75–9.

Fiorenza, E. S. (1977), 'The Quest for the Johannine School: The Apocalypse and the Fourth Gospel', *NTS* 23, 402–27.

—— (1983), *In Memory of Her: A Feminist Reconstruction of Christian Origins*. London, SCM Press, and New York, Crossroad.

——, ed. (1992), *But She Said: Feminist Practices of Biblical Interpretation*. Boston, Beacon Pr.

—— (1993a), *Discipleship of Equals*. London, SCM Press.

——, ed. (1993b, 1994), *Searching the Scriptures*, 2 vols. London, SCM Press.

—— (1995), *Jesus: Miriam's Child, Sophia's Prophet*. London, SCM Press.

Fitzmyer, J. A. (1965), 'The Aramaic "Elect of God" Text from Qumran Cave IV', *CBQ* 27, 348–72.

—— (1970), 'The Languages of Palestine in the First Century AD', *CBQ* 32, 501–31 (repr. in Porter (1991), 126–62).

—— (1981, 1985), *The Gospel according to Luke I-IX, X-XXIV* (AB). Garden City, NY, Doubleday.

Foerster, W. *et al.* (1965), '*Kyrios*, etc.', *TDNT* 3, 1039–1100.

Fogle, F. R., ed. (1965), *The Complete Poetry of Henry Vaughan*. New York, New York University Press.

Ford, J. M. (1997), *Redeemer – Friend and Mother: Salvation in Antiquity and the Gospel of John*. Minneapolis, Fortress.

Forestell, J. T. (1974), *The Word of the Cross: Salvation as Revelation in the Fourth Gospel* (AnBib. 57). Rome, Bib. Inst.

Forster, E. M. (1962), *Aspects of the Novel*. Harmondsworth, Penguin Books (orig. edn 1927).

Fortna, R. T. (1970), *The Gospel of Signs: A Reconstruction of the Narrative Source Underlying the Fourth Gospel* (SNTSMS 11). Cambridge, Cambridge University Press.

—— (1989), *The Fourth Gospel and its Predecessor*. Edinburgh, T. & T. Clark.

Fossum, J. A. (1985), *The Name of God and the Angel of the Lord* (WUNT 36). Tübingen, Mohr-Siebeck.

—— (1995), *The Image of the Invisible God: Essays on the Influence of Jewish Mysticism on Early Christianity* (NTOA 30). Freiburg, Universitätsverlag, and Göttingen, Vandenhoeck & Ruprecht.

France, R. T. (1982), 'The Worship of Jesus: A Neglected Factor in Christological Debate?', in Rowdon (1982), 17–36.

Freed, E. D. (1965), *Old Testament Quotations in the Gospel of John* (NovTSup 11). Leiden, Brill.

—— (1970), 'Did John Write Partly to Win Samaritan Converts?', *NovT* 12, 240–56.

Fuller, R. H. (1972), *The Formation of the Resurrection Narratives*. London, SPCK.

Funk, R. W. and Hoover, R. W. (1993), *The Five Gospels: The Search for the Authentic Words of Jesus*. New York, Macmillan.

Gager, J. G. (1983), *The Origins of Anti-Semitism: Attitudes toward Judaism in Pagan and Christian Antiquity*. Oxford and New York, Oxford University Press.

Gardner-Smith, P. (1938), *St John and the Synoptic Gospels*. Cambridge, Cambridge University Press.

Gasque, W. W. (1982), 'Jew', *ISBE* 2, 1056.

Glasson, T. F. (1963), *Moses in the Fourth Gospel* (*SBT* 40). London, SCM Press.

Gnuse, R. (1997), *No Other Gods: Emergent Monotheism in Israel* (*JSOTSup* 241). Sheffield, Sheffield Academic Press.

Goulder, M. D. (1991), 'Nicodemus', *SJT* 44, 153–68.

Grant, R. M., ed. (1970), *Theophilus of Antioch, Ad Autolycum* (*Oxord Early Christian Texts*). Oxford, Clarendon Press.

Grayston, K. (1984), *The Johannine Epistles* (*NCB*). London, Marshall, Morgan & Scott, and Grand Rapids, Eerdmans.

—— (1990), *The Gospel of John* (*Epworth Commentaries*). London, Epworth Press.

Green, J. B., and McKnight, S., eds (1992), *Dictionary of Jesus and the Gospels*. Downers Grove, Ill. and Leicester, Inter-Varsity Press.

—— and Turner, M., eds (1994), *Jesus of Nazareth, Lord and Christ: Essays in the Historical Jesus and New Testament Christology*. Grand Rapids, Eerdmans, and Carlisle, Paternoster.

Gruenler, R. G. (1986), *The Trinity in the Gospel of John*. Grand Rapids, Baker Book House.

Grundmann, W. *et al.* (1974), 'Chriō, etc.', *TDNT* 9, 493–580.

Guilding, A. (1960), *The Fourth Gospel and Jewish Worship*. Oxford, Oxford University Press.

Gunther, J. J. (1980), 'Early Identifications of Authorship of the Johannine Writings', *JEH* 31, 407–27.

—— (1981), 'The Relation between the Beloved Disciple and the Twelve', *TZ* 37, 129–48.

Gutiérrez, G. (1984), *We Drink from Our Own Wells: The Spiritual Journey of a People*. ET London, SCM Press.

Haenchen, E. (1984), *A Commentary on the Gospel of John* (Hermeneia), 2 vols. ET Philadelphia, Fortress.

Hahn, F. (1969), *The Titles of Jesus in Christology*. ET London, Lutterworth.

Haight, R. (1999), *Jesus: Symbol of God*. Maryknoll, NY, Orbis Books.

Hammer, R. (1995), *The Classic Midrash: Tannaitic Commentaries on the Bible* (*Classics of Western Spirituality*). New York and Mahwah, NY, Paulist Press.

Hanson, A. T. (1991), *The Prophetic Gospel: A Study of John and the Old Testament*. Edinburgh, T. & T. Clark.

Hanson, R. (1979), *Christian Priesthood Examined*. Guildford and London, Lutterworth.

Harris, M. J. (1992), *Jesus as God: The New Testament Use of Theos in Reference to Jesus*. Grand Rapids, Baker Book House.

Harvey, A. E. (1976), *Jesus on Trial: A Study in the Fourth Gospel*. London, SPCK.

Hayman, P. (1991), 'Manotheism – A Misused Word in Jewish Studies?', *JJS* 42, 1–15.

Hays, R. B. (1996), *The Moral Vision of the New Testament*. San Francisco, Harper.

Hedrick, C. W. (1999), *When History and Faith Collide*. Peabody, Mass., Hendrickson.

Hemer, C. J. (1986), *The Letters to the Seven Churches of Asia in their Local Setting* (*JSNTSup* 11). Sheffield, JSOT Press.

Hengel, M. (1974), *Judaism and Hellenism*, 2 vols. ET London, SCM Press.

—— (1986), *The Cross of the Son of God*. ET London, SCM Press.

—— (1989), *The Johannine Question*. ET London, SCM, and Philadelphia, Trinity Press International.

Hick, J., ed. (1977), *The Myth of God Incarnate*. London, SCM Press.
—— (1993), *The Metaphor of God Incarnate*. London, SCM Press.
Hooker, M. D. (1969), 'John the Baptist and the Johannine Prologue', *NTS* 16, 354–8.
—— (1991), *The Gospel according to St Mark*. London, Black.
Hoppe, L. J. (2000), review of Horbury (1998a), *CBQ* 62, 359–60.
Horbury, W. (1982), 'The Benediction of the *Minim* and Early Jewish-Christian Controversy', *JTS* 33, 19–61.
—— (1998a), *Jewish Messianism and the Cult of Christ*. London, SCM Press.
—— (1998b), *Jews and Christians in Contact and Controversy*. Edinburgh, T. & T. Clark.
Horsley, G. H. R. (1981), *New Documents Illustrating Early Christianity*, vol. 1. North Ryde, Australia, Ancient History Documentary Research Centre, Macquarie University.
—— (1992), 'The Inscriptions of Ephesos and the New Testament', *NovT* 34, 105–66.
Horsley, R. A. (1984), 'Popular Messianic Movements around the Time of Jesus', *CBQ* 46, 471–95.
Hoskyns, E. C. (1947), *The Fourth Gospel*, ed. F. N. Davey. London, Faber & Faber.
Hull, J. M. (2001), *In the Beginning there was Darkness: A Blind Person's Conversations with the Bible*. London, SCM Press.
Hunter, A. M. (1965), *The Gospel according to John*. Cambridge, Cambridge University Press.
Hurtado, L. (1998), *One God, One Lord: Early Christian Devotion and Ancient Jewish Monotheism*, 2nd edn. Edinburgh, T. & T. Clark (orig. edn, 1988).
—— (1993), review of Barker (1992), *Theology* 96, 319–20.
Jacobson, H. (1983), *The Exagoge of Ezekiel*. Cambridge, *et al.*, Cambridge University Press.
Jasper, A. (1998), *The Shining Garment of the Text* (*JSNTSup* 165). Sheffield, Sheffield Academic Press.
Jeremias, J. J. (1967), '*Mōusēs*', *TDNT* 4, 848–73.
—— (1969), *Jerusalem in the Time of Jesus: An Investigation into Economic and Social Conditions during the New Testament Period*. ET London, SCM Press.
—— (1971), *New Testament Theology*, vol. 1. ET London, SCM Press.
Jerumanis, P.-M. (1996), *Réaliser la communion avec dieu: croire, vivre et demeurer dans l'évangile selon S. Jean*. Paris, Librairie Lecoffre.
Johnson, L. T. (1989), 'The New Testament's Anti-Jewish Slander and the Conventions of Ancient Polemic', *JBL* 108, 419–41.
Kanagaraj, J. J. (1998), '*Mysticism' in the Gospel of John* (*JSNTSup* 158). Sheffield, Sheffield Academic Press.
Käsemann, E. (1968), *The Testament of Jesus*. ET Philadelphia, Fortess.
Katz, S. T. (1984), 'Issues in the Separation of Judaism and Christianity after 70 C.E.: A Reconsideration', *JBL* 103, 43–76.
Kazantzakis, N. (1988), *The Last Temptation of Christ*, London, Pocket Books.
Keith, G. (1997), *Hated without a Cause? A Survey of Anti-Semitism*. Carlisle, Paternoster.
Kelber, W. H. (1996), 'Metaphysics and Marginality in John', in Segovia (1996), 129–54.
Kelly, J. N. D. (1972), *Early Christian Creeds*, 3rd edn. London, Longman.
Kenney, E. J. and Clausen, W. V. (1982), *The Cambridge History of Classical Literature II. Latin Literature*. Cambridge, *et al.*, Cambridge University Press.
Kermode, F. (1986), 'The Uses of Error', in *Preached before King's: University Sermons in King's College Chapel 1983-97*, ed. G. Pattison, 30–5. Cambridge, King's College.

Kerr, A. R. (2002), *The Temple of Jesus' Body* (*JSNTSup* 220). Sheffield, Sheffield Academic Press.

Kimelman, R. (1981), 'Birkat Ha-Minim and the Lack of Evidence for an Anti-Christian Jewish Prayer in Late Antiquity', in Sanders (1981), 226–45.

King, J. S. (1984), 'Is Johannine Archaeology Really Necessary?', *EQ* 56, 103–11.

Klassem, W. (1996), *Judas: Betrayer or Friend of Jesus?*, London, SCM Press.

Kohler, K. (1905), 'New Testament', *Jewish Encyclopedia* 9, 246–54.

Krämer, G. *et al.* (1968), '*Prophētēs, etc.*', *TDNT* 6, 781–851.

Kraemer, R. S. (1991), 'Women's Authorship of Jewish and Christian Literature in the Greco-Roman Period', in Levine (1991), 221–42.

Krentz, E. (1975), *The Historical-Critical Method*. London, SPCK, and Philadelphia, Fortress.

Krey, D. W., and Smith, L., eds (2000), *Nicholas of Lyra: The Senses of Scripture*. Leiden, Boston, *et al.*, Brill.

Kümmel, W. G. (1973), *The New Testament: The History of the Investigation of its Problems*. ET London, SCM Press.

—— (1975), *Introduction to the New Testament*. ET London, SCM Press.

Kysar, R. (1976), *John, the Maverick Gospel*. Atlanta, John Knox Pr.

Ladd, G. E. (1975), *I Believe in the Resurrection of Jesus*. London, *et al.*, Hodder & Stoughton.

—— (1982), 'Eschatology', *ISBE* 2, 130–43.

Lake, K., tr. (1912–13), *The Apostolic Fathers* (*LCL*), 2 vols. London, Heinemann, and New York, Putnam's Sons.

—— and Oulton, J. E. L., trs (1926–32), *Eusebius: The Ecclesiastical History* (*LCL*), 2 vols. Cambridge, Mass. and London, Harvard University Press.

Lampe, G. W. H. (1961), *A Patristic Greek Lexicon*. Oxford, Clarendon Press.

Lefkowitz, M. R. (1991), 'Did Ancient Women Write Novels?', in Levine (1991), 199–219.

Légasse, S. (1997), *The Trial of Jesus*. ET London, SCM Press.

Levine, A.-J., ed. (1991), '*Women Like This*': *New Perspectives on Jewish Women in the Greco-Roman World* (*SBLEJL* 1), Atlanta, Scholars Press.

Lieu, J. (1986), *The Second and Third Epistles of John*. Edinburgh, T. & T. Clark.

—— (1999), 'Temple and Synagogue in John', *NTS* 45, 51–69.

Lightfoot, J. B. (1891), *The Apostolic Fathers*, ed. J. R. Harmer. London, Macmillan.

Lincoln, A. T. (2000), *Truth on Trial: The Lawsuit Motif in the Fourth Gospel*. Peabody, Mass., Hendrickson.

Lindars, B. (1971), *Behind the Fourth Gospel*. London, SPCK.

—— (1972), *The Gospel of John* (*NCB*). London, Oliphants/Marshall, Morgan & Scott.

—— (1981), 'Discourse and Tradition: The Use of the Sayings of Jesus in the Discourses of the Fourth Gospel', *JSNT* 13, 83–110.

—— (1983), *Jesus Son of Man: A Fresh Examination of the Son of Man Sayings in the Gospels in the Light of Recent Research*. London, SPCK.

—— (1986), 'Jesus Risen: Bodily Resurrection, but No Empty Tomb', *Theology* 89, 90–6.

—— (1990), *John* (*New Testament Guides*). Sheffield, JSOT Press (corr. repr. in Lindars *et al.* (2000), 29–108).

—— *et al.* (2000), *The Johannine Literature* (with an introduction by R. A. Culpepper). Sheffield, Sheffield Academic Press.

Lohse, E. (1968), '*Rabbi, rabbouni, etc.*', *TDNT* 6, 961–5.

—— (1981), *Die Texte aus Qumran: Hebräisch und Deutsch*, 3rd edn. Munich, Kösel-Verlag.

Longenecker, R. N. (1975), *Biblical Exegesis in the Apostolic Period*. Grand Rapids, Eerdmans.

Lowe, M. (1976), 'Who were the *Ioudaioi*?', *NovT* 18, 100–30.

Lowry, R. (1977), 'The Rejected-Suitor Syndrome: Human Sources of New Testament "Anti-Semitism"', *JES* 14, 219–32.

Luther, M. (1543), *Von den Juden und ihren Lügen*, see Sherman (1971).

Maccini, R. G. (1996), *Her Testimony is True: Women as Witnesses in the Fourth Gospel* (*JSNTSup* 125). Sheffield, Sheffield Academic Press.

McGrath, J. F. (2001), *John's Apologetic Christianity: Legitimation and Development in Johannine Christianity* (*SNTSMS* 111). Cambridge, Cambridge University Press.

McHugh, J. (1975), *The Mother of Jesus in the New Testament*. London, Darton, Longman & Todd.

McNamara, M. (1968), *Targum and Testament*. Shannon, Irish University Press.

Mahoney, R. K. (1974), *Two Disciples at the Tomb: The Background and Message of John 20. 1-10*. Bern, Herbert Lang, and Frankfurt am Main, Peter Lang.

Malatesta, E. (1978), *Interiority and Covenant* (*AnBib*. 69). Rome, Bib. Inst.

Malbon, E. S. (2000), *In the Company of Jesus: Characters in Mark's Gospel*. Louisville, Westminster John Knox Press.

Malina, B. J. and Rohrbaugh, R. L. (1998), *Social-Science Commentary on the Gospel of John*. Minneapolis, Fortress.

Marcus, R. (1953), *Philo: Supplement I* (*LCL*). London, Heinemann, and Cambridge, Mass., Harvard University Press.

Marjanen, A. (1996), *The Woman Jesus Loved: Mary Magdalene in the Nag Hammadi Library and related documents*. Leiden, *et al*., Brill.

Marrow, S. B. (2002), '*Kosmos* in John', *CBQ* 64, 90–102.

Marsh, C., and Moyise, S. (1999), *Jesus and the Gospels*. London and New York, Cassell.

Marsh, J. (1968), *Saint John* (Pelican Gospel Commentary). Harmondsworth, Penguin.

Marshall, I. H., ed. (1979), *New Testament Interpretation*, rev. edn. Exeter, Paternoster.

—— (1982), 'Johannine Theology' and 'John, Epistles of', *ISBE* 2, 1081–91, 1091–8.

—— (1990), *The Origins of New Testament Christology*, updated edn. Leicester, Apollos.

Martin, R. A. (1974), *Syntactical Evidence of Semitic Sources in Greek Documents* (*Septuagint and Cognate Stud*. 3). Cambridge, Mass., SBL/Scholars Press.

—— (1989), *Syntax Criticism of Johannine Literature, the Catholic Epistles, and the Gospel Passion Accounts*. Lampeter, Mellen.

Martínez, F. G. (1996), *The Dead Sea Scrolls Translated*, 2nd edn. Leiden, *et al*., Brill, and Grand Rapids, Eerdmans.

Martyn, J. L. (1979), *History and Theology in the Fourth Gospel*, 2nd edn. Nashville, Abingdon (orig. edn 1968).

Maynard, A. H. (1984), 'The Role of Peter in the Fourth Gospel', *NTS* 30, 531–48.

Meeks, W. A. (1967), *The Prophet-King: Moses Traditions and the Johannine Christology* (*NovTSup* 14). Leiden, Brill.

—— (1972), 'The Son of Man in Johannine Sectarianism', *JBL* 91, 44–72 (repr. in Ashton (1986), 141–73).

Meier, J. P. (1991, 1994, 2001), *A Marginal Jew: Rethinking the Historical Jesus*, 3 vols. New York, London, *et al*., Doubleday.

Menken, M. J. J. (2001), 'Scriptural Dispute between Jews and Christians in John: Literary Fiction or Historical Reality? John 9:13-17, 24-34 as a Test Case', in Bieringer *et al*. (2001), 445–60.

Metzger, B. M. (1971), *A Textual Commentary on the Greek New Testament*. Stuttgart, United Bible Societies.

Miller, E. L. (1989), *Salvation-History in the Prologue of John: The Significance of John 1:3/4* (*NovT Sup*. 60). Leiden, *et al*., Brill.

Mitchell, S. (1993), *Anatolia: Land, Men, and Gods in Asia Minor*, 2 vols. Oxford, Clarendon Press.

Mlakuzhyil, G. (1987), *The Christocentric Structure of the Fourth Gospel* (*AnBib* 117). Rome, Bib. Inst.

Moloney, F. J. (1978), *The Johannine Son of Man*, 2nd edn. Rome, LAS.

—— (1985), *Woman: First Among the Faithful*. London, Darton, Longman & Todd.

—— (1993), *Belief in the Word: Reading John 1-4*. Minneapolis, Fortress.

—— (1996), *Signs and Shadows: Reading John 5-12*. Minneapolis, Fortress.

—— (1998a), *Glory Not Dishonor: Reading John 13-21*. Minneapolis, Fortress.

—— (1998b), *The Gospel of John* (Sacra Pagina 4). Collegeville, Minn. Glazier/Liturgical Press.

Moltmann-Wendel, E. (1982), *The Women Around Jesus*. ET London, SCM Press.

Moody, D. (1953), 'God's Only Son: The Translation of John 3. 16 in the RSV', *JBL* 72, 213–19.

Morris, L. (1969), *Studies in the Fourth Gospel*. Exeter, Paternoster.

—— (1972), *The Gospel according to John*. London, Marshall, Morgan & Scott (2nd edn. Grand Rapids, Eerdmans, 1995).

—— (1986), 'Light', *ISBE* 3, 134–6.

Motyer, S. (1997), *Your Father the Devil? A New Approach to John and 'the Jews'*. Carlisle, Paternoster.

Moule, C. F. D. (1962), 'The Individualism of the Fourth Gospel', *NovT* 5, 171–90.

—— (1977), *The Origin of Christology*. Cambridge, *et al.*, Cambridge University Press.

Neirynck, F. (1977), 'John and the Synoptics', in de Jonge (1977), 73–106.

Nereparampil, L. (1978), *Destroy This Temple: An Exegetico-Theological Study of the Temple-Logion in Jn 2:19*. Bangalore, Dharmaran College.

Nestle–Aland (1993), *Novum Testamentum Graece*, ed. E. Nestle, B. Aland, K. Aland *et al.*, 27th edn. Stuttgart, Deutsche Bibelgesellschaft.

Neusner, J. *et al.*, eds (1987), *Judaism and their Messiahs at the Turn of the Christian Era*. Cambridge, *et al.*, Cambridge University Press.

——, tr. and ed. (1988), *The Mishnah*. New Haven and London, Yale University Press.

Newbigin, L. (1982), *The Light Has Come*. Grand Rapids, Eerdmans.

Newson, C. A., and Ringe, S. H., eds (1992), *The Women's Bible Commentary*. London, SPCK, and Louisville, Westminster John Knox Press.

Neyrey, J. H. (1988), *An Ideology of Revolt: John's Christology in Social-Science Perspective*. Philadelphia, Fortress.

Ng, E. Y. L. (2002), *Reconstructing Christian Origins? The Feminist Theology of Elisabeth Schüssler Fiorenza*. Carlisle, Paternoster.

Ng, W.-Y. (2001), *Water Symbolism in John*. New York, Bern, *et al.*, Peter Lang.

Nicholson, G. C. (1983), *Death as Departure: The Johannine Ascent-Descent Schema* (*SBLDS* 63). Chico, Calif. Scholars Press.

Nickelsburg, G. W. E. (1981), *Jewish Literature between the Bible and the Mishnah*. London, SCM Press.

Nicol, W. (1972), *The Sēmeia in the Fourth Gospel* (*NovT Sup* 32). Leiden, Brill.

Nissen, J., and Petersen, S., eds (1999), *New Readings in John: Literary and Theological Perspectives* (*JSNTSup* 182). Sheffield, Sheffield Academic Press.

Nock, A. D., and Festugière, A.-J., eds and trs (1945–54), *Corpus Hermeticum*, 4 vols. Paris, Budé.

O'Day, G. R. (1992), 'John', in Newson and Ringe (1992), 293–304.

Odeberg, H. (1929), *The Fourth Gospel Interpreted in its Relationship to Contemporaneous Religious Currents in Palestine and the Hellenistic-Oriental World*. Uppsala, Almqvist & Wiksell (repr. Chicago, Argonaut, 1968).

O'Neill, J. C. (1997; orig. edn 1979), 'The Lamb of God in the *Testaments of the Twelve Patriarchs*', in Evans and Porter (1997), 46–66.

Pagels, E. H. (1973), *The Johannine Gospel in Gnostic Exegesis: Heracleon's Commentary on John* (*SBLMS* 17). Nashville: Abingdon Press.

—— (1979), *The Gnostic Gospels*. London, Weidenfeld & Nicolson.

Pancaro, S. (1975), *The Law in the Fourth Gospel (NovTSup* 42). Leiden, Brill.

Parker, T. H. L., tr. (1959, 1961), *Calvin's Commentaries: The Gospel according to St. John*, 2 vols. Edinburgh, Oliver & Boyd and St. Andrew Press.

Pazdan, M. M. (1991), *The Son of Man: A Metaphor for Jesus in the Fourth Gospel (Zacch. Stud.*). Collegeville, Minn., Glazier/Liturgical Press.

Pelikan, J., ed. (1957, 1959), *Luther's Works*, vols. 22, 23: *Sermons on the Gospel of St. John, Chs. 1-8*. Saint Louis, Concordia.

Perkins, P. (2000), *Peter: Apostle for the Whole Church*. Edinburgh, T. & T. Clark.

Pesch, R. (1969), *Der reiche Fischfang (Lk 5, 1-11/Jo 21, 1-14). Wundergeschichte – Berufungsgeschichte – Erscheinungsbericht*. Düsseldorf, Patmos.

Pine-Coffin, R. S., tr. (1961), *Saint Augustine, Confessions*. Harmondsworth, Penguin Books.

Pippin, T. (1996), '"For Fear of the Jews": Lying and Truth-Telling in Translating the Gospel of John', *Semeia* 96, 81–97.

Pollard, T. E. (1970), *Johannine Christology and the Early Church*. Cambridge, Cambridge University Press.

Porter, S. E., ed. (1991), *The Language of the New Testament*. Sheffield, Sheffield Academic Press.

Pryor, J. W. (1992), *John, Evangelist of the Covenant People*. London, Darton, Longman & Todd.

Quast, K. (1989), *Peter and the Beloved Disciple (JSNTSup* 32). Sheffield, JSOT Press.

Quell, G. *et al.* (1964), 'Alētheia, etc.', *TDNT* 1, 232–51.

Rahlfs, A. (1935), *Septuaginta: Id est Vetus Testamentum graece*, 8th edn., 2 vols. Stuttgart, Württembergische Bibelanstalt.

Reinhartz, A. (1994), 'The Gospel of John', in Fiorenza (1994), 561–600.

—— (1998), 'The Johannine Community and Its Jewish Neighbours', in Segovia (1998), 111–38.

—— (2001), '"Jews" and Jews in the Fourth Gospel', in Bieringer *et al.* (2001), 341–56.

Reitzenstein, R. (1978), *The Hellenistic Mystery Religions*. ET Pittsburgh, Pickwick Press (orig. German edn 1910).

Rensberger, D. (1988), *Overcoming the World: Politics and Community in the Gospel of John*. London, SPCK and Louisville, Westminster John Knox Press (as *Johannine Faith and Liberating Community*).

—— (1998), 'Sectarianism and Theological Interpretation in John', in Segovia (1998), 139–56.

—— (1999), 'Anti-Judaism and the Gospel of John', in Farmer (1999), 120–57.

—— (2001), *The Epistles of John*. Louisville, London, *et al.*, Westminster John Knox.

Reynolds, J., and Tannenbaum, R. (1987), *Jews and Godfearers at Aphrodisias (PCPS Suppl.* 12). Cambridge, Cambridge Philological Society.

Richardson, A. (1959), *The Gospel according to Saint John*. London, SCM Press.

Ringe, S. H. (1999), *Wisdom's Friends: Community and Christology in the Fourth Gospel*. Louisville, Westminster John Knox Press.

Robinson, J. A. T. (1952), *The Body (SBT* 5). London, SCM Press.

—— (1962), 'The Destination and Purpose of St John's Gospel' and 'The New Look on the Fourth Gospel', in J. A. T. Robinson, *Twelve New Testament Studies (SBT* 34), 94–106, 107–25. London, SCM Press.

—— (1962/3), 'The Relationship of the Prologue to the Gospel of St John', *NTS* 9, 120–9.

—— (1976), *Redating the New Testament*. London, SCM Press.

—— (1985), *The Priority of John*. London, SCM Press.

Robinson, J. M., ed. (1977), *The Nag Hammadi Library in English*. San Francisco, London, *et al.*, Harper & Row.

Rowdon, H. H., ed. (1982), *Christ the Lord (Studies Presented to Donald Guthrie)*. Leicester, Inter-Varsity Press.

Ruckstuhl, E. (1977), 'Johannine Language and Style', in de Jonge (1977), 125–47.

Ruether, R. R. (1974), *Faith and Fratricide: The Theological Roots of Anti-Semitism*. New York, Seabury Press (citations in text are from 1997 printing by Wipf & Stock).

Ryle, H. S., and James, M. R., eds. (1891), *Psalmoi Solomōntos*. Cambridge, Cambridge University Press.

Sanders, E. P. *et al.*, eds (1981), *Jewish and Christian Self-Definition*, vol. 2: *Aspects of Judaism in the Graeco-Roman World*. London, SCM Press.

—— (1985), *Jesus and Judaism*. London, SCM Press.

—— (1992), *Judaism: Practice and Belief 63 BCE–66 CE*. London, SCM Press, and Philadelphia, Trinity Press International.

Sanders, J. N., and Mastin, B. A. (1968), *A Commentary on the Gospel according to St John*. London, A&C Black.

Sanders, J. T. (1971), *The New Testament Christological Hymns (SNTSMS 15)*. Cambridge, Cambridge University Press.

—— (1986), *Ethics in the New Testament*, 2nd edn. London, SCM Press.

—— (1987), *The Jews in Luke-Acts*. London, SCM Press.

Schillebeeckx, E. (1981), *Ministry: A Case For Change*. ET London, SCM Press.

Schlatter, D. A. (1902), *Die Sprache und Heimat des vierten Evangelisten*. Gütersloh, C. Bertelsmann.

Schnackenburg, R. (1968, 1980, 1982), *The Gospel according to St John*, 3 vols. ET London, Burns & Oates, and New York, Seabury/Crossroad.

Schneiders, S. M. (1993), 'Women in the Fourth Gospel and the Role of Women in the Contemporary Church', in Stibbe (1993b), 123–43.

—— (1999), *Written That You Might Believe: Encountering Jesus in the Fourth Gospel*. New York, Herder & Herder/Crossroad.

Schoon, S. (2001), 'Escape Roots as Dead Ends', in Bieringer *et al.* (2001), 144–58.

Schrenk, H. (1967), '*Eklektos*', *TDNT* 4, 181–92.

Schüssler, see Fiorenza, E. S.

Schwartz, G. (1991), *Rembrandt: His Life, his Paintings*. ET London, Penguin.

Schweizer, E. (1961), *Church Order in the New Testament*. ET London, SCM Press.

Scott, E. F. (1906), *The Fourth Gospel: Its Purpose and Theology*. Edinburgh, T. & T. Clark.

Scott, M. (1992), *Sophia and the Johannine Jesus (JSNTSup 71)*. Sheffield, JSOT Press.

Segal, A. (1977), *Two Powers in Heaven: Early Rabbinic Reports about Christianity and Judaism (Stud. Jud. Late Ant. 25)*. Leiden, Brill.

Segovia, F. F. (1981), 'The Love and Hatred of Jesus and Johannine Sectarianism', *CBQ* 43, 258–72.

—— ed. (1996), '*What is John?*' *Readers and Readings of the Fourth Gospel (SBLSS 3)*. Atlanta, Scholars Press.

——, ed. (1998), '*What is John?*' *II: Literary and Social Readings of the Fourth Gospel (SBLSS 7)*. Atlanta, Scholars Press.

Sherman, F., ed. (1971), *On the Jews and their Lies*, tr. M. H. Bertram in *Luther's Works*, vol. 47: *The Christian in Society* IV, 121–306. Philadelphia, Fortress.

Sherwin-White, A. N. (1986), 'Pilate, Pontius', *ISBE* 3, 867–9.

Smalley, S. S. (1978, 1998), *John: Evangelist and Interpreter*, 1st and 2nd edns. Carlisle, Paternoster.

—— (1994), *Thunder and Love: John's Revelation and John's Community*. Milton Keynes, Nelson Word Ltd.

Smith, D. M. (1976), 'Johannine Christianity: Some Reflections on its Character and Delineation', *NTS* 21, 222–48 (repr. in Smith (1987), ch. 1).

—— (1987), *Johannine Christianity*. Edinburgh, T. & T. Clark.

—— (1995), *The Theology of the Gospel of John*. Cambridge, Cambridge University Press.

Smith, T. V. (1985), *Petrine Controversies in Early Christianity* (*WUNT* 15). Tübingen, Mohr-Siebeck.

Snyder, G. F. (1971), 'John 13:16 and the Anti-Petrinism of the Johannine Tradition', *Biblical Research* 16, 5–15.

Staley, J. L. (1988), *The Print's First Kiss: A Rhetorical Investigation of the Implied Reader in the Fourth Gospel* (*SBLDS* 82). Atlanta, Scholars Press.

Stendahl, K., ed. (1958), *The Scrolls and the New Testament*. London, SCM Press.

Stibbe, M. W. G. (1991), 'The Elusive Christ', *JSNT* 44, 19–38 (repr. in Stibbe (1993b), 231–47).

—— (1993a), *John*. Sheffield, JSOT Press /Sheffield Academic Press.

——, ed. (1993b), *The Gospel of John as Literature: An Anthology of Twentieth-Century Perspectives*. Leiden, *et al.*, Brill.

—— (1994), *John's Gospel* (*New Testament Readings*). London, *et al.*, Routledge.

Strack, A. L., and Billerbeck, P. (1982, 1983), *Kommentar zum Neuen Testament aus Talmud und Midrasch: Das Evangelium nach Markus, Lukas und Johannes*, 8th edn. vols. 1 and 2. Munich, C. H. Beck'sche Verlag.

Streeter, B. H. (1924), *The Four Gospels: A Study of Origins*. London, Macmillan.

Talbert, C. H. (1992), *Reading John: A Literary and Theological Commentary on the Fourth Gospel and the Johannine Epistles*. London, SPCK.

Tasker, R. V. G. (1960), *John* (*Tyndale New Testament Commentaries*). Leicester, Inter-Varsity Press.

Taylor, V. (1966), *The Gospel according to St. Mark*, 2nd edn. London and Basingstoke, Macmillan.

Temple, W. (1939, 1940), *Readings in St. John's Gospel*, 2 vols. London, Macmillan.

Thackeray, H. St. J. (1926–65), *Josephus* (*LCL*), 10 vols. Cambridge, Mass. Harvard University Press, and London, Heinemann.

Theissen, G., and Mertz, A. (1998), *The Historical Jesus: A Comprehensive Guide*. London, SCM Press.

Thompson, M. B. (1998), 'The Holy Internet: Communication between Churches in the First Christian Generation', in Bauckham (1998b), 49–70.

Thompson, M. M. (1988), *The Humanity of Jesus in the Fourth Gospel*. Philadelphia, Fortress.

—— (2001), *The God of the Gospel of John*. Grand Rapids and Cambridge (UK), Eerdmans.

Thompson, M. R. (1995), *Mary of Magdala: Apostle and Leader*. New York and Mahwah, NJ, Paulist Press.

Thompson, S. (1985), *The Apocalypse and Semitic Syntax* (*SNTSMS* 52). Cambridge, *et al.*, Cambridge University Press.

Thyen, H. (1980), '"Das Heil kommt von den Juden"', in *Kirche (FS G. Bornkamm)*, ed. D. Luhrmann and G. Strecker, 163–84. Tübingen, Mohr-Siebeck.

Tomson, P. J. (2001), '"Jews" in the Gospel of John', in Bieringer *et al.* (2001), 301–40.

Trebilco, P. R. (1991), *Jewish Communities in Asia Minor* (*SNTSMS* 69). Cambridge, *et al.*, Cambridge University Press.

Trevett, C. (1996), *Montanism: Gender, Authority and the New Prophecy*. Cambridge, *et al.*, Cambridge University Press.

Trigg, J. W. (1983), *Origen: The Bible and Philosophy in the Third-Century Church*, London, SCM Press.

Trites, A. A. (1977), *The New Testament Concept of Witness* (*SNTSMS* 31). Cambridge, Cambridge University Press.

Turner, M. (1990), 'Atonement and the Death of Jesus in John: Some Questions to Bultmann and Forestell', *EQ* 62, 99–122.

Turner, N. (1976), *A Grammar of New Testament Greek*, ed. J. H. Moulton, vol. IV,

Style. Edinburgh, T. & T. Clark.

van Belle, G. (1994), *The Signs Source in the Fourth Gospel: Historical Survey and Critical Evaluation of the Semeia Hypothesis* (*BETL* 116). Leuven, Leuven University Press and Peeters.

VanderKam, J. C. (1992), 'Righteous One, Messiah, Chosen One, and Son of Man in 1 Enoch 37–71', in Charlesworth (1992), 169–91.

—— (1994), *The Dead Sea Scrolls Today*. Grand Rapids, Eerdmans.

—— (2001), *The Book of Jubilees* (*Guides to Apocrypha and Pseudepigrapha*). Sheffield, Sheffield Academic Press.

van Unnik, W. C. (1959), 'The Purpose of St. John's Gospel', *SE* 1, 382–411 = *TU* 73.

Vaughan, H., 'The Night', in Fogle (1965), 323–5.

Vermes, G. (1998), *The Complete Dead Sea Scrolls in English*. Harmondsworth, Penguin Books.

—— (1999), *An Introduction to the Complete Dead Sea Scrolls*, 3rd edn. London, SCM Press.

von Campenhausen, H. (1969), *Ecclesiastical Authority and Spiritual Power in the Church of the First Three Centuries*. ET London, Black.

von Rad, G. *et al.* (1965), 'Israēl, Ioudaios, Hebraios, etc.', *TDNT* 3, 356–91.

von Wahlde, U. C. (1981), 'The Witnesses to Jesus in John 5:31–40 and Belief in the Fourth Gospel', *CBQ* 3 (1981), 385–404.

—— (1982), 'The Johannine "Jews": A Critical Survey', *NTS* 28, 33–60.

—— (2001), '"You are of Your Father the Devil" in its Context: Stereotyped Apocalyptic Polemic in John 8:38–47', in Bieringer *et al.* (2001), 418–44.

Ware, K. (1983), 'Man, Woman, and the Priesthood of Christ', in T. Hopko (ed.), *Women and the Priesthood*, 9–37. Crestwood, NY, St. Vladimir's Seminary Press.

Weber, R. (1983), *Biblia Sacra Iuxta Vulgatam Versionem*, 3rd edn. Stuttgart, Deutsche Bibelgesellschaft.

Wenham, J. (1984), *Easter Enigma: Are the Resurrection Stories in Conflict?* Exeter, Paternoster.

Weren, W. (1999), *Windows on Jesus*. ET London, SCM Press.

Westcott, B. F. (1919), *The Gospel according to St John* (corr. repr.). London, John Murray (orig. edn 1880).

Westerholm, S. (1992), 'Pharisees', in Green and McKnight (1992), 609–14.

Whaling, F. (2002), 'Christian Theological Attitudes to Other Religious Traditions in a Plural World', *ExpT* 113, 101–19.

Wiles, M. (1960), *The Spiritual Gospel*. Cambridge, Cambridge University Press.

Wilken, R. L. (1983), *John Chrystostom and the Jews: Rhetoric and Reality in the Late 4th Century*. Berkeley, London, *et al.*, University of California Press.

Williams, A. L. (1935), *Adversus Judaeos: A Bird's-Eye View of Christian Apologiae until the Renaissance*. Cambridge, Cambridge University Press.

Williams, C. (2000), *I am He: The Interpretation of 'Anî Hû' in Jewish and Early Christian Literature* (*WUNT* 113). Tübingen, Mohr-Siebeck.

Williamson, R. (1989), *Jews in the Hellenistic World: Philo*. Cambridge, *et al.*, Cambridge University Press.

Windisch, H. (1964), 'Hellēn, etc.', *TDNT* 2, 504–16.

Woll, D. B. (1981), *Johannine Christianity in Conflict* (*SBLDS* 60). Ann Arbor, Scholars Press.

Wright, N. T. (1992, 1996), *Christian Origins and the Question of God*: vol. 1, *The New Testament and the People of God*. Minneapolis, Fortress; vol. 2, *Jesus and the Victory of God*. London, SPCK.

Yee, G. A. (1989), *Jewish Feasts and the Gospel of John* (*Zacchaeus Studies*). Wilmington, Del., Glazier.

Young, B. H. (1988), 'Targum', *ISBE* 4, 727–33.

Index of Biblical References

Genesis 29
1.1 87
1.3 88, 90
1.6 88
2.7 LXX 82f.
14 129
14.18 51
16.5 94
16.7–13 129
18 92
24.10–67 107
29.1–30 107
32.24–30 129

Exodus 29, 64
2.15–22 107
3 94
3.6 131
3.12 90
3.13–16 132
3.14 56, 131
6.7 141
7.1 130
12.22 79
12.46 79
14.19–25 55
16.15 56, 89
19.9, 19f. 92
20.2 131
20.3 133
20.21 130
21.6 133
23.20–2 129
24.10 95
28.41 64
29.38–42 69
29.43–6 88
33.11 144
33.20–33 92
34.6 94
40.34 93
40.34–8 88

Leviticus
4.32 69
19.18 124

Numbers
9.12 79
21.9 124
23.19 70
24.17 LXX 158

Deuteronomy
5.6 131
6.4 129
13.1–3 118
13.6 94
18.15–18 55
18.18 64
30.15, 19 138
32.29 132
32.46 89
33.1 130

Judges
9.13 51
11.34 LXX 95

Ruth
4.16 94

1 Samuel
15.1 64
24.6 64
28.13 133

2 Samuel
2.6 94
7.11–14 67
7.11–16 65

1 Kings 29
12.22 89
17.8–16 55
17.17–24 53
17.19 94
17.23 LXX 53
19.16 64
22.19–23 118, 129

2 Kings 29
2.8, 14 55
4.1–7 55
4.9 LXX 66
4.18–37 53
4.42–4 55
5 53
5.10 57
17.29–31 107

Chronicles 29, 136

Job
1.6 129
25.6 70
38.7 67

Psalms
1.6 142
2.7 67
7.7f. 130
8.4 70
8.5 133
23.1f. 131
25.5 68
25.10 94
27.9 68
30.2f. 72
33.6 88
35.23 72
45.6 133
45.6f. 134
51.2 104
69.9 77, 128
77.19f. 56
82.1 129, 133
82.6 (81.6 LXX) 133
86.11 142
88.1 73
89.3f. 65
89.14 94
89.19–37 67
89.33–7 65
97.7 133
104.15 51
106.16 66
107.20 88
107.30 55

119.17f., 43f. 89
144.3 70
147.16–18 88
148.5 88

Proverbs
6.23 89
8.22–31 88
9.5 56

Isaiah 92
1.2f. 119
2.3 89
6.1, 5 94
6.10 75
7.14 65
9.2–7 65
11.1–10 65
11.9f. 129
25.6–9 51
35.1–6 61
35.5f. 66
40.3 142
40.11 94
41.4 132
41.8 144
42.6 127
43.10 132
45.15, 21 68
48.12 132
49.6 127
49.60f. 129
51.10 56
52.7 130
52.13 75
52.13—53.12 75
53.1 75
53.7 69
53.12 69, 75
54.13 56
55.1 64
55.10f. 88
61.1 64
61.1–3 130
63.11 LXX 131

Jeremiah
1.5 66

2.4–37 119
2.9 119
14.14 118
23.5 65

Ezekiel 92
2.1 70
34.23f. 65
36.25–7 104
37.9f. 83
37.24 131
40—47 128
43.7 93

Daniel 92
3.25 67
7.13f., 18 70
7.22, 27 70
12.1 129

Hosea
1.1 89
2.1–13 119
4.1 119
4.1–19 119

Joel
3.17 (4.17 LXX)
   93
3.18 51

Amos
4.1 120
9.13 51

Micah
5.2 65, 66
6.1–8 119
7.5 94

Zechariah
6.12 LXX 158
9.9 75
13.9 LXX 73
14.20f. 67, 128

Malachi
3.1 68
3.1–4 67, 128
4.5 61, 68

Tobit
3.15 95
5.4 92
5.4—12.22 129
12.16 131
12.19 92
14.6 129

Wisdom
2.17f. 67
11.1 66
15.11 83
18.15f. 88

Ecclesiasticus
(Ben Sirach)
4.10 67
15.3 56
15.7 88
24.1–11 88
24.10 88
24.19 56
24.23 89
31.27 51

Baruch
3.12, 29–31 88
3.36f. 88
4.1 89

Matthew
1.21 68
1.23 134
2.2 113
2.5 66
2.11 134
3.7–10 125
4.3 137
5—7 7, 31
5.9 67
5.11f. 58
5.17 123
5.44 43
7.5 137
7.15 118
7.22 33
8.5–13 53
8.20 70
9.27–31 57
10.1 6
10.5–15 6
10.24f. 32
11.2f. 68
11.5 59, 61
11.25–7 30
11.27 137
12.9–14 54
13.47f. 60
13.55 20
13.57 63
14.28–31 101
15.24 137
16.16 37
16.17–19 101
16.18 140
16.21 51

16.23 121
17.23 51
18.17 140
20.28 144
21.11 63
23.13 137
23.15 67
23.33 121
24 7
24.5 131
26.6–13 109
26.47 116
26.51 101
26.59–66 116
26.61 77
26.62f. 74
26.63 37
27.14 74
27.18 116
27.25 117
27.29 113
27.40 77
27.41f. 113
27.55f. 109
27.57 104, 105
28.9 134
28.9f. 82
28.15 113
28.16–20 83
28.17 134
28.18 137
28.18–20 103
28.19 134

Mark
1.1 37, 41
1.11 137
1.16–30 60
1.17 60
1.29–31 43
1.41 33
2.1–12 54
2.6–12 119
2.11 29, 54
2.17 137
2.23–38 54
2.27 54
3.1–6 54, 119
3.22–7 118
3.28 70
4.14 91
5.22–4 54
5.22–43 35, 59
5.35–43 54
6.2 33
6.3 20
6.4 63
6.5 33

6.7–13 6
6.30–52 29, 55
6.37 29
6.50 131
7.1–13 119
7.3 113
7.19 125
7.24–30 53
8.22–6 57
8.23 57
8.28 61, 63
8.29 2, 66, 101,
   108
8.31 70, 73
8.33 121
8.38 137
9.11f. 61
9.12 73
9.31 70, 73
9.35 144
10.33f. 73
10.45 144
10.46–52 57
10.51 62
11.1–10 29
11.16 128
12.28–34 124
12.29 129
12.31 43
13 7, 31
13.2 127
13.6 131
13.9 58
13.22 118
13.26 70, 137
13.32 137
14.1—16.8 29
14.3, 5 29
14.3–9 109
14.22 60
14.29–31 100
14.32–42 78
14.36 137
14.43 116
14.47 101
14.55–64 116
14.57f. 77, 127
14.60f. 74
14.66–72 100
15.2 113
15.4f. 74
15.9 29
15.10 116
15.13f. 116
15.18 113
15.21 74
15.26 113
15.29 77

15.32   113
15.34   5
15.40f.   109
15.43   104
16.1   7

Luke
1.47   68
2.11   68
2.49   137
4.18f.   130
4.21   123
4.24   63
5.1   91
5.1–11   60
5.4–11   30
5.8   131
6.20–49   7
6.22   58
6.26   118
6.27, 35   43
7.1–10   53
7.3   113
7.11–15   35
7.11–17   59
7.12   95
7.16   63
7.19   68
7.22   59, 61
7.36–50   109, 110
7.38   30, 78
8.2f.   109
8.42   95
9.1–6   6
9.22   51
9.38   95
10.10–15   137
10.13   33
10.21f.   30, 137
10.38–42   59, 108
11.20   33
11.42–52   137
13.10–17   54
13.11–13   54
13.15f.   54
14.1–6   54
14.5f.   54
16.19–31   59
17.22–37   7
21.5–36   7
22.19   57
22.27   144
22.32   100
22.49f.   101
22.51   30
22.54   116
22.66   116
23.4   30

23.9   74
23.14   30
23.21   30
23.22   30
23.49   109
23.50f.   104
23.51   105, 113
24.4   30
24.7   51
24.16   110
24.26f.   74
24.30   60
24.31   110
24.34   82
24.36–49   30
24.39   82
24.43   82
24.46–9   103
24.50–2   83

John
1.1   63, 87, 90,
       91, 96, 97,
       132, 154
1.1–5   96
1.1–18   2, 84, 85,
       86, 87
1.2   132
1.3   89
1.3f.   159
1.4   53
1.5   81, 96
1.6   2
1.7   96, 155
1.7f.   2
1.9   58, 97, 143,
       160
1.10   96f.
1.11   74, 88, 97,
       115, 116
1.12f.   88, 141
1.13   159
1.14   27, 42, 75,
       88, 90, 91,
       92, 93, 94,
       96, 133, 154
1.15   2, 68, 96, 97
1.16   27, 42, 92,
       93, 94, 96,
       124
1.17   3, 41, 93,
       94, 96, 97,
       124
1.18   39, 63, 71,
       89, 94, 95,
       96, 97, 102,
       124, 133
1.19   114

1.19–25   157
1.19–35   96
1.19–51   2, 62
1.20   65
1.20f.   131
1.21   156
1.23   72, 123
1.24   105, 114
1.25   65
1.26   2
1.27   68
1.29   2, 41, 69,
       79, 80, 97
1.30   68, 96
1.32   2
1.32–4   30
1.33f.   67
1.34   2, 40, 69,
       157
1.35–40   19
1.36   41
1.38   40, 62
1.39   27
1.41   2, 40, 65
1.41f.   38
1.42   40, 100
1.43   62
1.45   3, 64, 97,
       100, 123
1.47   113, 115
1.47–51   39
1.49   62, 66, 67,
       113, 157
1.51   70, 71
Jn 2—12   33
2.1–11   3, 33,
       50–2
2.2   98
2.4   51, 52, 77,
       161
2.6   38, 52, 105,
       113, 126
2.10   50
2.11   33, 34, 50,
       61, 75, 77,
       93, 98, 118,
       154
2.13   105, 113,
       126
2.13–22   3, 67
2.15f.   128
2.16   128
2.17   77, 123,
       128
2.18   113
2.19   3, 77
2.19f.   47
2.20   105, 113

2.22   75, 77, 99,
       123
2.23   33, 34, 154
2.23f.   105
2.24   118
2.25   93, 98
Jn 3   32
3.1   104
3.1–3   104, 154
3.1–11   104
3.1–15   3
3.2   34, 61, 62,
       154
3.3–5   7, 8, 17,
       125, 153f.
3.3–8   97
3.5   145
3.8   8
3.9   106
3.10   104, 113
3.12f.   70, 71
3.12–21   77
3.13   32, 39, 70,
       76
3.14   3, 70, 71,
       75, 97, 124
3.14f.   80
3.16   79, 95, 97,
       124, 144
3.16f.   97
3.17   67, 69, 77
3.18   67, 76, 95
3.19   77, 80, 121,
       143
3.19–21   4, 58, 96
3.20f.   105
3.21   155
3.22   98
3.25   52
3.25–30   96
3.26   62, 155
3.28   65
3.29   155
3.31–4   63
3.36   42, 76
Jn 4.1–42   38, 154
4.2   47
4.4–16   57
4.4–42   3, 106–8
4.5f.   45
4.8   98
4.9   113
4.10   53
4.10–14   127
4.11   108
4.12   3
4.14   53, 124
4.15   108

4.16–19 107, 124
4.17f. 106
4.18 93
4.19 61, 63, 107
4.19f. 108
4.20f. 45
4.21–4 128
4.22 121, 128, 162
4.23 76
4.25 65, 108, 131, 157
4.26 131
4.27 98
4.28f. 108
4.29 63, 65, 108
4.31 62, 98
4.33 98
4.34 32
4.38 98
4.39 107, 108
4.41 96
4.42 53, 68, 69, 80, 97
4.44 63
4.46 35
4.46–54 33, 52–4
4.48 34, 52
4.50 52, 53, 96
4.53 33, 61, 103
4.54 34, 154, 156
Jn 5 10, 117, 119, 156
5.1 113, 126
5.1–9 54, 154
5.1–47 54f., 57
5.2 44, 113
5.2f. 54
5.8 29, 54
5.10 113
5.13 57
5.14 10
5.16 113
5.17 32, 39, 54, 130
5.17f. 93
5.18 114, 125
5.19 32, 54
5.21 96
5.22 54
5.23 124, 132
5.24 96
5.25 59, 67, 76
5.26 53
5.26f. 54, 124
5.27 70, 71
5.28 59

5.28f. 76, 154
5.30 54
5.34 69
5.36 33, 50
5.37 54
5.38 55
5.39 123
5.39f. 124
5.42 119
5.43 68
5.45f. 97
5.45–7 55
5.46 64, 123
Jn 6 32, 47, 55, 60, 154, 156
6.1–15 55
6.1–21 29
6.3 98
6.4 126
6.4–59 3
6.6 93, 98
6.7 29
6.8f. 100
6.10 27
6.11 60
6.14 33, 55, 64, 68
6.15 64
6.16–21 33, 55
6.20 56, 131
6.22–71 55
6.23 72
6.25 62
6.25–40 56
6.26–59 57
6.27 56, 157
6.31 56, 123
6.31f. 55
6.32 56, 64, 97, 131, 160
6.32f. 97
6.33 53, 56, 76
6.35 56, 61, 131
6.37 143
6.38 32, 76
6.39 76
6.39f. 154
6.40 76
6.41 76, 113, 115
6.41–51 3
6.42 113
6.44 56, 76
6.45 123
6.46 39
6.48 56, 131
6.48–51 61
6.49 55
6.50f. 76, 124

6.51 56, 77, 80, 131
6.51–8 6, 30, 41, 47, 57, 156
6.52 113, 115
6.53 56, 157
6.54 76
6.56–8 57
6.57f. 61
6.58 57, 76
6.59 62
6.62 32, 70, 76
6.63 57, 80, 139, 145
6.66 99
6.66–71 61
6.67 6, 30
6.67f. 102
6.68 80
6.68f. 66, 101, 102
6.69 61
6.70 100, 121
6.70f. 74, 77
6.71 6
Jn 7 77
7—10 117
7.1 113, 114
7.2 38, 127
7.3 33
7.7 97
7.10 126
7.13 114
7.14 62, 126
7.16 63
7.16f. 64
7.18 93
7.19 97, 123, 125
7.21–4 125
7.22 39
7.22f. 97, 125
7.26 65
7.27 65, 66, 68
7.28 62, 126, 160
7.30 75
7.30f. 78
7.31 65, 66, 68
7.32 4
7.33 75
7.35 40, 113
7.37 126, 127
7.37–40 64
7.38 123
7.39 75
7.40f. 157
7.41 40, 61, 65, 68

7.41f. 66
7.42 65, 68
7.45f. 4
7.50–2 104, 105
7.52 61
Jn 8 77, 119, 120, 121
8.12 58, 96, 120, 127, 131, 155
8.12–59 117, 120
8.16 160
8.17 39, 162
8.18 3
8.19 115, 118
8.20 62, 75
8.21f. 75
8.22 113
8.23 76, 93, 97, 114, 115, 118
8.23f. 115
8.24 76, 131
8.27 115
8.28 71, 75, 80, 131
8.29 96
8.30 115
8.31 96, 120
8.31f. 118
8.32 140, 160
8.33–41 118
8.37–47 119
8.41 124
8.42–4 120
8.43f. 115
8.44 114, 118, 119, 120, 124, 160
8.46 120
8.48 114, 118, 120
8.50 93
8.52 114, 120
8.53–8 3
8.54 93
8.56 39, 123
8.57 113
8.58 96, 131
8.58f. 132
8.59 4, 78, 118
Jn 9 57f., 119
9.1–12 154
9.2 62, 98
9.3 50
9.3f. 32, 57
9.5 58, 61, 80, 127

9.7 44
9.8–12 57
9.9 131
9.13 114
9.13–17 57, 118
9.15 114
9.16 33, 125
9.17 58, 63, 156
9.18 33, 113, 114
9.18–23 57
9.22 48, 58, 65,
    104, 114
9.24–34 57, 118
9.27 104
9.28f. 97
9.29 61, 66
9.33 58
9.34 33, 104
9.35–8 33, 58,
    157
9.36 72
9.37f. 61
9.38 72, 103, 133
9.38f. 160
9.39 68
9.39–41 58, 61
9.40 114
Jn 10 77, 102
10.1 155
10.1–18 127
10.3f. 97, 161
10.7 131
10.9 8, 131
10.10 68, 96, 143
10.11 74, 80, 131
10.12 97
10.15 74, 80
10.16 141, 143
10.17f. 74
10.22 126
10.22f. 44
10.24 65
10.25 50
10.30 80, 132
10.31 4, 78, 114
10.32 50, 61
10.33 114
10.34 39, 133,
    162
10.35 89, 123
10.36 66, 67, 77,
    127
10.37f. 50
10.39 4, 78, 108
10.42 115
Jn 11 4
11.1–44 3, 108
11.1–53 59

11.2 72, 108, 109
11.3 20
11.4 50, 59, 67
11.5 20, 108, 111
11.8 62, 114
11.9f. 96
11.11 144
11.16 20, 100
11.19 113, 121
11.21 72, 108
11.24 76, 108
11.25 59, 61, 81,
    131
11.27 65, 67, 72,
    108, 118
11.28 63
11.28–33 108
11.31 113, 121
11.32 108
11.33–7 121
11.39 27
11.40 50, 93
11.41f. 93
11.43f. 59
11.44 82
11.45 59, 115,
    121
11.45f. 4
11.47 33
11.47–52 114
11.50 61
11.50f. 80
11.50–3 78
11.51f. 40
11.52 141
11.53 78
11.54 115
11.55 113
Jn 12 4
12—13 29
12.1–8 78, 109
12.2 30
12.3 29, 30
12.4 78, 100
12.4f. 109
12.4–6 139
12.5 29
12.6 100, 124
12.11 59, 61, 115
12.12 126
12.13 68, 72,
    113, 123,
    127
12.13–16 66
12.14f. 123
12.16 75, 78, 98,
    99
12.18 33

12.20–2 40, 100
12.21 71
12.23 51, 67, 71,
    75
12.23f. 75
12.23–6 144
12.23–33 4
12.24 78
12.27–36 23
12.27 51
12.27f. 78
12.28 78
12.31 4, 80
12.31–3 97
12.32 75, 80, 143
12.32f. 75, 78
12.34 65, 69, 71
12.35 11
12.36 67
12.37 74
12.37–50 4
12.38 75, 158
12.40 158
12.40f. 75
12.41 93, 96, 123
12.42 48, 58,
    105, 115
12.42f. 104
12.43 50
12.46 77
12.46f. 68
12.47 69
12.48 76
Jn 13 4, 31, 109
13.1 51, 74, 78,
    79, 97, 116,
    161
13.2 100
13.4–15 98
13.6 99
13.6–10 100
13.7 99
13.10 126
13.11 74, 100
13.13 52
13.16 32, 152
13.18 74, 100,
    123
13.18–30 78
13.19 131, 132
13.23 18, 22
13.23f. 23
13.23–6 101
13.24 101
13.26 155
13.26f. 74
13.27 99
13.30 4, 100, 105

13.31f. 4, 71, 75
13.31–3 78
13.31—17.26 34
13.33 10, 39, 98
13.34 99, 124,
    144
13.34f. 43
13.35 99
13.36 99
13.37f. 100
13.38 99
Jn 14—17 4
14.1–3 99
14.2 143
14.2f. 76
14.3 76
14.5 99, 100
14.6 91, 131,
    142f., 160
14.8 96, 99
14.9 80, 132
14.9f. 93
14.10 80, 132
14.12 76, 99
14.13f. 99
14.16 99, 145
14.16f. 32
14.17 97, 99, 120
14.18 76
14.20 132
14.21 99
14.22 20, 99
14.23f. 99
14.24 64, 96
14.26 32, 76, 99,
    145, 163
14.27 99
14.28 93
14.31 77
Jn 15.1 160
15.1–8 141
15.3 77, 126
15.4–10 99
15.6 155
15.10 80
15.11 99
15.12 124, 139,
    144
15.12f. 43
15.13 80
15.13f. 144
15.14f. 98, 144
15.16 98
15.17 99, 124
15.18f. 43, 114
15.18–21 99
15.19 97
15.25 162

15.26 32, 76, 99, 163
15.27 99
Jn 16.1–4 99
16.2 43, 48, 58
16.7 76
16.7–15 99, 145
16.13 9, 32, 76
16.13f. 163
16.20–2 99
16.23f. 96
16.24, 26 99
16.27, 32 99
16.33 4f., 80, 97, 99
Jn 17 78, 127
17.1 4, 75
17.1–5 74
17.1–26 93
17.2 124
17.3 14, 31, 41, 65, 80, 125, 132, 160
17.4 74
17.5 93, 96, 131
17.6 98
17.6–8 31
17.8 99, 105
17.9–25 99
17.11 76, 124
17.12 74, 98, 100
17.13 76, 99
17.14 43, 64, 76, 93, 114
17.16 43, 93
17.17 66, 160
17.18 77, 98
17.19 66, 80, 160
17.21 132, 141
17.24 93, 96
17.25 124
17.26 96, 144
Jn 18—20 29, 31
18.2 100
18.5 100, 131
18.5f. 74
18.6 5, 108
18.8 99
18.8f. 74
18.10 27, 30, 102
18.10f. 101
18.11 74, 78
18.12 116
18.14 80, 114
18.15 23
18.15f. 19, 101
18.15–18 5

18.15–27 100, 102
18.17 131
18.20 62
18.25 131
18.25–7 5
18.28 44, 116
18.33 44, 113
18.33–7 66
18.34–7 74
18.35 113, 116
18.36–9 5
18.38 30, 160
18.38–40 114, 116
18.39 29
18.40 74
Jn 19.1–3 74
19.2f. 5
19.3 61
19.4 30
19.5 71
19.6 30, 117
19.6f. 5
19.7 114, 116
19.11 74, 100
19.13 44, 113
19.13–16 11
19.14 79
19.14f. 118
19.15 116, 117
19.17 74
19.19 5
19.19–21 66
19.19–22 74, 113
19.21f. 116
19.23 10, 66
19.23f. 5
19.24 123
19.25 109
19.25–7 109
19.26 161
19.26f. 5, 18, 25, 101
19.28 123
19.29 79
19.30 5, 74
19.31 116
19.33–6 79
19.34 80, 82
19.35 18, 27, 36, 160
19.36f. 123
19.38 104, 114
19.38–42 104, 105
19.40 38
Jn 20 5

20.1f. 81, 109f.
20.1–10 23
20.2 19, 23, 72, 110
20.2–10 19, 81
20.4 101
20.8 20, 100, 101
20.9 123
20.10 20, 110
20.11 110
20.11–18 81, 109f.
20.12 30
20.13 72, 110
20.15 72, 110
20.16 40, 62, 63
20.17 82, 83, 141
20.18 110
20.19 114
20.19–23 30, 81, 83
20.20 20, 145
20.21–3 103
20.22 82, 99
20.23 103
20.24 6, 30
20.24–9 81
20.25 20, 100
20.27 20, 82, 83
20.28 5, 20, 63, 72, 97, 100, 133
20.29 83, 100
20.30 50
20.30f. 19, 34, 83
20.31 5, 18, 37, 40, 65, 67, 68
Jn 21 26, 47, 81, 83, 103
21.1 155
21.1–8 35
21.1–14 60
21.2 6, 20, 23
21.3 128
21.4–11 30
21.5 98
21.6f. 60
21.7 19, 23, 72, 101
21.9–19 24
21.11 60
21.12 72
21.13 60
21.14 140, 154, 158
21.15–19 41, 60, 100, 101

21.19 103, 144
21.20 23
21.22 19, 76, 101, 128
21.24 19, 24, 27, 42, 152
21.24f. 24
21.25 5, 19

Acts 40, 102, 121, 161
1.1–11 76
1.2–11 83
1.4 82
1.13 23
2 83
2.16–21 123
2.22 33
2.22f. 117
2.36 117
3.1–10 54
3.1–11 23
3.14f. 117
3.22 64
4.10 117
4.13 23
4.13–19 23
4.16 33
5.1–11 120
5.36 64
6.14 77
7.37 64
7.56 70
8.14 23
8.32–5 69
9.2 142
9.36 25
9.36–42 59
10.2 52
10.9–16 126
10.40 51
10.41 82
11.14 52
12.2 23
13.5 91
13.10 120
14.3 92
14.8–11 54
15.28f. 126
16.15 52
16.25–34 103
20.7–12 59
20.28 102
21.38 64
22.11 93

Romans
1.1 41

1.1–3 37
1.18–25 143
3.23–5 93
5.15 92
5.21 93
9.5 134
10.15 130
14.14f. 126
15.19 33

1 Corinthians
1.23 74, 91
5.7 41
5.7f. 69
7.19 125
9.1 110
10.25–8 126
11.24f. 57
15.4 51
15.5 82
15.8 83

2 Corinthians
6.14–18 143
11.24f. 58
12.12 33

Galatians
5.6 125
5.11 74

Ephesians
1.3–14 92
1.13 91
4.10 83
4.11 102
5.8 67
5.8–14 143
5.22—6.9 139

Philippians 47
2.6 134
2.6–11 87
2.7f. 92
2.11 72
3.20 68

Colossians
1.15 134
1.15–19 44
1.15–20 87
2.9 92
2.11 125
3.11 125
3.18–4.1 139

1 Thessalonians
2.13 91
2.14–16 58, 117

1 Timothy
3.16 83, 87

2 Timothy
2.9 91
2.11–13 87

Titus
2.11–13 92
2.13 134

Hebrews 24, 47, 79, 137
1.1–4 91
1.2 44
1.3 83
1.8f. 134
2.6 70
2.9 83
11.17 95

12.2 74
13.20 83

James
1.2 138
4.4 120

1 Peter 79, 102
1.19 41, 69
2.9f. 143
2.23 74
3.18–22 83
4.12 138
5.2 102

2 Peter 102
1.1 134

1 John 24, 41–4, 48, 79
1.1 87
1.1–4 27, 42, 91
1.3 140
1.4 99
1.6f. 140
1.7 79
1.9 79
2.1f. 69
2.2 79, 80
2.7 124
2.15–17 43
2.18 120
2.19 8
2.28 76
3.13 43
3.14 42, 43
3.16–18 43
3.17f. 144
3.23 43

4.3 120
4.6 120
4.7–12 43, 144
4.9 95
4.14 68
4.21 43
5.21 143

2 John 21, 22, 24, 41–4, 48
–.1 24
–.5 43
–.7–9 8
–.12 99

3 John 21, 22, 24, 41–4, 48

Revelation 18, 22, 24, 41, 42, 44, 46, 48, 79
1.1, 4 24
1.9 24, 44
1.13 70
1.17 41
2.9 138
4.11 72, 133
5.6 69
7.14 69, 138
13.11–18 24
14.14 70
17.14 69
19.11–13 87
21.3 93, 128
21.22 128
22.8 24
22.16 41
22.17 64

Index of Ancient Authors and Texts

Note: The Qumran texts are shown in bold to distinguish them from the page numbers.

1. Christian and/or Gnostic Writings
Anti-Marcionite Prologue 21
Augustine 10, 91
Chrysostom 10, 11
Clement of Alexandria 28
Cyprian 10
Cyril of Alexandria 10, 152
Didache 136, 163
Dionysius the Great 11, 42
Epiphanius 21f., 153
Eusebius 11, 21, 22, 28, 42
Gaius 22
Heracleon 9, 10, 21
Hippolytus 22
Ignatius 7, 22, 46, 57
Irenaeus 9, 21, 22, 122
Jerome 11
Justin Martyr 8, 48, 99
Muratorian Canon 21
Nag Hammadi texts 138; *Dialogue of the Saviour* 136; *Gospel of Mary* 153, 159; *Gospel of Philip* 9, 157; *Gospel of Thomas* 136; *Gospel of Truth* 9; *Trimorphic Protennoia* 9
Odes of Solomon 14, 32, 159
Origen 9f., 11, 132, 162
Papias 21, 22
Polycarp 22
Ptolemaeus 9, 21
Tatian 9
Theodore of Mopsuestia 10
Theophilus of Antioch 8, 21, 56
Valentinus 9

2. Greek and Roman Authors
Apollonius Rhodius 55
Diodorus Siculus 52
Hesiod 92, 95
Homer, *Odyssey* 26, 92
Homeric Hymns (*h. Hom.*) 52, 55, 158
Martial 72
Ovid 92
Pausanias 52
Philostratus 53
Plato 42, 99, 162
Pliny 52

Suetonius 72, 162
Thucydides 32, 162

3. Jewish Authors and Writings
Babylonian Talmud 155; *b. Ber.* 48, 53; *Pesaḥim* 89
Jerusalem Talmud: *y. Ber.* 48
Josephus 29, 32, 58, 64, 136
Mishnah 117, 156; *Pirke Aboth (mAboth)* 51; *mSanh.* 162; *mSukkah* 127
Philo 14, 46, 51, 56, 89f., 130, 132, 137, 157
Pseudepigrapha 138; *2 Baruch 51, 156; 1 Enoch* 66, 71, 88, 137, 157; *4 Ezra (2 Esdras)* 65, 66, 67; *Jubilees* 29, 136; *Prayer of Joseph* 129, 162; *Psalms of Solomon* 65, 153; *Testaments of the Twelve Patriarchs* 14; *T. Benj.* 6; *T. Joseph* 69; *T. Jud.* 120; *T. Levi* 66, 120, 152
Qumran texts (Dead Sea Scrolls) 14, 65, 138, 153; **1QSa** 66, 67; **4Q161** 157; **4Q174 (4Q Flor.)** 67, 157; **4Q175** 118; **4Q339** 118; **4Q285** 157; **4Q400** 133; **11Q13** 129; *Community Rule* (**1 QS**) 43, 64, 119; *Damascus Document* (**CD**) 43, 66; *Hymns* 159; *New Jerusalem Scroll* 128; *see also* Index of Names and Subjects
Rabbinic texts 51; *Mekhilta on Ex. 156; Midrash on Dt.* 130; *Midr. Rabbah Eccles.* 156; see also Mishnah, Targums
Targums 51, 88, 90, 156, 159; Fragment 90; Palestinian (Neophyti 1) 90, 156; Targum on Isaiah 158; Targum Onkelos 156, 159; *see also* Index of Names and Subjects

4. Other Ancient Writings
Hermetica (Corpus Hermeticum) 14, 32, 90, 157
Mandaean texts 13f., 90, 138
Nag Hammadi texts *see* sect. 1
Samaritan texts: *Tibat Marqe (Memar Marqar)* 157
Sibylline Oracle 56

Index of Names and Subjects

Abraham   3, 39, 92, 118, 123, 125, 131, 144
Adler, W.   162
Agourides, S.   101
Akiba, R.   124, 162
Aland, B.   157, 158
Albright, W. F.   45, 156
Alexandrine School   9–11
allegorical exegesis   9f., 11, 12, 17, 160
Allison, D. C.   53
Alogoi   22, 153
Alter, R.   15
Andrew   6, 19, 21, 100, 102, 143
androcentrism   16f., 139f.
angel(s)   30, 67, 92, 29, 130, 131, 133f; of Darkness 119; of the Lord 134; of the Presence 29
Annas   5, 6, 36, 58, 161
'Anointed'   37, 39, 40, 41, 51, 64–7; see also messiah
anointing (of Jesus)   29, 78, 108, 109
Antichrist   120, 154
'anti-Jewish(ness)', 'anti-Judaism'   1, 3, 17, 112–22, 133, 134, 141f.
Antiochene School   9, 10f.
'anti-Semitism'   1, 112, 114, 117, 121, 122, 141
Apollonius of Tyana   53
apostle(s)   6, 21, 103, 110; see also John, Paul, Thomas, etc.
Appendix (Epilogue)   5, 19, 60, 76, 83, 102; see also Index of Biblical References (John 21)
Aramaic   40, 44, 62, 70, 71, 88, 90, 154, 155, 159; source 31f., 45f.
art, John's Gospel in   11, 12, 110
ascent (theme)   38, 39, 70, 75f., 83
Ashton, J.   13, 32, 153, 154, 161
Asiedu-Peprah, M.   3, 119, 120
Asklepios   53, 68
atonement   40, 69, 79f., 129; Day of, 162
audience (Gospel)   30, 37–41, 42, 44, 91, 129, 134
Aune, D.   70, 72, 161
Aus, R.   51
author(s)hip   13, 16, 17, 18–26, 42; 'ideal' 19, 102; implied 23; not a

woman 17, 24f., 153

Bamford, C.   145, 152
baptism   8, 10, 125, 140, 156; of Jesus 6, 30
Baptist see John the Baptist
Barclay, J. M. G.   43, 46, 124
Barclay, W.   52
Barker, M.   162
Barrett, C. K.   15, 22, 40, 49, 50, 52, 62, 63, 66, 69, 71, 84, 87, 90, 91, 93, 105, 118, 132, 153, 156, 157, 158, 159, 160
Barton, J.   16
Barton, S. C.   44, 146
Bassler, J. M.   106
Bauckham, R.   19, 24, 31, 44, 131, 160, 158
Beare, F. W.   161
Beasley-Murray, G. R.   69, 103, 158, 160, 161
Beck, N. A.   112, 117
Becker, J.   154
'beloved disciple'   6, 12, 18–26, 72, 81, 82, 101, 102, 111; not a woman, 24f.
Berger, K.   15
Berkowitz, L.   153
Bernard, J. H.   158, 160
Bertram, M. H.   12
Bethlehem   66
Bieringer, R.   17
birkat ha-minim   48, 58
Black, M.   45
Blackburn, B.   53, 154
blind/newly sighted man   33, 57f., 63, 72, 103f., 154, 157
blindness (motif)   58
Boers, H.   107
Boismard, M.-É.   3, 15, 33
Bond, H. K.   161
Borgen, P.   132
Bornhäuser. K.   161
Borsch, F. H.   157
Bousset, W.   13
Boyarin, D.   90, 159
Bradley, I.   79
bread   56, 124, 145; see also discourse(s)
Bridegroom   17, 50, 107f., 155
Brodie, T. L.   62, 110, 153, 159

Brown, R. E.   3, 4, 15, 16, 17, 19, 22, 31, 42, 47, 48, 51, 58, 66, 72, 84, 86, 87, 88, 101, 103, 104, 105, 109, 126, 140, 153, 154, 156, 157, 158, 160, 161
Bruce, F. F.   78, 110, 152
burial (of Jesus)   78, 81f., 105, 109
Bultmann, R.   13f., 16, 19, 31, 32, 33, 45, 77, 81, 86, 88, 90, 101, 102, 105, 115, 154, 158, 159, 160, 161
Burney, C. F.   45, 159
burning bush   56, 90, 130, 131
Burridge, R.   153, 163
Butler, S.   26

Caiaphas   5, 6, 40, 80, 111, 114
Caird, G.   15
Calvin, J.   12
Cana   34, 45, 77, 98; miracle (wine miracle) 3, 11, 12, 33f., 35, 50–2, 55, 60, 61, 75, 154
Capernaum   54
Carnley, P.   158
Carson, D.   15, 22, 39, 44, 49, 62f., 123, 124, 154, 157, 161
Carter, W.   95
Casey, M.   1, 39, 45, 47, 112, 122, 124–7, 129, 162
Cassem, N. H.   97
Cerinthus   22
characters   16, 44, 98–112
charis   93f., 97, 124; see also grace
Charlesworth, R. H.   20, 56, 115, 129, 156, 157, 158, 159
Chief Priest(s) see High/Chief Priest(s)
'Christ' see 'Anointed'; messiah
Christology see incarnation, logos, sophia, theios anēr, theos, titles, etc.
Church   78, 83, 85, 107, 110, 127, 140f., 142; Gentile 101; and Mary 160f.; unity of 10, 60, 135
Chyutin, M.   128
circumcision   39, 123, 125
Cohn-Sherbok, D.   112, 115, 122
Collins, R. F.   105, 160
Coloe, M. L.   127
Colwell, E. C.   155, 162
'coming (one)'   67f., 96, 97
'community', Johannine   15, 17, 41–4, 48, 49, 138, 139
confrontational dialogues   117–21, 130
controversy motif see rib
Conway, C. M.   98, 106, 161
Conzelmann, H.   159
covenant   122, 125, 141
Crawford, S. W.   128
creation   9, 39, 87f., 90, 96, 97, 130
Creed, Nicene   11
Crossan, J. D.   137

crucifixion   18, 27, 74, 81, 116f.; see also death, 'glorification'
Cullmann, O.   51, 153
Culpepper, R. A.   11, 16, 21, 42, 85, 98, 99, 160, 161

Dalman, G.   72, 156
darkness see light
date of composition   15, 46–9
Davey, J. E.   93
David   65, 66, 131, 157
Davies, M.   16, 71
Davies, W. D.   53
D'Costa, G.   158
Dead Sea Scrolls see Qumran
death (of Jesus)   4, 57, 75, 77–81, 97, 117, 141, 146
Decalogue   124
Dedication, Feast of   3, 126, 127
de Jonge, H. J.   115
de la Potterie, I.   94
de Lyra, Nicholas 11f.
'departure' (motif)   4, 75f.
descent theme   32, 70
Deuteronomic prophet   (prophet like Moses) 39, 55, 56, 64, 68, 118
devil   42, 100, 112, 114, 118, 119, 120, 121, 138; see also Satan
Diaspora (Dispersion)   40, 46, 90, 124
dietary laws   123, 125f.
Dionysos   51f.
disciples   6, 19, 33, 34, 36, 43, 62, 66, 75, 81, 82f., 97, 98–103, 105, 114, 118, 138, 139, 140, 141, 154, 161
discipleship   103, 144
discourse(s)   7, 86; Bread of Life 57, 154; Farewell (Supper) 7, 42, 47, 76, 78, 80, 103, 111; Good Shepherd, 77, 78; see also Revelation discourses/sayings
discourse source   31f.
divinity of Jesus   56, 61, 63, 71, 93, 95, 129–34
Dodd, C. H.   2, 3, 14, 28, 33, 38, 52, 53, 81, 86, 89, 90, 153, 157
Dokka, T. S.   15
Domitian   48, 72
doxa   93, 97, 159; see also glory
dualism, dualities   9, 14, 31, 38, 41, 43, 121, 138f.
Dunn, J. D. G.   39, 126, 127, 162, 163

Eagle image (for John)   1, 10, 84, 152; for Rome, 65
Edwards, R. B.   15, 42, 44, 48, 57, 78, 87, 94, 103, 112, 137, 140, 160
ego eimi see 'I am' sayings
'Elect One'   71, 130, 157
Eliezer b. Jose, R.   89

Elijah   33, 52, 53, 55, 59, 61, 63, 156
Elisha   33, 52, 53, 55, 57, 58, 59, 61, 63
'ĕlohim   129f., 130, 133
Emmaus episode   60, 82
emperor, Roman   68, 71, 72, 116, 133
Ensor, P. W.   32, 45, 155
Ephesus   21, 22, 46, 48, 49
Epilogue see Appendix
erga   33, 50, 55; see also 'work(s)'
Eriugena   1, 145, 152
eschatology   42, 76, 158
eternal life see life
Etheridge. J. W.   159
ethical teaching, ethics   7, 43, 120, 121, 124, 138, 139
Eucharist   12, 30f., 41, 51, 57, 60, 140
Eve, E.   155
'exclusivism'   142f.

faith   34, 37, 61, 68, 83, 100, 103, 107, 118, 140; confessions, 61–73, 100, 108, 111, 140
faiths, world   142f.
Farmer, W. R.   17, 117
Farewell Discourses see discourse(s)
Father (God)   3, 5, 41, 43, 54, 56, 61, 74, 78, 83, 85, 93, 94, 95, 99, 102, 124, 127, 128, 130, 137, 140, 142, 158
Faure, A.   13
feasts (festivals), Jewish   3, 11, 38, 40, 113, 123, 126f., 136
feeding miracle   29, 33, 55–7, 60f., 126
Fehribach, A.   17, 107, 140, 161
feminist criticism   16f.
Fergusson, D. A.   14, 143, 145
Fiorenza, E. S.   16f., 25f., 42, 106, 111, 160
fish miracle   30, 60
Fitzmyer, J. A.   161
flesh   7, 30, 56, 80, 92, 133, 138f.
Fogle, F. R.   160
foot washing   4, 6, 78, 98, 100f., 102, 109, 111, 144
Ford, J. M.   163
Forestell, J. T.   79
Forster, E. M.   111
Fortna, R. T.   43, 154
Fossum, J. A.   134
Freed, E. D.   154
friendship   144, 146, 163
fulfilment   134; see also Scripture(s)
Fuller, R. H.   158

Galilee   6, 35, 44, 55, 64, 81, 83, 109, 126
Gardner-Smith, P.   14f., 28f.
Gasque, W. W.   161
genre   29

Gentiles   37, 38, 39, 40, 41, 44, 53, 125, 129, 130, 135, 141
Glasson, T. F.   97
'glorification'   74f., 78, 93, 99, 136
Glory, Book of   4
glory of God   39, 50, 78, 92, 93, 130, 155, 158; of Jesus 4, 27, 50f., 75, 92, 93, 97
Gnosticism, Gnostics   9, 14, 86f., 92, 136, 157, 99, 110, 158, 159, 161; see also Index of Ancient Authors (sects 1 and 4)
Gnuse, R.   162
God: doctrines of   124; love 41, 97, 144, 145; Name 132, 134, 162; 'seeing' God, 94f.; self-revelation 86, 89, 94, 124, 131, 146; transcendence 130; see also Father, glory, Jesus, theos, YHWH
Goulder, M. D.   105
grace   85, 92, 93, 97, 124
Grayston, K.   42, 48, 133, 143
'Greeks', coming of   6, 40, 100
Gruenler, R.G.   163
Grundschrift   13
Gunther, J. J.   22, 153
Gutiérrez, G.   17

Hadrian   68
Haenchen, E.   84, 87, 92, 160
Hahn, F. 66
Haight, R.   143, 145, 163
Hanina ben Dosa, R.   53, 155
Hanson, A. T.   123, 158
Hanson, R.   103
Harris, M. J.   133, 162
Harvey, A. E.   3
Hayman, P.   162
Hays, R. B.   139
Hebrew   41, 45f., 90, 93, 94, 113, 127, 154, 163
Hebrew Bible   5, 38f., 51, 53, 56, 64, 67, 70, 87, 89, 94, 107, 118, 89, 94, 107, 118, 123, 129, 131, 133, 138; see also Scripture(s), Index of Biblical References
Hedrick, C. W.   163
Hellenism, Hellenistic ideas   23, 28, 37, 44, 46
Hemer, C. J.   155
Hengel   21, 153, 158
'hermeneutic of suspicion'   17, 140
Hermes   14, 158
Herodians   121
Hick, J.   145
High/Chief Priest(s)   3, 5, 40, 64, 90, 114, 116, 161
High-Priestly Prayer   4, 47, 66, 76, 78, 152
Hillel, R.   124, 162

historical criticism 12–15, 17f.; accuracy (of John) 14, 36, 135f.
Holocaust 17
'Holy One' 66, 73, 101
Hooker, M. D. 78, 86, 162
Horbury, W. 66, 155, 162
Horsley, G. H. R. 46, 131
Horsley, R. 157
Hoskyns, E. C. 63, 103
'hour' (of Jesus) 4, 51, 78, 80
Hull, J. M. 58
Hunter, A. M. 52
Hurtado, L. 133, 158, 162
'hymn', postulated 84, 85f., 92, 96

'I am' sayings 56, 61, 74, 93, 131f.
incarnation 85, 86, 91–3, 139, 145, 163; see also logos
individualism 140f.
Ioudaioi 38, 113f., 121f.; see also 'Jews, the'
Isis 68, 131
Israel 38, 109, 110, 115f, 119; see also 'King of Israel'
Israel (angel) 129, 162
Israēlitēs 113

Jacob 3, 39, 123, 129, 157; ladder 71; well 45
James (son of Zebedee) 6, 22, 23, 156
Jamnia 40, 47, 48, 97, 115, 117
Jasper, A. 16
Jeremias, J. J. 130, 154, 161
Jerumanis, P.-M. 132
Jerusalem 6, 20, 46, 54, 57, 65, 81, 82, 101, 102, 109, 136; New, 93, 128
Jesus: elusiveness 4; identity 33; 'on trial' 3; 'portraits' of 36, 136–8; relation to God 37, 61, 67, 72f., 93, 94–6, 127, 129, 132–4, 137, 140, 141, 142; speech-style, 7, 70, 136; worship, 108; 131, 132, 134; see also baptism, crucifixion, death, divinity, foot washing, logos, love command, messiah, pre-existence, prophet, Resurrection Narratives, Revealer, Son, teacher, titles, 'work(s)'
Jewish Christianity 19, 58, 101, 102
'Jewishness', criteria for 162
'Jews, the' 3f., 5, 12, 17, 33, 36, 39, 43, 47, 52, 55, 56, 57, 75, 97, 102, 104, 112–22, 123, 124, 125, 141f., 146
Johannan b. Zakkai, R. 128
Johannine Epistles: authorship 18, 21, 22, 153; date 8; relation to John 41–3, 48; see also Index of Biblical References
Johnson, L. T. 120
John, son of Zebedee (apostle) 6, 13, 15, 18, 21–4, 27, 46, 143

John the Baptist 2, 3, 19, 28, 29, 30, 36, 38, 54, 65, 67, 68, 84–7, 96, 100, 108, 123, 125
John the Elder 20, 21, 153
Joseph of Arimathea 5, 7, 104, 105, 109, 111
Judaea, Judaeans 114f., 141f., 161
Judaism 39, 52, 58, 102, 135, 141f.; see also 'Jewishness', monotheism, synagogue, Torah, etc.
Judas (Iscariot) 4, 29, 61, 74, 78, 99f., 104, 105, 109, 111, 115, 121, 138, 139, 160
Judas (not Iscariot) 6, 20, 21, 99

Käsemann, E. 77, 78
Kanajaraj, J. J. 95
Katz, S. T. 155
Keith, G. 117
Kelber, W. H. 161
Kelly, J. N. D. 11
Kermode, F. 15, 160
Kerr, A. R. 126, 127
Kimelman, R. 155
King, J. S. 15
Kingdom (of God) 7, 33, 104, 154
'King of Israel' 62, 67, 68, 75
'King of the Jews' 5, 29, 113
kingship of Jesus 5, 64, 66, 73, 74, 79, 97, 109, 115, 134
Klassem, W. 160
Knox, J. 78
Kohler, K. 1
kosmos 96f.; see also 'world, the/this'
Kraemer, R. S. 26
Krentz, E. 13
Krey, D. W. 12
Kümmel, W. G. 13, 153
kyrios title 71f., 158; see also Lord
Kysar, R. 6

Ladd, G. E. 158
Lamb (of God) 2, 41, 69, 73, 79, 127, 128
lame man 33, 54f., 57, 113
Lampe, G. W. H. 71
language 45; see also style
Last Supper 6, 18, 23, 25, 30, 57, 98f., 103, 139
law, Jewish 38, 39, 40, 64, 85, 89, 94, 97, 120, 123, 124; see also dietary laws, purity laws, Torah
Lazarus 4, 6, 12, 20, 21, 30, 33, 47, 59, 77, 82, 108, 144
Lefkowitz, M. R. 26
Légasse, S. 158
liberationist criticism 16f., 140

Lieu, J.   153
life, life-giver   53, 57, 80, 81, 89, 91, 96,
   124, 142, 145
light   13, 89, 90, 91, 105, 127, 130, 145;
   and darkness 4, 41, 58, 81, 96; image
   for Jesus 58, 80, 81, 86, 87, 127, 143;
   Prince of 119
Lincoln, A. T.   3, 48, 119
Lindars, B.   15, 34, 35, 47, 60, 70, 80,
   106, 140, 153, 154, 158, 161
literary approaches   15–17
logos 11, 37, 41, 58, 86, 87–92, 96, 97,
   115f., 130, 132, 134, 137, 138, 140,
   154 and *memra* 159; and Philo 51, 56,
   89; and Stoicism 8, 38; in the *Hermetica*
   14, 9; *see also* Word
Lohse, E.   156, 157
Longenecker, R. N.   123
Lord, Jesus as   62, 71–3, 137; of the
   Spirits 66, 130
love command   124, 139, 144
Lowe, M.   114
Lowry, R.   112
Luckmann, T.   15
Luke (Gospel): relation to John   28, 35,
   47, 109; to Mark 29; *see also* Synoptics;
   Index of Biblical References
Luther, M.   12, 122

Maccini, R. G.   17, 108
McGrath, J. F.   43
McHugh, J.   161
McNamara, M.   159
Mahoney, R. K.   101
Malatesta, E.   132
Malbon, E.   1, 37, 98
Malchus 27
Malina, B. J.   43, 44, 157
Mandaeans   13f., 32, 90; *see also* Index
   of Ancient Authors (sect. 4)
manna   55, 56, 57, 124, 156
Marjanen, A.   110
Mark (Gospel): relation to John   28f., 30,
   35, 47, 54, 109; *see also* Synoptics;
   Index of Biblical References
Marrow, C.   163
Marsh, C.   163
Marsh, J.   1, 23, 63
Marshall, I. H.   13, 42, 71, 140
Martha   4, 6, 12, 27, 30, 33, 59, 63,
   67f.,72, 100, 108f., 111, 121, 143
Martin, R. A.   45
Martínez, F. G.   14, 157
Martyn, J. L.   43, 48, 58, 115, 155
Mary Magdalene   5, 12, 61, 62f., 72, 81,
   82, 83, 109f., 111, 140; as *apostola
   apostolorum* 109f.; not the 'beloved
   disciple' 25

Mary (of Bethany)   6, 12, 30, 33, 59, 78,
   108f., 111, 121, 143
Mary of Klopas   25, 109, 160
Mary (Virgin) *see* mother of Jesus
Mastin, B. A.   20
Matthew (Gospel): 'anti-Semitism'   121;
   relation to John 47; to Mark and Luke
   29f.; *see also* Synoptics; Index of Biblical
   References
Maynard, A. H.   102
Meeks, W. A.   32, 43, 44, 105, 130
Meier, J. P.   137
Melchizedek   51, 129
Memra   90, 95, 130, 159
Menken, M. J. J.   118
messianic age (end time)   51, 55, 61, 76,
   128
   sign(s) 59, 61
messiah   2, 41, 64–7, 73, 74, 97, 107,
   122, 130, 131, 132, 134, 137, 154, 157,
   158
Metzger, B. M.   156, 160
miracles   3, 5, 6, 33–5, 49–61, 66, 119,
   136; *see also* Cana, lame man, etc.
Mitchell, S.   46
Mlakuzhyil, G.   16
Moloney, F. J.   3, 16, 17, 62, 68, 71, 85,
   106, 108, 110, 127, 155, 156
Moltmann-Wendel, E.   110
monogenēs   95
monotheism   122f., 129–35, 141, 162
Montanists   9, 22, 24
moral teaching *see* ethical teaching
Morris, L.   14, 22, 52, 153, 159
Moses   3, 29, 33, 39, 52, 55, 56, 57, 61,
   63, 64, 90, 92, 94f., 97, 121, 123, 124,
   125, 130, 131, 144, 157, 162; prophet
   like *see* Deuteronomic prophet
mother of Jesus (Virgin Mary)   6, 12, 22,
   25, 102, 109, 111, 140, 160f.
Motyer, S.   39f., 43, 44, 119, 120, 126,
   127, 161
Moule, C. F. D.   72
Moyise, S.   163
Muratorian Canon   21, 152, 153
music, John in   12

Naaman   53, 57
Nag Hammadi   9; *see also* Index of
   Ancient Authors
'Narrative christology'   61; criticism   16;
   'ethics', 146; 'theology', 49, 73, 146
Nathanael   6, 62, 67, 100, 115
Nazi(s)   112, 119, 122, 162
Neirynck, F.   15, 153
Nereparampil, L.   128
Nero   24, 68
Neusner, J.   66, 122

Newbigin, L. 91
'new look' 14, 35
newly sighted man see blind/newly sighted man
Ng, E. Y. L. 17
Nickelsburg, G. W. E. 157
Nicodemus 3, 5, 7, 28, 34, 36, 62, 76, 77, 104–6, 109, 111, 143, 154
Nicol, W. 15, 154
Nicolson, G. C. 158

O'Day, G. R. 17, 107
Odeberg, H. 13, 156
Offenbarungsreden see discourse(s); Revelation discourses/sayings
official (royal) 28, 33f., 35, 52–4, 103, 111
Old Testament 31, 124; see also Hebrew Bible; Index of Biblical References
oral tradition(s) 15, 26, 27, 36, 46

Pagels, E. 9
Pancaro, S. 97
Paraclete 4, 22, 42, 76, 82, 99, 145, 163; see also Spirit
parallelism 32, 86
Parker, T. H. L. 12
parousia 76
Passion Narrative 4f., 6, 19, 20, 29, 31, 39, 77, 80, 116f., 122, 143
passion (of Jesus) 4, 5, 31, 51, 73–80, 97, 123, 136
Passover 3, 4, 6, 55, 79, 126f., 162
patriarchs, exalted 129, 130, 133, 137
'patriarchy' 16, 139f.
Paul (apostle) 20, 83, 91, 92, 122, 135, 156
Pauline letters 40, 44, 47, 58, 79, 92, 102, 143; see also Index of Biblical References
Pazdan, M. M. 71
Pelikan, J. 12
Pentecost 83, 123, 162
Perkins, P. 160
persecution 23f., 58, 104, 138, 160
'pesher' 123
Peter (apostle) 5, 19, 21, 23, 24, 29, 30, 60, 66, 81, 82, 99, 100–2, 111, 117, 121, 143, 144, 156, 157, 158
Pharisees 3, 4, 47, 57f., 59, 104f., 114, 118, 121, 125, 161
Philip 6, 20, 62, 99, 100, 111
Pilate 5, 29, 38, 71, 74, 111, 113, 117, 118, 143, 161
Pippin, T. 119
Platonic thought 13, 38
polemic 39, 94, 119f., 122
Pollard, T. E. 11

Polycrates 21
Prayer 74, 123; see also High-Priestly Prayer
pre-existence 68, 75, 89, 93, 96, 131, 137
Proem 2, 38, 157
Prologue 2, 9, 21, 27, 32, 37, 47, 53, 58, 61, 65, 75, 78, 81, 84–7, 115, 133, 140, 142
prophet, Jesus as 55, 58, 61, 63f., 66, 73, 107
prophets 54, 64, 66, 74, 86, 89, 94, 119, 123, 131, 157; false, 118; see also Deuteronomic prophet
Pryor, J. W. 115, 125
purification, purified cult 52, 67, 128
purity laws 123, 126, 128
purpose (of John) 14, 36, 37–41

'Q' (Gospel source) 30, 52, 162f.
qal waḥomer 54
Quast, K. 24, 101
Qumran 14, 32, 38, 64, 65, 67, 118, 123, 128, 129, 142, 152, 157, 162; texts see Index of Ancient Authors (sect. 3)

rabbinic discipleship 62, 98; exegesis 39, 94; texts see Index of Ancient Authors (sect. 3)
rabbi(s) 47, 62f., 89, 124
Rabboni 62, 82, 156
Raphael, archangel 92, 129
reader-response criticism 16
redeemer 13f., 32, 92, 159; Jesus as 31, 38, 65
Reinhartz, A. 17, 140, 155
Reitzenstein, R. 13
Religionsgeschichtliche Schule 13
Rembrandt 12
Rensberger, D. 17, 43, 104, 105, 155, 161
'replacement theology' 112, 122–8, 134, 141; see also supersession
Resurrection Narratives 4, 7, 19, 31, 61, 84; of Jesus 5, 20, 31, 51, 59, 73, 75, 76, 79, 81–3, 97, 123, 154
revealer 39, 58, 71, 85, 94–6, 137
Revelation, book of 18, 22, 24, 41f., 44, 46, 48, 93, 131
Revelation discourses/sayings 31f., 131, 136, 159
Reynolds, J. 46
rib (controversy) 119, 121, 130
Richardson, A. 91, 96
Ringe, S. H. 163
Robinson, J. A. T. 14, 15, 38, 40, 45, 47, 92, 96
Robinson, J. M. 9

Rohrbaugh, R. L.   43, 157
Roman Catholic Church   12, 103, 110
Romans, Rome   65, 113, 116, 142; see
   also emperor, trial
Ruckstuhl, E.   154
Ruether, R. R.   112, 115, 116

Sabbath   3, 38, 39, 54, 113, 116, 123,
   125, 126, 130
Sachkritik   18
sacraments   see baptism, Eucharist
sacrifice(s)   40, 79, 127, 128; Jesus' death
   as 79f., 96, 146
Sadducees   47, 121
Samaritan(s)   38, 44, 45, 68, 107, 120,
   128, 154, 157; woman 3, 6, 12, 25, 36,
   53, 63, 68, 100, 106–8, 111, 131, 143,
   154
Sanders, E. P.   128, 161, 162
Sanders, J. N.   20
Sanders, J. T.   43, 87, 117, 161
Sanhedrin   6, 104, 116, 117, 161
sarx see flesh
Satan   4, 120, 121, 129, 138, 157; see
   also devil
saviour   65, 68f, 73, 80, 97, 134, 145
Schillebeeckx, E.   17
Schlatter, D. A.   13
Schnackenburg, R.   11, 15, 22, 47, 60,
   64, 66, 86, 94, 96, 105f., 107, 116, 153,
   157, 159, 160
Schneiders, S. M.   17, 24–6, 106, 107
Schoon, S.   161
Schüssler see Fiorenza
Scott, M.   17, 25, 89, 106, 160
Scott, E. F.   38
scribes   121, 137
Scripture(s), Jewish   3, 12, 31, 38, 67, 68,
   87, 104, 110, 119, 121, 122, 123f.;
   fulfilment 5, 39, 51, 65, 74, 79, 123,
   134, 141; inspiration, 10, 122f.
seamless robe   6, 10, 36, 66
'sectarianism'   15, 43f., 138
Segovia, F. F.   16, 155
Sēmeia see 'signs'
Sēmeiaquelle   33–5
Semitisms, Semitizing Greek   41, 45, 67,
   71, 155
Septuagint   14, 45, 53, 64, 66, 67, 72,
   73, 75, 82f., 89, 95, 119, 123, 131, 132,
   133, 158
Servant, Isaianic   69, 75, 157
shekinah   39, 88, 130, 158
Shema   129
shepherd (theme)   39, 65, 102, 127, 131,
   134, 145
Sherman, F.   12
'signs' (sēmeia)   3, 33–5, 50–3, 154

sin, forgiveness of   80, 103; see also
   atonement
Smalley, S. S.   14, 38, 42, 153
Smith, D. M.   32, 155, 161
Smith, L.   12
Smith, T. V.   101
Snyder, G. F.   101
social-scientific analysis   15, 43, 49
Son of David   66
Son of God   37, 40, 41, 62, 67f., 73,
   95f., 108, 137, 140
Son of Man   58, 69–71, 73, 76, 103,
   130, 137, 157
Son, only(-begotten)   11, 95f., 133
'Son, the'   30, 67, 95, 102
sophia see wisdom/sophia
sources   20, 25, 28–35, 86f., 91f.
Spirit   2, 8, 30, 32, 39, 67, 75, 76, 80,
   83, 97, 103, 104, 139, 141, 145, 158,
   163; of Falsehood, 119f.; of Truth, 99f.
Squitier, K. A.   153
Staley, J. L.   16
Stibbe, M. W. G.   4, 16, 118
Stoicism, Stoics   8, 38, 87, 89, 163
Streeter, B. H.   28, 30
style   7, 34, 41, 42, 70
supersession   3, 52, 126f., 135; see also
   'replacement theology'
symbolism   7, 28, 51, 60, 134, 145; see
   also bread, life, light, etc.
synagogue   40, 41, 47, 103; conflict with
   15, 17, 43, 48, 58, 104, 115
Synoptics, John's relation to   6f., 15, 22,
   23, 28–31, 32, 35, 44, 47, 52–4, 59, 70,
   74, 79, 81f., 97, 98, 100, 102, 113, 117,
   118f., 121, 125, 136, 138, 139, 163

Tabernacles, Feast of   3, 126, 127
Taheb   157
Talbert, C. H.   85, 96, 153
tamid   69
Tannenbaum, R.   46
Tasker, R. V. G.   22
Taylor, V.   155, 162
teacher, Jesus as   61–3, 73
Temple   3, 31, 39, 40, 67, 75, 123, 127f.,
   162; action ('cleansing'), 3, 6, 10, 34,
   59, 127f.; destruction, 40, 47, 123, 127,
   128
Temple, W.   1, 78
'testimony'   2, 62
testimony, eyewitness   24, 25, 27, 36; see
   also witness
theios anēr   34, 53
theos   95, 96, 97, 130
Thomas   5, 6, 20f., 30, 61, 63, 72f., 81,
   82, 83, 97, 99, 100, 111, 133
Thompson, M. B.   44

Thompson, M. M. 92
Thompson, M. R. 160
Thompson, S. 155
Thyen, H. 161
titles (for Jesus) 2, 41, 61–73, 108, 133
topography 44f.
topos 120
Torah 40, 47, 56, 57, 66, 89, 94, 122, 123, 124, 125, 142, 162; *see also* law
tradition *see* oral tradition(s)
Trebilco, P. R. 46
Trevett, C. 9
trial (of Jesus) 36, 71, 117, 121
Trigg, J. W. 10
Trinity 11, 135, 145
'triumphal entry' 29, 75, 123
truth 2, 4, 5, 7, 8, 9, 14, 27, 32, 41, 91, 92, 93, 97, 120, 137, 138, 142, 145, 146
Turner, N. 154, 155
Twelfth Benediction *see birkat ha-minim*
'Twelve, the' 6, 22, 30, 100, 102
typology 123, 126, 127

van Belle, G. 35, 154, 162
VanderKam, J. C. 152, 153
van Unnik, W. C. 40
Vaughan, H. 106, 108
Vermes, G. 14, 64, 66, 118, 129, 133, 152
Virgin Birth 10, 56, 92, 159
von Campenhausen, H. 103
von Rad, G. 161
von Wahlde, U. C. 99, 114, 120

Ware, K. 110
water 2, 7, 42, 57, 80, 104, 107, 124, 127; walking on 29, 33, 55, 130

Wenham, J. W. 83
Weren, W. 163
Westcott, B. W. 13, 44
Westerholm, S. 161
Whaling, F. 143
Wiles, M. 10
Wilken, R. L. 11
Williams, C. 132, 157, 158, 162
Williamson, R. 90
wine miracle *see* Cana
Wirkungsgeschichte 8
wisdom/*sophia* 39, 56, 57, 86, 88f., 91f., 130, 140, 153
witness 2, 19, 27f., 41, 96, 81, 111
Woll, D. B. 43
women 6, 25f., 29, 82, 106–12, 140, 142, 144
Word, Jesus as 2, 8, 10, 37, 63, 75, 81, 84–93, 139, 145, 158, 159; *see also logos*
'work(s)' 32, 33, 50, 61, 57, 77
'world, the/this' 4, 9, 42, 43, 81, 96f., 99, 114, 115, 118, 138f., 163; ruler of 80, 81, 138, 145
worship 128, 141, 160; of Jesus 60, 133, 134, 135
Wright, N. T. 162

Yaoel 134
Yavne *see* Jamnia
Yee, G. A. 126
YHWH 56, 72, 75, 90, 107, 119, 129, 130, 131, 132, 133
Young, B. H. 159

Zeus 68, 95
Zimmerli, W. 159
Zoroastrianism 138